FROM JESUS TO CHRIST

FROM JESUS TO CHRIST

Eleven lectures given in Karlsruhe between 4 and 14 October 1911

TRANSLATED BY CHARLES DAVY AND
EDITED BY FREDERICK AMRINE

INTRODUCTION BY ROBERT MCDERMOTT

RUDOLF STEINER

RUDOLF STEINER PRESS

CW 131

Rudolf Steiner Press
Hillside House, The Square
Forest Row, RH18 5ES

www.rudolfsteinerpress.com

Published by Rudolf Steiner Press 2024

Originally published in German under the title *Von Jesus zu Christus* (volume 131 in the *Rudolf Steiner Gesamtausgabe* or Collected Works) by Rudolf Steiner Verlag, Dornach. Based on shorthand notes that were not reviewed or revised by the speaker. This authorized translation is based on the seventh revised German edition (1988), edited by Hella Wiesberger

Published by permission of the Rudolf Steiner Nachlassverwaltung, Dornach

© Rudolf Steiner Nachlassverwaltung, Dornach, Rudolf Steiner Verlag 1988

This translation © Rudolf Steiner Press 2024

A catalogue record for this book is available from the British Library

ISBN 978 1 85584 669 2

Cover by Morgan Creative
Typeset by Symbiosys Technologies, Visakhapatnam, India
Printed and bound by 4Edge Ltd., Essex

Contents

Publisher's Note … … ix
Introduction, by Robert McDermott … … x

LECTURE 1

KARLSRUHE, 5 OCTOBER 1911

Two directions of European intellectual development: the Jesus principle of Jesuitism and the Christ principle of Rosicrucianism. The trinity: conscious spiritual life, subconscious soul life, unrecognized natural life—Spirit, Son (Logos), Father—imagination, will, feeling. The spirit initiation of the Rosicrucians and the will initiation of the Jesuits.

Pages 1-15

LECTURE 2

KARLSRUHE, 6 OCTOBER 1911

The Christian-Rosicrucian initiation. Rosicrucianism and spiritual science. The doctrine of reincarnation and karma in the Rosicrucian initiation and with Droßbach, Widenmann and Lessing on the one hand and in Buddhism on the other. The loosening of the etheric body through the Rosicrucian path of knowledge. The path to experiencing the Christ-Event through ongoing revelation. The personal experience of images from the Gospels in Rosicrucian initiation. The encounter with the Guardian of the Threshold and the story of Jesus' temptation. The fear and the Mount of Olives. The difference to the Jesuit path.

Pages 16-30

LECTURE 3

KARLSRUHE, 7 OCTOBER 1911

Three sources of knowledge for the Christian mysteries: the Gospels, the research of clairvoyants, faith as a path to self-knowledge and of Christ. The transfer of the karmic office of judge to Christ. Jesus of Nazareth was a true human being, not an adept like Apollonius of Tyana. The relationship of the Christ individuality to the body of Jesus of Nazareth in contrast to the relationship of the Apollonius individuality to its body. The Fall and the compensation through Christ. Two witnesses of faith: Pascal and Solovyov.

Pages 31-49

LECTURE 4

KARLSRUHE, 8 OCTOBER 1911

The replacement of faith by the vision of Christ. The experience of the Logos in pre-Christian and post-Christian times. Richard Wagner's intuition of the Mystery of Golgotha as an example of the necessary devotional attitude towards the truths of the spiritual world. The traditional Gospels and the Akashic Record. Jerome and the Gospel of Matthew. The path from the inner emotional experience of Christ to Christian initiation.

Pages 50-64

LECTURE 5

KARLSRUHE, 9 OCTOBER 1911

The letters of Paul. The question of the decay of the physical body at death. The connection between the form of the physical body and ego consciousness. Greek culture: The highest love for the physical body. Buddha consciousness: the disdain for the physical body. Ancient Hebrew antiquity: The reproduction of the form of the physical body through the generations. The Book of Job.

Pages 65-80

LECTURE 6

KARLSRUHE, 10 OCTOBER 1911

The core question of Christianity: the Resurrection. The initiations in the Mysteries and the Gospels. Paul's view of history after the experience of Damascus. Christ, the second Adam. The corruptible body of Adam and the incorruptible body of the second Adam. The physical body and the form of the human being, the phantom. The connection between the visibility of the physical body and the luciferic influence.

Pages 81-98

LECTURE 7

KARLSRUHE, 11 OCTOBER 1911

The only one-time embodiment of Christ in a physical body. The ego nature of man. The difficult understanding of the Resurrection. The physical body as a mirror for the soul's experiences. The destruction of the phantom of the physical body: the Fall of man. The resurrected body of Christ as the pure phantom of the physical body. The re-establishment of man's lost principles. The rescued human phantom.

Pages 99-112

LECTURE 8
KARLSRUHE, 12 OCTOBER 1911

The two Jesus boys. The Zarathustra individuality. The influence of the Buddha forces. The ego of the Nathan Jesus boy. The twelve-year-old Jesus in the temple. The thirty-year-old Jesus at the Baptism in the Jordan. Ashes and salt. The spiritual body of Christ: the resurrected phantom. For Paul the scripture in Damascus is fulfilled.

Pages 113-126

LECTURE 9
KARLSRUHE, 13 OCTOBER 1911

The relationship of the individual to the Christ-Impulse. Earlier theosophy in Bengel and Oetinger, the objectivity of the luciferic influence (sin, lies, error) and the objectivity of Christ's redemptive act. The exoteric path to Christ through the Lord's Supper and the Gospels. Communion in the spirit through the power of meditation and concentration as an esoteric path.

Pages 127-142

LECTURE 10
KARLSRUHE, 14 OCTOBER 1911

The relationship of the Christ-Impulse to every single human soul. The esoteric path to Christ through initiation. The seven stages of Christian initiation and their goal. Receiving the phantom of the Resurrected Christ. The karmic judgment of Christ. The doctrine of reincarnation. The clarification of the view backwards through the second Christ-Event. About Jeshu ben Pandira and the Bodhisattva. The bringer of good through the Word. The voluntary sacrifice of Christ's act of Redemption.

Pages 143-162

PUBLIC LECTURE
KARLSRUHE, 4 OCTOBER 1911

The historical Jesus research of the nineteenth century. Arthur Drews. The Gospels as historical documents? Christianity as a mystical fact. The mysteries of antiquity. Aristides as a student of the mysteries. Two completely different types of mysteries: the Egyptian and Greek mysteries—the Persian mysteries or

Mithra mysteries. The primeval man Adam and original sin. Pauline Christianity. The Gospels are not biographies, but descriptions of initiation.
Pages 163-182

APPENDICES:
1. Rosicrucianism *185*
2. Gotthold Ephraim Lessing *186*
3. The Etheric and Astral Bodies *190*
4. Immanuel Kant *192*
5. Gnosis/Gnosticism *194*
6. Helena Blavatsky *196*
7. Cosmic Evolution *198*
8. The Hierarchies *200*
9. Ahriman and Lucifer *202*
10. The Kant-Laplace Hypothesis *204*

Notes 205

Rudolf Steiner's Collected Works 213

Significant Events in the Life of Rudolf Steiner 231

Index 247

Publisher's Note

In his lecture of 7 May, 1923 in Dornach ('The Easter Thought, the Ascension Revelation and the Pentecost Mystery' in GA 224), Rudolf Steiner says about the lecture cycle *From Jesus to Christ*: '... which was held in Karlsruhe, and which, because certain truths, which many people want to remain concealed, were once spoken out of an esoteric sense of duty, was the most hostile. Indeed, one could say that from certain quarters the hostility towards anthroposophy began precisely with this cycle'.

INTRODUCTION

Background and Purpose of these Lectures
The ten lectures in this volume assume Steiner's description of the evolution of consciousness,* and especially the transformation of human consciousness due to the Mystery of Golgotha, so named by Rudolf Steiner to refer to the Crucifixion and Resurrection of Christ. Steiner's purpose is not only historical; he is eager to show the relevance of the Mystery of Golgotha for the time when he was writing and lecturing, especially for Europe of the twentieth century. If he were lecturing now, he would surely emphasize that an understanding of the Mystery of Golgotha is even more urgent than a century ago.

In the months prior to these lectures, Rudolf Steiner was in an intense conflict with Annie Besant, president of the Theosophical Society, who had announced the founding of the Order of the Rising Star (later renamed Order of the Star in the East) which C. W. Leadbeater was establishing with Besant's support. Leadbeater named Jiddu Krishnamurti, age 16, the World Teacher, or Jesus Christ, reborn. In response, Steiner emphatically stated that Christ could incarnate only once. At age 21, Krishnamurti renounced the title given to him by Leadbeater. Subsequently, Krsishnamurti proved to be an influential spiritual teacher in India and the West.

In June, in direct response to Besant and Leadbeater, Rudolf Steiner delivered three lectures with the title *The Spiritual Guidance of*

---

* For Rudolf Steiner's account of the evolution of consciousness, see especially *An Outline of Esoteric Science*, trans., Catherine E. Creeger, introduction, Clopper Almon (Hudson, NY: SteinerBooks, 1977), Ch. 4: 'Cosmic Evolution and the Human Being', 117-280, and Stewart C. Easton, *Man and World in the Light of Anthroposophy* (Hudson, NY: SteinerBooks, 2024—originally published 1975, 20-121).

the Individual and Humanity, one of the clearest accounts of Steiner's teaching on the relationship of Jesus of Nazareth, a human being, and Christ, the divine Logos. These three lectures were one of only two sets of lectures that Steiner revised. He was eager to make them especially relevant for his relations to the Theosophical Society and worthy to endure. In October, continuing with the same intent and at greater length, he delivered the ten lectures in this volume with the revealing title, *From Jesus to Christ*. In addition to explaining the transformative impact of the Mystery of Golgotha on the evolution of consciousness, Steiner was determined to communicate to his followers, presumably all members of the German Section of the Theosophical Society of which he was head, that his teaching was focused primarily on Christ and secondarily on Krishna and Buddha, the primary focus of the Theosophical Society. By means of clairvoyant 'reading' of the Akashic Record, Steiner was able to explain the radical shift in consciousness as a result of the Mystery of Golgotha, continuing to the present and increasingly for thousands of years to come. The many themes in these lectures all serve to establish the transformation of human consciousness as a result of the Mystery of Golgotha.

Throughout his life as an esoteric teacher (1900-1925), Rudolf Steiner taught an understanding of the Incarnation of Christ in contrast to the words enshrined in the Nicaean Creed—'by the power of the Holy Spirit, He was incarnate of the Virgin Mary and was made man'. Steiner maintained that Christ did not 'become man', but rather, at the baptism of Jesus, Christ, a fully divine being, entered the human being Jesus of Nazareth. By so doing, Christ served as the 'I' of Jesus, in place of the Zarathustra 'I' who entered Jesus at age twelve—as a result of which Jesus was able to lecture to the rabbis in the Temple. Steiner similarly taught that the Logos in the Prologue to John's Gospel refers to Christ, the Word, who was 'in the beginning'. In his lectures *The Bhagavad Gita and the Epistles of Paul* (1912), Steiner explains that Paul, on the road to Damascus, in an experience that Steiner describes as an initiation, experienced the Risen Christ. Steiner was eager to convince his audience of theosophists that while it is important to study and revere Krishna and Buddha, it is essential for the evolution of humanity to love and experience the transformative effect of Jesus who was joined by Christ, taught, healed, was crucified, resurrected and ascended to the spiritual world to reign at one with God the Father. Steiner repeated frequently that Christ is a cosmic being devoted eternally to the evolution of humanity. He agrees with the affirmation of the Nicaean Creed: 'His kingdom will have no end.'*

Steiner's audience in Karlsruhe, southwest Germany, probably held an ambivalent relationship to Christianity. Steiner wished his audience to understand the relationship between religion (specifically Christianity†) and esotericism (specifically anthroposophy, or spiritual science). He stated:

> We shall best come to a more precise understanding of our subject—modern religious life on the one hand and the anthroposophical deepening of spiritual life on the other—if we glance at the origins of both religious life and esoteric spiritual life in recent centuries. For as regards spiritual development in Europe during this period, we can discern two directions of thought that have been cultivated with the utmost intensity: on the one hand an exaggeration of the principle of Jesus, and on the other, a most careful, conscientious preservation of the principle of Christ. (1)‡

Steiner in effect helped his audience understand that the intellectual milieu of the time was working against their attaining a living knowledge of Christ, and especially of Christ's resurrection. As the universe is understood 'as a collaboration of atoms... there is no place for the Being of Christ in this cosmogony, indeed no place for anything spiritual.' (136)

---

* See Rudolf Steiner, *The Mystery of the Trinity*, revised second edition, trans., James H. Hindes (Hudson, NY: SteinerBooks, 2016), especially p. 71, and James H. Hindes, *Renewing Christianity* (Hudson, NY: SteinerBooks, 1995), especially Chapter 3: 'God and Christ Jesus'.

† See Rudolf Steiner, *Christianity as Mystical Fact*, trans., intro., Andrew Welburn, afterword, Michael Debus (Hudson, NY: Steinerbooks, 1997).

‡ Page numbers for quotations from these lectures are given in parentheses following each quotation.

Physical Body and Ego according to Ancient Greeks, Hebrews, and Buddhists

As in all Rudolf Steiner's writings and lectures, in these lectures he strives to show that the spiritual is primary, both logically and temporally. Students of Steiner are fond of quoting the maxim, 'matter is never without spirit, spirit is never without matter', but it seems to me that this quotation is not true to Steiner's understanding of matter or spirit. Steiner does hold that matter is never without spirit but he also holds that spirit exists prior to matter, in important respects is independent of matter, and in the end of time will presumably prevail without matter. He does not accept either the modern Western materialist idea that matter exists without spirit—or simply, spirit does not exist—nor the Buddhist idea of the co-arising of matter and spirit. The accurate term for Steiner's position with respect to material creation is panentheism, according to which the divine precedes and permeates creation but unlike pantheism, is not co-extensive with matter. Before and after matter, there is and will be spirit forever.

Steiner often celebrates the Greek love of the ideal physical form. He states that the Greeks felt 'that the highest tribute someone could offer to the Gods was to clothe them with this human form that they themselves valued so much.' (76) This positive attitude toward the physical is the opposite of Steiner's description of the Buddhist view, namely, to overcome suffering due to attachment, the physical needs to be negated. Steiner considers the Hebraic view of matter to be between the Greek and Buddhist:

> This old, Judaic mode of thought, standing midway between Greek thought and Buddhism, does not involve, as Greek thought does from the outset, a predisposition to tragedy in face of the phenomenon of death, but a tragic feeling is indirectly present in it. It is truly Greek for the hero to say: 'Better a beggar in the upper world'—i.e. with the human bodily form—'than a king in the realm of shades', but a Hebrew could not have said it without something more. For the Hebrews know that when in death their bodily form falls away, they remain united with God. (77)

Steiner prizes the ancient Greek ideals of the body and ideal form as well as Hebraic consciousness of Providence as necessary (though incomplete) contributions to the development of the historical (or evolutionary) context for the Incarnation of Christ, or more fully, for the Mystery of Golgotha. Although the contributions of the Greek and Hebraic traditions were deep and positive, they did not sufficiently prepare for the Incarnation of Christ. In fact, just the reverse. Steiner stated in these lectures, and in other sets of lectures on the Gospels from 1911 to 1915, that Christ incarnated when the culture of the Roman Empire was at its lowest ebb: 'Human feelings and perceptions changed altogether at the turning-point of the old and new epochs, a point marked by the events of Palestine.' (135)

According to Steiner, the consciousness of the ancient Hebrews was characterized by 'a folk-group-ego'. Consciousness had not yet penetrated as far as to attain a separate individuality in each person. Hebraic consciousness was closer to the Buddhists than to the Greeks. In sum, the Greeks experienced the beginning of ego-consciousness; the Hebrews experienced the ego of the Hebrew People; the Buddhists denied the ego whether of a people or of an individual. Buddhists focused on individuals rather than, as with the Hebrews, a people, but saw the need to deny the value and even the unqualified existence of an ego. According to Buddhist teaching, the apparent ego that claims the attention of each individual human being is *maya*, illusion—not in its effect on each person but ontologically (what is real).

Steiner then offers this summary of the consciousness of the ancient Greeks, Hebrews, and Buddhists:

> The Greeks said: 'I value my ego so greatly that I look with horror on what will happen to it after death'. The Buddhists said: 'That which is the cause of the external human form must fall away from humans as soon as possible'. The Hebrews said: 'I am united with God; that is my fate, and as long as I am united with Him, I bear my fate. I know nothing else than the identification of my ego with the Divine Ego.' (77)

With the aid of Gotthold Lessing's influential book *Education of the Human Race*,* Steiner views each culture in sequence in light of its

---

* Gotthold Ephraim Lessing, *The Education of the Human Race*. Trans., F.W. Robertson. Fordham University Modern History Sourcebook.

contribution to the evolution of humanity. This is where, or how, Steiner's account of the evolution of consciousness exhibits a nineteenth-century European bias: Steiner agrees with Lessing's view of the Old Testament as God's first gift to human evolution, the New Testament as the second, and the third, 'an independent feeling in the human soul for the true, the good, and the beautiful'. (20) As he often does, in these lectures Steiner speaks positively of Buddha but not with respect to the evolution of consciousness. In this view, Buddha contributed to the work of Christ and the enlightenment of individuals but does not advance the essentially Christian ideals of individuality, love, and freedom. For those ideals, the 'I' must be affirmed and developed in ways that are not affirmed in core Buddhist teaching. Steiner stated:

> For such things as I have quoted from the heart of Buddhism—for example, the conversation between King Milinda and the Buddhist sage Nagasena—testify clearly that the nature of the ego cannot be spoken of in Buddhism as we must speak of it. For a genuine follower of Buddhism, it would indeed be heretical to speak of the nature of the ego as we must represent it. On this very account, we must ourselves be clear regarding the nature of the ego. (100)

Now that a wide and deep dialogue between Buddhism (particularly the Mahayana and Vajrayana schools) and Christianity (not yet Buddhism and anthroposophy*) is advancing, the Christian and European understanding of Hinduism and Buddhism will need greater openness and insight. On the Buddhist side, the writings and lectures of His Holiness the Dalai Lama are the best source of dialogue with anthroposophy. Arthur Zajonc, professor emeritus of physics, Amherst College, and former general secretary of the Anthroposophical Society in America, was privileged to discuss deep spiritual topics with His Holiness the Dalai Lama.

---

* Such a dialogue would do well to begin with Hermann Beckh, *Buddha's Life and Teaching*. Trans. Katrin Binder. Edited, foreword by Neil Franklin (Forest Row, U.K.: Temple Lodge, 2019—originally published 1916). Beckh, a scholar of Sanskrit, Tibetan, and Pali, was an anthroposophist and a correspondent with Rudolf Steiner during the years 1911-15 when Steiner was lecturing on the Gospels, including the relationship between Buddha and Christ.

Four Parts of the Human Being

As Frederick Amrine explains in Appendix 3, 'The Etheric and the Astral Bodies,' 'The individual etheric body is precipitated out of a vast cosmic ether'; it is grasped by Imagination. The astral body, which is experienced by Inspiration, 'is Steiner's early, theosophical term for the subtle body that corresponds generally to "soul" or "psyche".' In these lectures, in order to better explain the relationship between Jesus and Christ, particularly in relation to the crucifixion of Jesus and the resurrection of Christ (including Jesus), Steiner also describes the functions of the ego and the physical body. The relationship of these four parts of the human body at death provides the surest way to understand and remember them: the physical body that is burned or buried loses its appearance and function, but because the other bodies were dependent on the physical body for their functions, the physical body has a lasting effect. For three days after the death of the physical body, the etheric body hovers over the physical body and then performs two essential functions: it communicates the essential contents of its life to both the astral (soul) and to the etheric realm that surrounds Earth. The astral body in turn communicates its total content to the 'I'/ego. This process lasts approximately one-third of the number of years that the deceased ('so-called dead') person lived. The ego, the sole surviving part of the deceased person, is guided by spiritual beings toward the 'cosmic midnight hour', when it will transition from the end of its previous life to preparation for its next life.

*The Phantom and the Resurrection**

While Steiner was delivering these lectures on the relationship of Jesus and Christ, he probably assumed that his audience had in mind his description of the four-part human being—physical, etheric, astral, and 'I' or spirit. It would be surprising, however, if his audience would have had in mind a clear understanding of 'phantom', a term that Steiner introduces for the form of the physical body. Steiner introduced this concept in these lectures for the first—and it seems for the last—time. The term phantom is discussed most extensively in

---

* I am grateful to Rev. James Hindes for advice concerning this section.

Sergei O. Prokofieff's *The Mystery of the Resurrection*, particularly in its Appendix: 'The Forces of the Phantom and Stigmatization'.* These pages on the phantom are at least as difficult to understand as the references to phantom in *From Jesus to Christ*. Fortunately, in 2006, *Perspectives*, the quarterly journal of the Christian Community in the UK, published a full issue on the Resurrection, including a discussion of the phantom.† Subject to correction, here is my summary of Steiner's understanding of the phantom and its significance for the Resurrection and the human physical body.

It probably makes most sense to begin not with the evolution of the phantom in relation to Old Saturn or its future in relation to Vulcan, but specifically as part of the experience of Paul on his way to Damascus. Steiner considers Paul, by virtue of his spiritual (karmic) preparation and his experience on the road to Damascus, to be the surest teacher of the mystery of the Resurrection. According to Steiner, Paul 'wishes to say' that because the pure phantom of Christ arose out of the grave at death, 'what had been taken from [human beings] through the luciferic influence can be given back to them through its presence as the Risen Body of Christ'. (109)

> [Paul] experienced something that he knew could be experienced only when the Scriptures were fulfilled; when a perfect human phantom, a human body risen from the grave in a supra-sensible form, would appear in the spiritual atmosphere of the Earth. And that is what he saw! (126)

What exactly is this 'perfect human phantom' which seems to appear in Steiner's sentences where we might expect a reference to either the

---

* Sergei O. Prokofieff, *The Mystery of the Resurrection in the Light of Anthroposophy*, trans. Simon Blaxland-de Lange (Forest Row, U.K.: Temple Lodge Publishing, 2010). In addition to the inherent difficulty of explaining Steiner's concept of the phantom, this Appendix is complicated by Prokofieff's determination to separate the stigmata of Judith von Halle 'from the real tasks that Rudolf Steiner has placed before us'. Judith von Halle (b. 1972), trained as an architect, is an anthroposophist, and a stigmatist.

† Except for Sergei O. Prokofieff, important anthroposophical authors such as Stewart Easton, Rudolf Frieling, and Edward Smith, and others who offer explanations of the Resurrection, do not discuss the phantom.

etheric body or resurrected body of Christ? Because the divine Christ was the ego of Jesus, from his baptism until his crucifixion, luciferic forces exercised no influence on Jesus. After his crucifixion and death, his phantom was in the tomb. This explains why Mary Magdalen initially failed to recognize the crucified Christ. It made possible the resurrection as a counter to death—in Paul's famous phrase, 'death, where is thy sting?' Prior to the death of Jesus, all human physical bodies were permeated by luciferic influence, except the Nathan (Luke) Jesus who was joined by the ego of Christ at the baptism by John. The phantom of Jesus, permeated by Christ, rose from the grave. Note that Christ, a divine being, did not and could not die.

As the description of Mary Magdalen at the tomb—and in the process of recognizing Jesus—with the exclamation 'Master!' has challenged scholars, preachers, and laypersons throughout the history of Christianity, Steiner's words, which I take to be a solution of this sublime process—though not a reduction of the mystery—deserves to be quoted in full:

> The important thing is not what Christ taught, but what he gave: His Body! For the Body that rose from the grave of Golgotha had never before entered into human evolution. Never before had there been present on Earth, through someone's death, what came to be present as the Risen Body of Jesus Christ. Previously, after humans had passed through the gate of death and had gone through the period between death and a new birth, they had brought to Earth with them the defective phantom, given over to deterioration. No one had ever caused a perfect phantom to arise. (111)
>
> The disciples who looked into the grave found the linen cloths in which the body had been wrapped, but the phantom, on which the evolution of the ego depends, had risen from the grave. It is not surprising that Mary Magdalen, who had known only the earlier phantom when it was permeated by earthly elements, did not recognize the same form in the phantom, now freed from terrestrial gravity, when she saw it clairvoyantly. It seemed to her different. (125)

Steiner is recommending that the phantom of Jesus Christ, experienced by Mary Magdalen and then by the disciples seven times*

---

* Rudolf Frieling, *New Testament Studies*, ed., Tony Jacobs-Brown (Edinburgh: Floris Books, 1994): 'The Seven Easter Stories in the Gospels'.

between the Resurrection and Ascension, should be thought of as the Resurrected Christ. As a phantom, Christ appeared to be both physical and invisible, such that it could pass through the wall of a closed room and appear to eat food. We surely do not need to remind ourselves that the Resurrection is a mystery. That said, it might be slightly more intelligible if we can grasp the meaning of the phantom—invisible and yet in the shape, and with some of the functions, of a physical body. It has long seemed to me more efficacious and reverent to picture the resurrected Christ as an etheric or resurrected body rather than as a physical body in need of oxygen and occupying space. Although 'phantom' with respect to the resurrected Christ is a rather inelegant term, it supplies a missing piece of a profound mystery. Like many of Steiner's statements about the Mystery of Golgotha, his account of the evolution of the phantom at least appears to be (and probably is) in conflict with orthodox Christian thinking and devotion. It might nevertheless be time to focus on it as a way to imagine Christ's Resurrection—without which Christianity and anthroposophy are without foundation.

It remains to be seen whether Christians and specifically anthroposophists will earn the privilege of sharing in the experience of Christ's phantom that graced Mary Magdalen and ten apostles—all but Judas who hung himself after betraying Jesus, and Thomas who, it seems, unlike Mary and the other apostles, had not developed supersensible sight.* It also remains to be seen whether, or the extent to which, Christians will be able to understand and hold the concept of the Son of Man and its role in the Mystery of Golgotha. Along with the phantom, the Son of Man as described by Rudolf Steiner and further explained especially by Christian

---

* Although the account of the Son of Man in Wilhelm Kelber, *Christ and the Son of Man* (Edinburgh: Floris Books, 1997) is extremely complex, it is nevertheless the clearest description from an anthroposophical perspective that I have found. For a brief history that omits Steiner's account entirely, see Frederick Houk Borsch, *The Christian and Gnostic Son of Man*. Studies in Biblical Theology (Naperville, IL: Alec R. Allenson, 1970).

Community priests,* provides a way of contemplating the relation of Christ to Jesus during the Crucifixion, Resurrection, and thereafter eternally.

Roman Catholic and Anthroposophical Practice
Because Steiner was intensely aware of all the ways that materialist thinking can prevent a true experience of the deed of Christ by ordinary thinking, he shared dozens of exercises by which Christians, and specifically anthroposophists, might overcome these unsuspected epistemological limitations. He was especially aware that scripture scholars of late nineteenth and early twentieth centuries were missing the deep truths revealed at a level inaccessible to ordinary, even learned, textual analyses. While he respected the dedicated scientific research and creativity that interpreters brought to the study of the Gospels, he lamented that this scholarship 'succeeded only in losing the Bible'. (87) In response to the reduction of the Bible to the level of ordinary texts, Steiner offered both exoteric and esoteric methods by which biblical scholars and laypersons might access the revelations of the inspired Gospel authors. He particularly tried to lead his audiences to a relationship to the Risen Christ, and thereby to their own resurrection.

Throughout dozens of lectures on the Gospels, and perhaps most pointedly in these lectures, aptly titled *From Jesus to Christ*, Steiner's emphasis is primarily on Christ and secondarily on Jesus, as well as primarily on esotericism and secondarily on religion. In general, he sees religious teaching and practices as preparatory to esotericism, especially anthroposophical research and exercises. He rather forcefully contrasts practices, such as Jesuit training (according to his understanding), that focus on the life of Jesus in ways that might detract from a focus on Christ. In the following statement he

---

* Rudolf Steiner guided a group of Lutheran priests and seminarians in the establishment of the Christian Community. See Rudolf Steiner, *First Steps in Christian Religious Renewal: Preparing the Ground for the Christian Community* (CW 342), trans., Marsha Post., intro., Christopher Bamford (Hudson, NY: SteinerBooks, 2010).

contrasts 'Jesuitism' (based on his view of the *Spiritual Exercises* of Ignatius Loyola*) with Rosicrucian esotericism:

> In Jesuitism, we encounter a dangerous exaggeration of the principle of Jesus. In the other movement, which for centuries has existed in Europe as Rosicrucianism, we have an intimate movement toward Christ that above all seeks carefully for the ways of truth. (2)

Among many spiritual practices that Steiner recommended, he especially emphasized Holy Communion, receipt of the consecrated bread usually referred to as the Eucharist. In his lectures on the Gospel of St John, he explained and recommended practices known as Christian Initiation.† Steiner reminded his audience of theosophists in 1911 that 'the writer of the Apocalypse and of the Gospel of St John, at his advanced age, could speak the words "Children, love one another!" out of the essence of Christianity, but the same words from the mouth of another person may be a mere phrase.' (82) The difference, of course, is the result of the myriad practices prescribed by Christianity and other religious traditions—including especially Roman Catholicism, the Christian denomination with which Steiner had personal contact and which he admired and criticized.‡ Steiner also admitted that exoteric Christian practices can prepare the soul for growth in esoteric (especially anthroposophical) transformation. Steiner states:

> One of these exoteric ways is through the Gospels, through the New Testament. The contents of the Gospels, when they are received into our souls and permitted to work upon us, can in fact bring about for

---

* Ignatius Loyola, *Spiritual Exercises* (1548). See various Ignatian websites for the wide range of exercises, almost entirely at variance from Steiner's critique of 'Jesuitism'.

† See Rudolf Steiner, Lecture 11: 'Christian Initiation', *The Gospel of St. John* (Hudson, NY: SteinerBooks, 2022), trans., Maud Monges, revisions and notes, Frederick Amrine, intro., Robert McDermott.

‡ As Steiner recounted in his autobiography, in his youth he served the priest at the Roman Catholic mass (an excellent way to learn reverence) and as an adult he had important conversations with Roman Catholic monks.

> each one of us an inner experience, and this inner experience may indeed be called the Christ-Experience. (50)

Steiner's lectures which include comments on Roman Catholic teachings and practice have contributed to the perception—intensely advanced by Sergei O. Prokofieff—that Steiner and anthroposophy necessarily conflict with Catholic practice. In my view, it would be more helpful if Steiner's (and Prokofieff's) comments on Catholic teaching and practice would have the form 'both-and', or 'Catholic on the way to anthroposophical', rather than the either/or statements in these and some other lectures. A more balanced assessment of Steiner's relationship to Christianity would include his spiritual guidance of the founding of the Christian Community.* In summary, in addition to many exoteric practices, it was Rudolf Steiner's primary mission to teach esoteric practices designed to reveal the Mystery of Golgotha to human lives awake to its transformative effect. Anthroposophic practice involves the transformation of thinking, feeling and will, which presupposes a foundation in reverence and humility. The key is effort, constant striving. Steiner closes these lectures with the words of Goethe, 'the great forerunner'. As Frederick Amrine notes, the words that Steiner quotes—'He who never gives up striving, he it is whom we can redeem'—'are spoken by the angels after Faust's death and resurrection'.

Robert McDermott
October 2024

---

* See footnote to p. xx above. See also a vast library of theological writings by scholarly Christian Community priests, including Frederick Rittlemeyer, Emil Bock, Wilhelm Kelber, Rudolf Frieling, Evelyn Francis Cabel, Friedrich Hiebel, Hans-Werner Schroeder, Michael Debus, Tom Ravetz, and James Hindes. See also books by an Anglican priest: A. P. Shepherd, *Rudolf Steiner: Scientist of the Invisible* (Rochester, Vermont: Inner traditions, 1990—originally published 1954), and *The Battle for the Spirit: The Church and Rudolf Steiner* (Anastasi, 2012—originally published 1964).

LECTURE 1

KARLSRUHE, 5 OCTOBER 1911

THE object of these lectures is to place before you an idea of the Christ-Event in so far as it is connected with the historical appearance of the Christ in the person of Jesus of Nazareth. So many questions of spiritual life are bound up with this subject that the choice of it will enable us to make a wide survey of the realm of anthroposophy and its mission, and to discuss the significance of the anthroposophical movement for the spiritual life of the present time. We shall also have the opportunity of learning what the content of religion is. And since this content must spring from the common heritage of humanity, we shall seek to know it in its relation to the deeper sources of religious life, and to what the sources of esoteric science have to tell us concerning the foundation of all religious and philosophic endeavours. Much that we shall have to discuss will seem to lie very far from the theme itself, but it will all lead us back to our main purpose.

We shall best come to a more precise understanding of our subject—modern religious life on the one hand and the anthroposophical deepening of spiritual life on the other—if we glance at the origins both of religious life and of esoteric spiritual life in recent centuries. For as regards spiritual development in Europe during this period, we can discern two directions of thought that have been cultivated with the utmost intensity: on the one hand an exaggeration of the principle of Jesus, and on the other a most careful, conscientious preservation of the principle of Christ. When we place before our minds these two recent streams of the last centuries, we must see in the exaggeration of the principle of Jesus a great and dangerous error in the spiritual life of those times, and on the other side a movement of deep significance, a movement which seeks above all the true paths and is careful to avoid the paths of error. From the outset, therefore, in our judgement of two entirely different spiritual movements, we have to ascribe serious errors to one of them and the most earnest efforts to reach the truth to the other.

The movement that interests us in connection with our anthroposophical point of view, and which we may call an extraordinarily dangerous error in a certain sense, is the movement known in the external world as Jesuitism.[1] In Jesuitism, we encounter a dangerous exaggeration of the principle of Jesus. In the other movement, which for centuries has existed in Europe as Rosicrucianism, we have an intimate movement towards Christ that above all seeks carefully for the ways of truth.

Ever since a Jesuitical current arose in Europe, much has been said and written in exoteric life about Jesuitism. Those who wish to study spiritual life from its deeper sources will thus be concerned to see how far Jesuitism signifies a dangerous exaggeration of the principle of Jesus. If we wish to arrive at a true characterization of Jesuitism, we must get to know how the three chief principles of earthly evolution, which are indicated in the most varied ways in the different worldviews, find practical expression in human life, including exoteric life. Today we will first of all turn entirely away from the deeper significance and characterization of these three fundamental streams, which run through all life and all evolution, and will review them from an external point of view.

First of all, we have the cognitional element in our life of soul. Now, whatever may be said against the abstractions of a one-sided intellectual search for truth, or against the alienation from life of many scientific, philosophical, and theosophical endeavours, people who are clear in their own minds as to what they will and what they can will, know that cognition belongs to the most deeply rooted activities of the soul. For whether we seek knowledge chiefly through thinking, or more through sensation or feeling, cognition always signifies a taking account of the world around us, and also of ourselves. Hence, we must say that whether we are satisfied for the moment with the simplest experiences of the soul, or whether we wish to devote ourselves to the most complicated analysis of the mysteries of existence, cognition is the primary and most significant question. For it is basically through cognition that we form a picture of the content of the world—a picture we live by and from which our entire life of soul is nourished. The very first sensory impression, in fact the whole life of the senses, must be included in the realm of cognition, along with the highest formulations of the intellect.

Under cognition we must include also the impulse to distinguish between the beautiful and the ugly, for although it is true in a certain sense that there is no disputing about taste, yet cognition is involved when someone has adopted a certain judgement in a question of taste and can distinguish between the beautiful and the ugly. Again, our moral impulses—those which prompt us to do good and abstain from evil—must be seen as moral ideas, as cognition, or as impulses to do the one and avoid the other. Even what we call our conscience, however vague the impulses from it may be, comes under the heading of cognition. In short, the world we are consciously aware of, whether it be reality or *maya*[2]; the world we live in consciously, everything we are conscious of—all this can be embraced under the heading: cognitive spiritual life.

Everyone, however, must acknowledge that under the surface of this cognitive life something else can be discerned; that in our everyday existence our life of soul gives evidence of many things that are not part of our conscious life. When we wake up in the morning, our life of soul is always strengthened and refreshed and newly born from sleep. During the unconsciousness of sleep, we have gained something that is outside the realm of conscious cognition, but comes from a region where our soul is active below the level of consciousness.

In waking life, too, we must admit that we are impelled by impulses, instincts, and forces that throw up their waves into our conscious life, while they work and have their being below it. We become aware that they work below consciousness when they rise above the surface that separates the conscious from the subconscious. And indeed, our moral life also makes us aware of a subconscious life of soul of this kind, for we can see how in the moral realm this or that ideal comes to birth. It takes only a little self-knowledge to realize that these ideals do rise up into our life of soul, but that we are far from always knowing how our great moral ideals are connected with the deepest questions of existence, or how they belong to the will of God, in which they must ultimately be grounded. We might indeed compare our life of soul in its totality with a deep ocean. The depths of this oceanic life of soul throw up waves to the surface, and those that break out into the realm of air, which we can compare with normal consciousness, are brought within the range of conscious cognition. All conscious life is rooted in a subconscious life of soul.

Fundamentally, the whole evolution of humanity can be understood only if this kind of subconscious life of soul is acknowledged. For what does the progress of spiritual life signify save that many things that have long dwelt down below take form for the first time when they are brought to surface level? So, it is, for example, when an inventive idea arises in the form of an impulse towards discovery. Subconscious psychic life, as real as our conscious life, must therefore be recognized as a second element in our life of soul.

If we place this subconscious psychic life in a realm that is at first unknown—but not unknowable—we must contrast it with a third element. This element is immediately apparent to external, exoteric observation, for if we turn our attention to the outer world through our senses, or approach it through our intellect or any form of mental activity, we come to know all sorts of things. But a more exact consideration of the whole realm of cognition compels us to admit that behind everything we can know about the world at large something else lies hidden: something that is certainly not unknowable, but in every epoch has to be described as something not yet known. And this not-yet-known, which lies below the surface of the known in the mineral, plant, and animal kingdoms, belongs as much to ourselves as it does to external nature. It belongs to us in so far as we absorb and elaborate in our physical organism the materials and forces of the outer world; and inasmuch as we have within us a portion of nature, we have also within us a portion of the unknown in nature. So, in the world wherein we live we must distinguish a triad: our conscious spiritual life; our subconscious life of soul below the threshold of consciousness; and what, as the unknown in nature and at the same time in the human being, lives in us as part of the great, unknown nature.

This triad emerges directly from a rational observation of the world. And if looking away from all dogmatic statements, from all philosophical or theosophical traditions, in so far as these are clothed in conceptual definitions or schemas, we may ask: How has the human mind always expressed the fact that this triad is present not only in the immediate environment, but in the whole world to which humans themselves belong? We must then reply: We give the name of spirit to all that can be known within the horizon of the conscious. We designate as the Son or the Logos[3] what works in the subconscious and throws up only its waves from down below. And to what belongs equally to the unknown in nature, and to the part of our own being which is of one kind with nature, the name of the principle of the Father has always been given, because it was felt to express the relation of the third principle to the other two.

Besides what has now been said concerning the spirit, the Son, and the principle of the Father, it can be taken for granted that other differentiations we have formerly made, and also the differentiations made in this or that philosophy, have their justifications. But we can say that the most widely accepted idea of this differentiation corresponds with the account of it given here.

Now let us ask: How can we characterize the transition from that which belongs to the spirit, and so plays directly into the conscious life of the soul, to the subconscious element that belongs to the principle of the Son? We shall best grasp this transition if we realize that into ordinary human consciousness there plays clearly and distinctly the element we designate as will, in contrast to the elements of ideation and feeling. If we rightly interpret the Bible saying, 'The Spirit is willing, but the flesh is weak' [Matthew 26:41], it indicates that everything grasped by consciousness lies in the realm of the spirit, whereas by 'the flesh' is meant everything that lies more in the subconscious. As to the nature of the will, we need only think of what plays up as waves from the depths of the ocean of the life of the soul and enters into our consciousness only when we form concepts of it.

Only when we transform into concepts and ideas the dark impelling forces that are rooted in the elemental part of the soul—only then do they enter the realm of the spirit; otherwise they remain in the realm of the principle of the Son. And since the will plays through our feelings into the life of ideas, we see quite clearly the breaking out into the conscious of the waves from the subconscious ocean. In our threefold life of soul, we have two elements, ideation and feeling, which belong to conscious life, but feeling descends directly into the realm of the will, and the nearer we come to the impulses of will, the further we descend into the subconscious, the dark realms into which we sink completely when consciousness is engulfed in deep, dreamless sleep.

The genius of language is often much further along than the conscious human spirit, and thus it signifies things in the right manner that would probably be quite falsely designated if human beings could entirely master language with consciousness. Thus for example certain feelings are expressed in language so that already in the word the relationship of feeling to will is brought to expression, so that we cannot at all mean an impulse of will, but rather only a content of feeling, and yet we use the word 'will' in language. This is because the genius of language, in certain feelings that lie more deeply, and about which one no longer gives precise account, uses the word 'will'. That is for example the case when we speak of things being 'contrary to our will' [*Widerwillen*]. Then one does not at all need to have the impetus to do this or that; it is not at all necessary for the transition to the will to be made. Then relationships of feeling are expressed that lie deeper, about which we no longer give account, in the realm of the will in the unconscious life of soul. Because it is this way, that the element of will descends into the realm of the unconscious life of the soul, we must take note that this realm of will stands in an entirely different relationship to the humans and their individual, personal being from the realm of cognition, the realm of the Spirit. And then when we use our words to distinguish Spirit and the Son then we can say that we can awaken in ourselves the sense that human beings must stand in a different relationship to the Spirit from the Son. How can this be understood?

Even in exoteric life, it is quite easy to understand. Certainly, the realm of cognition has given rise to all kinds of debate, but if people would only come to understand one another concerning the concepts and ideas they formulate for themselves, controversy over questions of cognition would gradually cease. I have often emphasized that we no longer dispute over mathematics, because we have raised mathematics entirely into consciousness. The things we dispute about are those not yet raised into consciousness: we still allow our subconscious impulses, instincts, and passions to play into them. So, we see that in the realm of cognition we have to do with something more universally human than anything to be found in the subconscious realm. When we meet other people and enter into the most varied relationships with them, it is in the realm of conscious spiritual life that understanding should be possible. And a mark of a healthy life of soul is that it will always wish and hope to reach an understanding with the other person concerning things that belong to conscious spiritual life. It will be unhealthy for the soul if that hope is lost.

On the other hand, we must recognize the element of will, and everything in another person's subconscious, as something which should on no account be intruded upon; it must be regarded as their innermost sanctuary. We need consider only how unpleasant to a healthy life of soul is the feeling that the will of another is being placed under compulsion. It is not only aesthetically, but morally unpleasant to see the conscious psyche of anyone eliminated by hypnotism or any other powerful means; or to see the will power of one person working directly on the will of another. The only healthy way to gain influence over another person's will is through cognition. Cognition should be the means whereby one soul comes to an understanding with another. A person must first translate his wishes into a conceptual form; then they may influence another person's cognition, and they should touch his will only by this indirect route. Nothing else can be satisfactory in the highest, most ideal sense to a healthy life of soul. Every kind of forcible working of will upon will must evoke an unpleasant impression.

In other words, human nature strives, in so far as it is healthy, to develop in the realm of the spirit the life it has in common with others, and to cherish and respect the realm of the subconscious, in so far as it comes to expression in the human organism, as an inviolable sanctuary that should rest in the personality, the individuality, of each individual, and should not be approached save through the door of conscious cognition. So at least a modern consciousness, attuned to our epoch, must feel if it is to know itself to be healthy.

In later lectures, we shall see whether this was so in all periods of human evolution. What has been said today will help us to think clearly about what is outside us and what is within us, at least for our own period. This leads to the conclusion that fundamentally the realm of the Son—embracing everything that we designate as the Son or Logos—must be awakened in each individual as a quite personal concern; and that the realm of common life, where individuals may be influenced by one another, is the realm of the Spirit.

We see this expressed in the grandest, most significant way in the New Testament accounts of the attitude of Jesus Christ towards His first disciples and followers. From all that is told concerning the Christ-Event, we can gather that the followers who had hastened to Jesus during his lifetime were bewildered when His life ended with the Crucifixion; with that form of death which, in the land where the Christ-Event took its course, was regarded as the only possible expiation for the greatest crimes. And although this death on the cross did not affect everyone as it did Saul, who later became Paul, and as Saul had concluded that someone who suffered such a death could not be the Messiah, or the Christ—for the Crucifixion had made a milder impression on the disciples, one might say—yet it is obvious that the writers of the Gospels wished to give the impression that Jesus Christ, through His subjection to the shameful death on the Cross, had forfeited some of the effect He had had on the hearts of those around Him.

But something else is connected with this account. The influence that Jesus Christ had acquired—an influence we must characterize more exactly during these lectures—was restored to Him after the Resurrection. Whatever may be our present thoughts about the Resurrection, we shall have to discuss it here in the light of esoteric science; and then, if we simply go by the Gospel narratives, one thing will be clear: for those to whom Christ appeared after the Resurrection, He had become someone who was present in a quite special way, different entirely from His previous presence.

In speaking on the Gospel of St John, I have already pointed out how impossible it would have been for anyone who knew Jesus not to recognize Him after three days, or to confuse Him with someone else, if He had not appeared in an altered form. The Evangelists wish particularly to evoke the impression that the Christ appeared in this altered form. But they also wish to indicate something else. For the Christ to exert influence on human souls, a certain receptivity in those souls was necessary. And this receptivity had to be acted on not merely by an influence from the realm of the Spirit, but by the actual sight of the Being of Christ.

If we ask what this signifies, we must realize that when a person stands before us, his effect upon us goes beyond anything of which we are conscious. Whenever a human being or other being works upon us, unconscious elements affect our life of soul; they are produced by the others indirectly through consciousness, but they can produce them only if they stand before us in their reality. What Christ brought about from person to person after the so-called Resurrection was something that worked up from the unconscious psychic faculties of the disciples into their life of soul: an acquaintance with the Son. Hence the differences in the portrayal of the risen Christ; hence, too, the variations in the accounts, showing how the Christ appeared to one or other person, according to the disposition of the person concerned. Here we see the Being of Christ acting on the subconscious part of the souls of the disciples; hence, the appearances are quite individual, and we should not complain because they are not uniform.

If, however, the significance of the Christ for the world was to be His bringing to all of us something common to all of us, then not only this individual working of the Son had to proceed from the Christ, but the element of Spirit, which can encompass something that belongs to all of us, had to be renewed by Him. This is indicated by the statement that after the Christ had worked upon the human Logos-nature, He sent forth the Spirit in the form of the renewed or 'Holy Spirit'. Thus was created that element common to all of us that is characterized when we are told that the disciples, after they had received the Spirit, began to speak in the most diverse tongues. Here we are shown how the common element resides in the outpouring of the Holy Spirit. And something else is indicated: how different this outpouring of the Spirit from the simple imparting of the power of the Son is, for in the Acts of the Apostles we are told that certain persons to whom the Apostles came had already received the baptism according to John, and yet they had now to receive for the first time the Spirit, symbolically indicated by the laying on of hands. In the characterization of the Christ-Event, we are made very precisely aware of the difference between the working we have to designate as that of Christ, which acts upon the subconscious impulses of the soul and so must have a personal, inward character, and the spiritual element, which represents something common to all humanity.

It is this spiritual element that those who have named themselves 'Rosicrucians'[4] have sought to preserve most carefully, as far as human weakness permits. The Rosicrucians have always wished to adhere strictly to the rule that even in the highest regions of initiation, nothing must be worked upon except the spiritual element which, as common between individuals, is available in the evolution of humanity. The initiation of the Rosicrucians was an initiation of the Spirit. It was never an initiation of the will, for the human will was to be respected as a sanctuary in the innermost part of the soul. Hence individuals were led to those initiations which were to take them beyond the stage of Imagination, Inspiration, and Intuition,[5] but always so that they could recognize within themselves the response that the development of the spiritual element was to call forth. No influence was to be exerted on the will.

We must not mistake this attitude for one of indifference towards the will. The point is that by excluding all direct working upon the will, the purest spiritual influence was imparted indirectly through the Spirit. When we come to an understanding with another individual with regard to entering on the path of knowledge of the Spirit, light and warmth are radiated from the spiritual path, and they then enkindle the will, but always by the indirect path through the Spirit—never otherwise.

In Rosicrucianism, therefore, we can observe in the most eminent sense that impulse of Christianity which finds twofold expression: on the one hand in the element of the Son, in the working of Christ which goes down deeply into the subconscious; on the other, in the working of the Spirit, which embraces all that falls within the horizon of our consciousness. We must indeed bear the Christ in our will; but the way in which individuals should come to an understanding with each other in life concerning the Christ can be found only—in the Rosicrucian sense—through a conscious psychic life that penetrates ever more deeply into the esoteric.

In reaction against many other spiritual streams in Europe, the opposite way was taken by those who are usually called Jesuits. The radical, fundamental difference between what we justifiably call the Christian way of the spirit and the Jesuit way of the spirit, which gives a one-sided exaggeration to the principle of Jesus, is that the intention of the Jesuit way is to work directly, at all times, upon the will. The difference is clearly shown in the method by which the pupil of Jesuitism is educated. Jesuitism is not to be taken lightly, or merely exoterically, but also esoterically, for it is rooted in esotericism. It is not, however, rooted in the spiritual life that is poured out through the symbol of Pentecost, but rather it seeks to root itself directly in the Jesus-element of the Son, which means in the will; and thereby it exaggerates the elements of Jesus in the will.

This will be seen when we now inquire into the esoteric part of Jesuitism, its various spiritual exercises. How were these exercises arranged? The essential point is that every single pupil of Jesuitism goes through exercises which lead into the esoteric life, but into the will, and within the field of esotericism they hold the will in severe discipline; they 'break it in', one might say. And the significant fact is that this discipline of the will does not arise merely from the surface of life, but from something deeper, because the pupil has been led into the esoteric, but precisely in the way just indicated.

If now, leaving aside the exercises of prayer preparatory to all Jesuit exercises, we consider these esoteric exercises, at least in their chief points, we find that the pupil has first to call up a vivid imagination of Jesus Christ as the King of the Worlds—mark this carefully: an imagination! And no one would be received into the degrees of Jesuitism who had not gone through such exercises, and had not experienced in their soul the transformation that such psychic exercises means for the whole person. But this Imaginative presentation of Jesus Christ as King of the Worlds has to be preceded by something else. Pupils have to call up for themselves, in absolute solitude and seclusion, a picture of humans as they were created in the world, and how by falling into sin they incurred the possibility of the most terrible punishments. And it is strictly prescribed how one must picture such humans; how if they were left to themselves they would incur the utmost of torturing penalties. The rules are extraordinarily severe. With all other concepts or ideas excluded, this picture must live uninterruptedly within the soul of the future Jesuit, the picture of God-forsaken humans, humans exposed to the most fearful punishments, together with the feeling: 'That am I, since I have come into the world and have forsaken God, and have exposed myself to the possibility of the most fearful punishments'! This must call forth the fear of being forsaken by God, and detestation of humans as they are according to their own nature.

Then, in a further imagination, over against the picture of outcast, God-forsaken humans, must be set the picture of the God full of pity who then became Christ, and through His acts on Earth atones for what humans have brought about by forsaking the divine path. In contrast to the imagination of the God-forsaken human, there must arise that of the all-merciful, loving Being, Jesus Christ, to whom alone it is due that humans are not exposed to all possible punishments working upon their souls. And, just as vividly as a feeling of contempt for the forsaking of the divine path had first to become fixed in the soul of the Jesuit pupil, so must a feeling of humility and contrition now take hold of him in the presence of Christ.

When these two feelings have been called forth in the pupils, then for several weeks they have to practise severe exercises, picturing to themselves in imagination all details of the life of Jesus from his birth to the Crucifixion and Resurrection. And all that can arise in the soul emerges when the pupils live in rigorous seclusion and, except for necessary meals, let nothing else work upon their souls than the pictures that the Gospels give of the compassionate life of Jesus. But these pictures do not merely appear before him in thoughts and ideas; they must work upon his soul in vivid, living imaginations.

Only individuals who really know how the human soul is transformed through imaginations that work with full living power—only they know that under such conditions, the soul is in fact completely changed. Such imaginations, because they are concentrated in the most intense, one-sided way, first on sinful humanity, and secondly on the compassionate God, and then only on the pictures from the New Testament, evoke precisely, through the law of polarity, a strengthened Will. These pictures produce their effect directly, at first hand, for any reflection upon them must be dutifully excluded. It is solely a matter of holding before one's mind these imaginations, as they have just been described.

What then follows is this. In the further exercises, Jesus Christ—and now we may no longer say Christ but exclusively Jesus—is represented as the universal King of the Worlds, and thereby the element of Jesus is exaggerated. Jesus is only an element of this world. Because Christ had to be incarnated in a human body, the purely spiritual took part in the physical world; but over against this participation stand the monumental and most significant words: 'My kingdom is not of this world' [John 18:36]! We can exaggerate the Jesus element by making Jesus into a king of this world, by making Him what He would have become if He had not resisted the tempter who wished to give Him 'all the kingdoms of the world and the glory thereof' [Matthew 4:9, Luke 4:6]. Then Jesus of Nazareth would have been a king who, unlike other kings who possess only a portion of the Earth, would have had the whole Earth under his sway. If we think of this king portrayed in this guise, his kingly power so increased that the whole Earth is his domain, then we should have the very picture that followed the other exercises through which the personal will of each Jesuit pupil had been sufficiently strengthened.

To prepare for this picture of 'King Jesus', this Ruler over all the kingdoms of the earth, the pupil had to form an imagination of Babylon and the plain around Babylon as a living picture, and, enthroned over Babylon, Lucifer with his banner. This picture had to be visualized with great exactitude, for it is a powerful imagination: King Lucifer, with his banner and his hosts of luciferic angels, seated amidst fire and dense smoke, as he sends out his angels to conquer the kingdoms of the Earth. And the whole danger that issues from the 'banner of Lucifer' must first of all be imagined by itself, without casting a glance upon Jesus Christ. The soul must be entirely engrossed in the imagination of the danger that issues from the banner of Lucifer. The soul must learn to feel that the greatest danger to the world's existence that could be conjured forth would be a victory for the banner of Lucifer. And when this picture has had its effect, the other imagination, 'The banner of Jesus', must take its place. The pupil must now visualize Jerusalem and the plain around Jerusalem; King Jesus with His hosts, how He sends out His hosts, how He conquers and drives off the hosts of Lucifer and makes Himself King of the whole Earth—the victory of the banner of Jesus over the banner of Lucifer!

These are the strength-giving imaginations for the will that are brought before the soul of Jesuit pupils. This is what completely changes their will; makes them such that in their will, because it is trained esoterically, they turn away from everything else and surrender absolutely to the idea: 'King Jesus must become the Ruler upon Earth, and we who belong to His army have to employ every means to make Him Ruler of the Earth. To this we pledge ourselves, we who belong to His host assembled on the plain of Jerusalem, against the host of Lucifer assembled on the plain of Babylon. And the greatest disgrace for a soldier of King Jesus is to forsake His banner.'

These ideas, gathered up into a single resolution of the will, can certainly give the will immense strength. But we must ask: What is it in the life of soul that has been directly attacked? The element that ought to be regarded as intrinsically holy, the element that ought not to be touched—the element of will. In so far as this Jesuit training lays hold of the element of will, while the idea of Jesus seizes the element of will completely, in so far is the concept of the dominion of Jesus exaggerated in the most dangerous way—dangerous because through it, the will becomes so strong that it can work directly upon the will of another. For where the will becomes so strong through imaginations, which means by esoteric methods, it acquires the capacity for working directly upon the will of another, and hence also along all the other esoteric paths to which such a will can have recourse.

Thus we see how in recent centuries we encounter these two movements, among many others: one has exaggerated the element of Jesus and sees in 'King Jesus' the sole ideal of Christianity, while the other looks solely at the element of Christ and carefully sets aside anything that could go beyond it. This second outlook has been much calumniated because it maintains that Christ has sent the Spirit, so that, indirectly through the Spirit, Christ can enter into human hearts and minds. In the development of civilization during the last few centuries, there is hardly a greater contrast than that between Jesuitism and Rosicrucianism, for Jesuitism contains nothing of what Rosicrucianism regards as the highest ideal concerning human worth and human dignity, while Rosicrucianism has always sought to guard itself from any influence which could in the remotest sense be called Jesuitical.

In this lecture I wished to show how even so lofty an element as the principle of Jesus can be exaggerated and then becomes dangerous, and how necessary it is to sink oneself into the depths of the Being of Christ if we wish to understand how the strength of Christianity must reside in esteeming, to the very highest degree, human dignity and human worth, and in strictly refraining from groping our clumsy way into the inmost human sanctuary. Rosicrucianism, even more than Christian mysticism, is attacked by the Jesuit element, because the Jesuits feel that true Christianity is being sought elsewhere than in the setting that offers merely 'King Jesus' in the leading role. But the imaginations here indicated, together with the prescribed exercises, have made the will so strong that even protests brought against it in the name of the Spirit can be defeated.

Lecture 2

KARLSRUHE, 6 OCTOBER 1911

Yesterday I tried to give you a picture of a form of initiation that ought not to exist, according to our valuation of human nature. This initiation, as we have seen it in Jesuitism, leads to the acquisition of certain esoteric faculties, but if we bring a cleansed and purified esoteric vision to bear upon these faculties, they cannot be considered good. It will now be my task to show that the Rosicrucian way is characterized by all that high regard for human nature that we recognize as equally our own. But we must first be clear on certain points.

From explanations given previously in various forms, we know that the Rosicrucian initiation is essentially a development of the Christian initiation, so that we can speak of it as a Christian-Rosicrucian initiation. In earlier courses of lectures, the purely Christian initiation, with its seven degrees, and the Rosicrucian initiation, also with seven degrees, have been compared. But now we must note that with regard to initiation, the principle of the progress of the human soul must be strictly maintained.

We know that the Rosicrucian initiation had its proper beginning somewhere about the thirteenth century. At that time, it was recognized by those individualities who have to guide the deeper destinies of human evolution as the right initiation for the more advanced human souls. This shows that the initiation of the Rose-Cross takes full account of the continuous progress of the human soul and must therefore pay particular attention to the fact that since the thirteenth century, the human soul has developed further. Souls which are to be led to initiation in our day can no longer adopt the standpoint of the thirteenth century. I want specially to point this out because in our time there is such a strong desire to label everything with some mark or other, with some catchword. From this bad habit, and not for any justified reason, our anthroposophical movement has been given a label that could lead gradually to something like a calamity.

It is true that within our movement the principle of Rosicrucianism can be found in all completeness, so that we can penetrate into the sources of Rosicrucianism. So it is that persons who by means of our anthroposophical training penetrate into these sources can properly call themselves Rosicrucians. But it must be emphasized just as strongly that outsiders have no right to designate as Rosicrucian the anthroposophical stream we represent, simply because our movement has been given—consciously or unconsciously—an entirely false label. We are no longer standing where the Rosicrucians stood in the thirteenth century and on through the following centuries, for we take into account the progress of the human soul. Hence the way indicated in my book, *How to Know Higher Worlds*,[6] as the way best adapted for gaining access to the higher worlds must not without further explanation be equated with what may be called the Rosicrucian way. Through our movement, we can penetrate into true Rosicrucianism, but our movement extends over a far wider domain, for it embraces the whole of theosophy; hence it should not be labelled Rosicrucian. Our movement must be described simply as the 'anthroposophy of today', the anthroposophical spiritual science of the twentieth century. Outsiders, particularly, will fall—more or less unconsciously—into some kind of misunderstanding if they describe our movement simply as Rosicrucian. But an outstanding achievement of Rosicrucianism since the dawn of modern spiritual life in the thirteenth century has been to establish a rule which must also be ours: the rule that all modern initiation in the deepest sense of the word must recognize and treasure the independence of the most holy element in our inner life, our centre of will, as indicated yesterday. The esoteric methods there described are designed to overcome and enslave the human will and to set it on a predetermined course; hence, a true esotericism will rigorously avoid them.

Before characterizing Rosicrucianism and present-day initiation, we must mention a decisively relevant point: the Rosicrucianism of the thirteenth, fourteenth, and even of the sixteenth and seventeenth centuries has again had to be modified for our time. The Rosicrucianism of those earlier centuries could not reckon with a spiritual element that has since entered into human evolution. Without this element today, we can no longer understand rightly the fundamentals of all those spiritual streams which arise from the ground of esotericism, including therefore any theosophical stream. For reasons we shall see more exactly in the course of these lectures, the teaching of reincarnation and karma, of repeated earthly lives, was excluded for many centuries from the external, exoteric teachings of Christianity. In the thirteenth century, the teaching of reincarnation and karma had not yet entered, in the most eminent sense, into the first stages of Rosicrucian initiation. One could go far, up to the fourth or fifth degree; one could go through what was called the Rosicrucian *studium*—the acquiring of Imagination, the reading of the esoteric script, the finding of the philosopher's stone—and one could experience something of what is called the mystical death. One could reach this stage and acquire exceptionally high esoteric knowledge, but without needing to achieve full clarity concerning the illuminating teachings of reincarnation and karma.

We must be clear at the present moment that human thinking progresses and now embraces forms of thought which, if only we follow them out logically—and this can easily be done on the external, exoteric level—lead unconditionally to a recognition of repeated earthly lives and so to the idea of karma. The words spoken through the lips of Strader in my second Rosicrucian drama,[7] *The Soul's Probation*, are absolutely true: namely that logical thinkers of today, if they are not to break with everything that the forms of thought of the last century have brought in, must come finally to a recognition of karma and reincarnation.

This is something deeply rooted in present-day spiritual life. Just because this knowledge has been slowly prepared and has these deep roots, it emerges little by little, as though independently, in the West. It is indeed remarkable how the necessity of recognizing repeated earthly lives has independently made itself felt—though certainly only by outstanding individual thinkers. We need only call attention to certain facts that are quite forgotten, intentionally or unintentionally, in our present-day literature. Take, for example, what comes out so wonderfully in Lessing's *Education of the Human Race*.[8] We see how Lessing, that great mind of the eighteenth century who at the zenith of his life gathered up his thoughts and wrote *The Education of the Human Race*, came as though by inspiration to the thought of repeated earthly lives. So does the idea of repeated earthly lives find its way, as though by inner necessity, into modern life. It has to be taken into consideration, but certainly not in the way that ideas of this kind are considered in our history books or in cultured circles nowadays. For in such cases, one takes recourse to the familiar formula that when a clever man grows old, excuses must be made for him. So it is said that although we may appreciate Lessing in his earlier works, we must allow that in later years, when he came to the idea of repeated earthly lives, he had become somewhat feeble.

In more recent times, the idea occurs sporadically. Droßbach,[9] a nineteenth-century psychologist, spoke of it in the only way then possible. Without esotericism, simply by observing nature, he tried in his own way as a psychologist to establish the idea of repeated earthly lives. Again, in the middle of the last century, a small society offered a prize for the best essay on the immortality of the soul. This was a remarkable occurrence in German spiritual life, and it is very little known. Moreover, the prize went to an essay by Widenmann,[10] which tried to prove the immortality of the soul in the sense of repeated earthly lives: certainly an imperfect attempt, but it could not be otherwise in the 'fifties of the last [eighteenth] century, when the necessary forms of thought had not developed far enough.

One could quote various other instances where the idea of repeated earthly lives springs up, as though in response to a postulate, a demand, of the nineteenth century. Hence in my little book, *Reincarnation and Karma*,[11] and also in my book, *Theosophy*,[12] the ideas of repeated Earth-lives and of karma could be worked out in relation to the thoughts of natural science, but with reference to human individuality in contrast to the animal species.

We must, however, be clear on one essential point: there is an immense difference between the way in which Westerners have come to this idea simply through thinking, and the way in which it figures in Buddhism, for instance. It is most interesting to see how Lessing came to the idea of repeated earthly lives. The result can of course be compared with the idea of repeated earthly lives in Buddhism, and even given the same name; but the way taken by Lessing is very different and is not generally known. How did he come to this idea?

We can see this quite clearly if we go through *The Education of the Human Race*. There is no doubt that human evolution gives evidence of progress in the strictest sense. Lessing argued that this progress is an education of humanity by divine providence. God gave into human hands a first elementary book, the Old Testament. Thereby a certain stage of evolution was achieved. When the human race had gone further, it was given the second elementary book, the New Testament. And then Lessing sees in our time something that goes beyond the New Testament: an independent feeling in the human soul for the true, the good, and the beautiful. This marks for him a third stage in the education of the human race. The thought of the education of humanity by the divine powers is worked out in a lofty style.

Lessing then asks himself: What is the one and only way to explain this progress? He cannot explain it otherwise than by allowing every soul to participate in each epoch of human evolution, if human progress is to have any meaning at all. For it would have no meaning if one soul lived only in the epoch of Old Testament civilization and another soul only in the epoch of the New Testament. It has meaning only if souls are taken through all the epochs of civilization and share in all the stages of human education. In other words, if the soul lives through repeated earthly lives, the progressive education of the human race makes good sense. So the idea of repeated earthly lives springs up in Lessing's mind as something that belongs to human destiny.

In a deeper sense, the following underlies his thinking. If a soul was incarnated at the time of the Old Testament, it took into itself whatever it could take; when it reappears at a later time, it carries the fruits of its previous life into the next life, and the fruits of that life into the one following, and so on. Thus the successive stages of evolution are interlocked. And whatever a soul achieves is achieved not only for itself, but for all humanity. Humanity is a great organism, and for Lessing reincarnation is necessary in order that the whole human race can progress. Thus it is historical evolution, the concern of humanity as a whole, that he takes as his starting point, and from there he is impelled to a recognition of reincarnation.

It is different if we trace out the same idea in Buddhism. There, people are concerned merely with themselves, with their own psyches. Individuals say to themselves: I am placed in the world of maya; desire brought me into it, and in the course of repeated incarnations I shall free myself as an individual soul from the necessity of living again on Earth. This applies to the single individual; all the attention is focused there. That is the great difference: whether a person looks at the process from within, as in Buddhism, or from without, as Lessing does. His gaze takes in the whole of human evolution. In both cases, the same idea emerges, but in the West the path to it is quite different. While the Buddhist limits himself to concern for the individual, Westerners are concerned with the whole of humanity. They feel themselves bound up with everyone as a single organism.

What is it that has taught Westerners the necessity of realizing, above all, that their concern is with all of humanity? The reason is that into the sphere of the heart, into their world of feeling, they have received the words of Jesus Christ concerning human solidarity: that it is beyond all nationality, beyond all racial characteristics, and that humanity is a great organism.

Hence it is interesting to see how Droßbach, although his thinking is still imperfect, because the scientific ideas of the first half of the nineteenth century had not yet produced the corresponding forms of thought, does not take the Buddhistic path, but rather a universal, cosmic one. Droßbach starts from the thoughts of natural science and observes the soul within the cosmic. He cannot think otherwise of the soul than as a seed which goes through an external form and reappears in other external forms, and so is reincarnated. With him, this idea turns into fantasy, for he thinks that the world itself must be transformed, whereas Lessing thought correctly of short periods of time. Widenmann, too, in his prize essay, brings the immortality of the soul into logical connection with the question of reincarnation.

So we see that these ideas appear quite sporadically, and it is right that in spite of faulty modes of thinking they should spring up in minds such as these, and in others also. The great evolutionary change that the human soul has undergone from the eighteenth to the twentieth century is such that everyone today who begins the study of world progress must above all assimilate those forms of thought which lead quite naturally to the acceptance and making credible of the ideas of reincarnation and karma. Between the thirteenth and eighteenth centuries, human thought was not sufficiently advanced to come by itself to a recognition of reincarnation. One has always to start from the stage reached by the most highly developed thought of the period. Today the starting point must be the form of thinking that, on the basis of natural science, regards the idea of repeated earthly lives as logical—which means hypothetically true. So do the times advance.

Without describing the Rosicrucian path in detail today, we will bring out what is essential both to it and to the way of knowledge at the present time. The characteristic of both in the abstract sense is that everyone who gives advice and guidance for initiation will value in the deepest sense the independence and inviolability of the sphere of the human will. Hence the essential point is that through a special kind of moral and spiritual culture, the ordinary interweaving of the physical body, etheric body, astral body, and ego must be changed.[13] And those directions which are given for the training of the moral feelings, as also those for concentration in thinking, for meditation—all strive in the end towards the one goal of loosening the spiritual texture which binds together the physical and etheric bodies, so that the etheric body does not remain so firmly fitted into the physical body as it naturally is. All the exercises strive after this lifting out, this loosening, of the etheric body. Thereby another union between the astral body and the etheric body is brought about. It is because in ordinary life the etheric body and the physical body are so firmly united that the astral body cannot normally feel or experience what is going on in the etheric body. Because the etheric body has its seat within the physical body, our astral body and our ego perceive only what the physical body brings them from the world and enables them to think of through the instrument of the brain. The etheric body is too deeply embedded in the physical body for it to be experienced in ordinary life as an independent entity, as an independent instrument of cognition, or as an instrument of feeling and willing.

The efforts in concentrated thinking, according to the instructions given nowadays—and given also by the Rosicrucians—the efforts in meditation, the cleansing of the moral feelings: all these finally produce the effect on the etheric body described in my book, *How to Know Higher Worlds*. As we use our eyes for seeing and our hands for grasping, so eventually we shall use the etheric body with its organs, but for looking into the spiritual, not the physical, world. The way in which we gather together and concentrate our inner life works for the independence of the etheric body.

It is necessary, however, that we should first permeate ourselves, at least tentatively, with the idea of karma. And we do this when we establish a certain moral equilibrium, a balance of the psychic forces of feeling. A person who cannot to a certain extent grasp the thought that 'in the long run I myself am to blame for my impulses', will not be able to make good progress. A certain equanimity and understanding with regard to karma, even if only a purely hypothetical understanding, are necessary as a starting point. Persons who never get away from their ego, who are so dependent upon their narrowly limited ways of feeling and perception that when things go wrong, they always blame others and never themselves; persons who are always filled with the idea that the world, or a part of their environment, is against them; people who never get beyond the results of applying ordinary thinking to whatever can be learnt from exoteric theosophy—such people will find progress particularly difficult. Hence it is well that in order to develop equanimity and calmness of soul, we should make ourselves familiar with the idea that when something does not succeed, particularly on the esoteric path, we must blame not others, but rather ourselves. This does most to help our progress. What helps least is always wanting to lay the blame on the world outside, or always wanting to change our training methods.

Our attitude in such matters is more important than it perhaps appears. It is better to test carefully, at all times, how little we have learnt, and to seek the fault in ourselves when progress is not made. It is a quite significant advance when we can make up our minds always to seek the fault in ourselves. Then we shall see that we are making progress not only in farther off things, but also in matters of external life. Those who have some experience in this field will always be able to testify that by accepting the blame for their own non-success, they have found something that makes precisely their external life easy and bearable. We shall get on much more easily with our environment when we can truly grasp this fact. We shall rise above much grumbling and hypochondria, above complaining and lamenting, and pursue our way more calmly. For we should reflect that in every true modern initiation, he who gives advice is under the strictest obligation not to penetrate into the innermost sanctuary of the soul. With regard to this innermost part of the soul, therefore, we have from the start to undertake something for ourselves, and we should not complain that we are perhaps not getting the right advice. The advice may be right and yet the results may not be satisfactory, if we fail to make the resolve I have indicated.

This equanimity, this calmness, once we have made our choice— and the choice should come only from a serious resolve—is a good ground for meditation concerned with thoughts and feelings. In everything founded on Rosicrucianism, an important point is that in meditation and concentration we are always directed not to dogma, but rather to the universally human. The deviation of which we spoke yesterday takes its start from subject matter that is first given to the aspirant for holding in his mind. But what if this subject matter had first to be tested by esoteric cognition? What if it were not in any way firmly established in advance? We must take our stand on Rosicrucian principles, one of which is that we are not in a position to decide about anything that is supported only by external documents, for example, the accounts of what took place as the Event of Golgotha. We must come to know these things first by the esoteric path; we may not assume them beforehand. Hence, we should start from the universally human, from that which can be justified by every soul.

A glance into the great world, marvelling at the revelation of light in the Sun, feeling that what our eyes see of light is only the external veil of the light, its external revelation, or, as is said in Christian esotericism, the glory of light, and then yielding oneself up to the thought that behind the external sensible light something quite different is hidden—all this is fundamentally human. To think of, to gaze on, the light spread out through infinite space, and then clearly to feel that in this infinitely extended element of the light something spiritual must live, something which weaves this web of light in space; to concentrate upon these thoughts, to live in them—here we have something universally human, presented not through dogma, but through universal feeling. Or again, to perceive the warmth of nature, to feel how through the universe, along with the warmth, something moves in which there is spirit. Then, out of certain relationships in our own organism with the feeling of love, to concentrate on the thought of how warmth can exist spiritually, how it lives pulsing through the world. Then, to sink oneself into what we can learn from intuitions given to us by modern esoteric teaching. Then to take counsel with those who know something in this realm as to concentrating in the right way upon universal thoughts, cosmic thoughts. And further, the ennobling, the cleansing, of moral perceptions, whereby we come to understand that what we feel to be moral is reality. So we rise above the prejudice that these moral feelings are something transitory; we realize that they live on, are stamped into us as moral realities. We learn to feel the responsibility of being placed in the world as conscious beings, together with our moral feelings.

All esoteric life is fundamentally directed towards universally human experiences of this kind.

I will now describe how far we can go through exercises that take their start in this way from human nature, if only we devote ourselves to a clear-sighted examination of our own human nature. From this beginning, we come to a loosening of the connection between the physical body and the etheric body, and to a new kind of knowledge. We give birth, as it were, to a second individual within ourselves, so that we are no longer so firmly connected with the physical body as before. And in the finest moments of life we feel the etheric and astral bodies as though enclosed in an external sheath, and thereby know ourselves to be free from the instrument of the physical body. That is what we attain. We shall then be led to see our physical body in its true being, and to recognize how it affects us when we are within it. We become aware of the whole working of the physical body upon us only when we have in a certain sense come out of it, like the snake that after casting its skin can look upon the skin from outside, though feeling it as a part of itself. Through the first stages of initiation, we learn in like manner to feel ourselves free from the physical body, and learn to recognize it. At this moment quite special feelings will steal over us, which may be described as follows. (There are so many different experiences along the path of initiation that it has not yet been possible to describe them all. In *How to Know Higher Worlds* you will find much on the subject, but there is a great deal more.)

The first experience, open to nearly everyone who turns from ordinary life to pursue the path of knowledge, leads us to say, in accordance with our feeling: 'This physical body as it is, as it appears to me, has not been formed by myself. Most certainly I have not made this physical body, through which I have been brought to be what I am in the world. Without this body, the ego, which I now regard as my great ideal, would not have arisen within me. I have become what I am only through having kept my physical body riveted upon me.'

At first, all this gives rise to something like resentment, bitterness, against the cosmic powers. It is easy to say, 'I will not cherish this resentment.' But when there arises before us in melancholy majesty a picture of what we have become through being bound up with the physical body, the effect is overwhelming. We feel something like bitter hatred for the cosmic powers on this account. But now our esoteric training must be so far advanced that we overcome this hatred and on a higher level can say with our whole being, with our individuality which has already come down into repeated incarnations, that we ourselves are responsible for what our physical body has become. When we have mastered the bitterness, we experience the perception, already often described: 'Now I know I am that very thing which appears there as the changed form of my physical being. That I am myself. But because my physical being was crushing me to death, I knew nothing of it.'

We stand here before the significant meeting with the Guardian of the Threshold.[14] But if we come so far, if through the strenuousness of our exercises we experience what has just been said, then from out of what is common to human nature we recognize that we are as we are in our present form as the result of preceding incarnations. But we also recognize that we can experience the deepest pain and must work our way out beyond this pain to the overcoming of our present existence. And for everyone who is sufficiently far advanced and has experienced these feelings in all their intensity, who has looked upon the Guardian of the Threshold, there arises of necessity an Imaginative picture, a picture not painted by arbitrariness, as in Jesuitism, from passages in the Bible, but a picture that each person experiences through having felt, in a general human sense, what they are. Through these experiences, we will quite naturally come to know the picture of the Divine Ideal Human Being, who like us lived in a physical body, and who like us in this physical body felt all that a physical body can bring about. The Temptation, and the picture of it as presented to us in the synoptic Gospels, the leading of Jesus Christ to the mountain, the promise of all external realities, the desire to cling to these outer realities, the temptation to remain attached to matter: in short, the temptation to remain with the Guardian of the Threshold and not to pass beyond him appears to us in the great Imaginative picture of Jesus Christ standing on the mountain, with the tempter beside Him—a picture that would have arisen before us even if we had never heard of the Gospels. And then we know that he who wrote the story of the Temptation depicted his own experience of seeing, in the spirit, Jesus Christ and the tempter. Then we know it is true in the Spirit that the writer of the Gospel has described something that we ourselves can experience even if we knew nothing of the Gospels. Thus we shall be led to a picture which is similar to the picture in the Gospels. We gain for ourselves what stands in the Gospels. Nothing is forced upon us; everything is drawn forth from the depths of our own nature. We proceed from the universally human and bring forth the Gospels afresh through our esoteric life. We feel ourselves at one with the writers of the Gospels.

Then there arises within us another feeling, a next step along the esoteric path. We feel how the tempter has grown into a powerful Being who is behind all the phenomena of the world. Yes, we learn indeed to know the tempter, but by degrees we learn in a certain way to value him. We learn to say: 'The world spread out before us, whether it be *maya* or something else, has its right to exist; it has revealed something to me.' Then comes a second feeling, a quite definite one for every person who fulfils the conditions of a Rosicrucian initiation. The feeling arises: 'We belong to the Spirit who lives in all things, and with whom we have to reckon. We cannot in the least comprehend the Spirit if we do not surrender ourselves to it.' Then fear comes over us. We experience fear such as every real knower must undergo; a feeling for the greatness of the cosmic spirit who pervades the world. We are in the presence of this greatness and we feel our own powerlessness. We feel also what we might have become in the course of the Earth's history, or in that of the cosmos. We feel our own impotent existence so far removed from divine existence. We feel fear in face of the ideal we must come to resemble, and fear of the magnitude of the effort that should lead us to that ideal. As through esotericism we must feel the whole magnitude of the effort, so must we feel this fear as a struggle we take upon ourselves, a wrestling with the Spirit of the Cosmos. When we feel our own littleness, and the necessary struggle laid upon us to attain our ideal, to become one with what works and weaves in the world—when we experience this with fear, then only may we lay fear aside and betake ourselves to the path, to the paths which lead us to our ideal.

And if we feel this completely and rightly, there comes before us yet another significant Imagination. If we had never read a Gospel, if humanity had never had such an external book, a spiritual picture would nevertheless rise before our clairvoyant sight. We are led out into the solitude that stands clearly before the inner eye, and we are brought before the picture of the Ideal Human Being who in a human body experienced all the immeasurable fears and anguish that we ourselves can taste in this moment. The picture of Christ in Gethsemane stands before us, as He experienced fear to an overwhelmingly intensified degree, the fear that we ourselves must feel on the path of initiation, the fear that wrung from His brow the bloody sweat. That is the picture we encounter at a certain point on our esoteric path, independently of all external documents. So we have, standing before us like two great pillars on the esoteric path, the story of the Temptation experienced spiritually, and the scene on the Mount of Olives experienced spiritually. And then we understand the words: Watch and pray, and live in prayer, so that you will never be tempted to remain standing at any one point, but will continually stride forward.

This means that first of all we experience the Gospel; we experience everything so that we could write it down just as the writers of the Gospels have described it. For we do not need to take these two pictures from the Gospel; we can take them out of our own inner consciousness; we can bring them forth out of the Holy of Holies of the soul. No teacher is needed to come and say: 'You must place before yourself in imagination the Temptation, and the scene on the Mount of Olives.' We need only bring before ourselves what can be developed in our consciousness through meditation, purification of our common human feelings, and so on. Then, without constraint from anyone, we call forth the Imaginations which are contained in the Gospels.

In the Jesuit spiritual movement, the pupil had the Gospels given to him first, and afterwards he experienced what the Gospels describe. The way we have indicated today shows that when we have taken the path of the spiritual life, we experience esoterically what is connected with our own life, and thereby can experience through ourselves the pictures, the Imaginations, of the Gospels.

Lecture 3

KARLSRUHE, 7 OCTOBER 1911

We must now turn our attention to the relation between ordinary religious consciousness and the knowledge that can be gained through higher clairvoyant powers concerning the higher worlds in general, and in particular—this is especially relevant to our theme—concerning the relation of Jesus Christ to these higher worlds.

It will be clear to you all that the evolution of Christianity so far has been such that most persons have not been able to attain through their own clairvoyant knowledge to the Mysteries of the Christ-Event. It must be granted that Christianity has entered into the hearts of countless human beings, and to a certain degree its essential nature has been recognized by countless souls; but these hearts and souls have not been able to look up to the higher worlds and so to receive clairvoyant vision of what really took place in human evolution through the Mystery of Golgotha[15] and everything connected with it. Hence the knowledge that can be gained through clairvoyant consciousness itself, or through a person having accepted on one or other ground the communications of the seer concerning the mysteries of Christianity, must be carefully distinguished from the religious inclination to Christ and the intellectual leanings towards Him of a person who knows nothing of clairvoyant investigation.

Now you will all agree that during the centuries since the Mystery of Golgotha, there have been individuals of all degrees of intellectual culture who have accepted the mysteries of Christianity in a deeply inward way, and from what has been said lately in various recent lectures you will have felt that this is quite natural, for—as has been emphasized again and again—it is only in the twentieth century that a renewal of the Christ-Event will take place, for this is when a certain general heightening of human powers of cognition begins. It brings with it the possibility that in the course of the next 3,000 years, and without special clairvoyant preparation, more and more persons will be able to attain a direct vision of Jesus Christ.

This has never happened before. Until now there have been only two—or later on today we may perhaps discover three—sources of knowledge concerning the Christian mysteries for persons who could not rise by training to clairvoyant observation. One source was the Gospels and all that comes from the communications in the Gospels, or in the traditions connected with them. The second source of knowledge arose because there have always been clairvoyant individuals who could see into the higher worlds, and through their own knowledge brought down the facts of the Christ-Event. Other persons followed these individuals, receiving from them a 'never-ending Gospel', which could continually come into the world through those who were clairvoyant. These two seem at first to be the only two sources in the evolution of Christian humanity up to the present time.

And, now from the twentieth century onwards, a third begins. It arises because for more and more people an extension, an enhancement, of their cognitional powers, not brought about through meditation, concentration and other exercises, will occur. As we have often said, more and more persons will be able to renew for themselves the experience of Paul on the road to Damascus. Hence, we can say of the ensuing period that it will provide a direct means of perceiving the significance and the Being of Jesus Christ.

Now the first question that will naturally occur to you is this: What is the essential difference between the clairvoyant vision of Christ that has always been possible as a result of the esoteric development described yesterday, and the vision of Christ which will come to people, without esoteric development, in the next 3,000 years, beginning from our twentieth century?

There is certainly an important difference. And it would be false to believe that what the seer through his clairvoyant development sees today in the higher worlds concerning the Christ-Event, and what has been seen clairvoyantly concerning the Christ-Event since the Mystery of Golgotha, is exactly the same as the vision which will come to an ever greater and greater number of people. These are two quite different things. As to how far they differ, we must ask clairvoyant research how it is that from the twentieth century onwards Jesus Christ will enter more and more into ordinary human consciousness. The reason is as follows.

Just as on the physical plane in Palestine, at the beginning of our era, an event occurred in which the most important part was taken by Christ Himself—an event which has its significance for the whole of humanity—so in the course of the twentieth century, towards the end of the twentieth century, a significant event will again take place, not in the physical world, but in the world we usually call the world of the etheric. And this event will have as fundamental a significance for the evolution of humanity as the event of Palestine had at the beginning of our era. Just as we must say that for Christ Himself the event of Golgotha had a significance that with this very event a God died, a God overcame death—we will speak later concerning the way this is to be understood; the Deed had not happened before and it is an accomplished fact which will not happen again—so an event of profound significance will take place in the etheric world. And the occurrence of this event, an event connected with the Christ Himself, will make it possible for people to learn to see the Christ, to look upon Him.

What is this event? It consists in the fact that a certain office in the cosmos, connected with the evolution of humanity in the twentieth century, passes over in a heightened form to the Christ. Esoteric, clairvoyant research tells us that in our epoch Christ becomes the Lord of Karma for human evolution. This event marks the beginning of something that we find intimated also in the New Testament: He will come again to separate, or to bring about the crisis for, the living and the dead. Only, according to esoteric research, this is not to be understood as though it were a single event for all time that takes place on the physical plane. It is connected with the whole future evolution of humanity. And whereas Christianity and Christian evolution were hitherto a kind of preparation, we now have the significant fact that Christ becomes the Lord of Karma, so that in the future it will rest with Him to decide what our karmic account is, how our credit and debit in life are related.

This has been common knowledge in Western esotericism for many centuries, and is denied by no esotericist who knows these things. But recently it has been verified again with the utmost care, by every means available to esoteric research. We will now enter more exactly into these matters.

Ask all those who know something of the truth about these things, and you will find everywhere one fact confirmed, but a fact which only at this present stage in the development of our movement could be made known. Everything which can make our souls receptive to such a fact had first to be gathered together. You can find in esoteric literature information concerning these matters if you wish to search for it. However, I shall take no account of the literature; I shall only bring forward the corresponding facts.

When certain conditions are described, including those I have dealt with myself, a picture has to be given of the world we enter on passing through the gate of death. Now there are a great many individuals, especially those who have gone through the development of Western civilization—these things are not the same for all peoples—who experience quite a definite event in the moment following the separation of the etheric body after death. We know that on passing through the gate of death, we separate ourselves from the physical body. The individual is at first still connected for a time with their etheric body, but afterwards they separate their astral body and also their ego from the etheric body. We know that they take with them an extract of their etheric body; we know also that the main part of the etheric body goes another way; generally it becomes part of the cosmic ether, either dissolving completely—this happens only under imperfect conditions—or continuing to work on as an enduring, active form. When the individual has stripped off their etheric body, they pass over into the *Kamaloka*[16] region for the period of purification in the world of soul. Before this, however, they undergo a very special experience that has not previously been mentioned, because, as I said, the time was not ripe for it. Now, however, these things will be fully accepted by all who are qualified to judge them.

Before entering *Kamaloka*, individuals experience a meeting with a quite definite being who presents them with their karmic account. And this being, who stood there as a kind of bookkeeper for the karmic powers, had for many individuals the form of Moses. Hence the medieval formula which originated in Rosicrucianism: Moses presents us in the hour of death—the phrase is not quite accurate, but that is immaterial here—Moses presents us in the hour of our death with the record of our sins, and at the same time points to the 'stern law'. Thus individuals can recognize how they have departed from this stern law which they ought to have followed.

In the course of our time—and this is the significant point—this office passes over to Jesus Christ, and individuals will ever more and more meet Jesus Christ as his judge, their karmic judge. That is the super-sensible event. Just as on the physical plane, at the beginning of our era, the event of Palestine took place, so in our time the office of karmic judge passes over to Jesus Christ in the higher world next to our own. This event works into the physical world, on the physical plane, in such a way that individuals will develop towards it the feeling that by all their actions they will be causing something for which they will be accountable to the judgement of Christ. This feeling, now appearing quite naturally in the course of human development, will be transformed so that it permeates the soul with a light that little by little will shine out from the individual himself, and will illuminate the form of Christ in the etheric world. And the more this feeling is developed—a feeling that will have stronger significance than the abstract conscience—the more will the etheric form of Christ be visible in the coming centuries. We shall have to characterize this fact more exactly in the next few days, and we shall then see that an entirely new event has come to pass, an event which works into the Christ-development of humanity.[17]

With regard to the evolution of Christianity on the physical plane, let us now ask whether for the non-clairvoyant consciousness there was not also a third way, over against the two already given. Such a third way was in fact always there, for all Christian evolution. It had to be there. The objective evolution of humanity is not directed in accordance with human opinions, but in accordance with objective facts.

Concerning Jesus Christ, there have been many opinions in the course of the centuries, or the Councils and Church assemblies and theologians would not have disputed so much among themselves. In no period, perhaps, have so many people held various views regarding Christ as in our own. Facts, however, are not determined by human opinions, but by the forces actually present in human evolution. These facts could be recognized by many more people simply through noticing what the Gospels have to say, if people had the patience and perseverance to look at things really without prejudice, and if they were not too quick and biased in considering the objective facts. Most people, however, do not want to form a picture of Christ according to the facts, but rather one that suits their own likings and represents their own ideal. And it must be said that in a certain respect, theosophists of all shades of opinion do this very thing today. When, for example, certain highly developed individuals who have attained an advanced stage of human evolution are spoken of in theosophical literature as masters, or adepts, this is a truth that cannot be disputed by anyone who knows the facts. It applies to individuals who have had many incarnations; through exercises and holy life, they have pressed on in advance of humanity and have acquired powers that the rest of humanity will acquire only in the future.

It is natural and right that a student of theosophy who has acquired some knowledge concerning the masters, the adepts, should feel the highest respect for such lofty individuals. If we go on to contemplate so sublime a life as that of Buddha, we must agree that Buddha should be looked on as one of the highest adepts. And we shall then be able to gain through our minds and feelings an inward relationship to such a person.

Now because theosophists approach the figure of Jesus Christ on the ground of this theosophical knowledge and feeling, they will naturally feel a certain need—and a very comprehensible need—to connect with Jesus Christ the same concept that they have formed of a master, of an adept, perhaps of Buddha; and they may be impelled to say: 'Jesus of Nazareth must be thought of as a great adept!' This preconceived opinion would turn upside down any knowledge of the real nature of Christ. And it would be no more than a preconceived opinion; only a prejudice, although an understandable one. How shall someone who has won the deepest, most intimate relationship to Christ not place the bearer of the Being of Christ in the same rank as the master, the adept, or the Buddha? Why should he not? This must seem to us quite comprehensible. Perhaps to such a person it would seem like a depreciation of Jesus of Nazareth if we were not to do so. But by applying this concept to Jesus of Nazareth, we are led away from directing our thought according to the facts, at least as these facts have found their way to us through tradition. Anyone who examines without bias the traditional records—disregarding all opinions offered by Church Councils and Fathers and so on—will not fail to recognize one fact: Jesus of Nazareth cannot be called an adept.

Where in tradition do we find anything which allows us to apply to Jesus of Nazareth the concept of the adept as we have it in theosophical teaching? In the first periods of Christianity, one thing was emphasized: that Jesus of Nazareth was a man like any other, a weak man like any other. And those who uphold the saying, 'Jesus was truly man' understand most nearly who it was that came into the world. Thus if we pay proper heed to the tradition, no idea of 'adept' is to be found there. And if you remember all that has been said in past lectures concerning the development of Jesus of Nazareth—the history of the Jesus child in whom up to his twelfth year Zarathustra lived, and the history of the other Jesus child in whom Zarathustra then lived up to his thirtieth year—you will certainly say: Here we have to do with a special man, a man for whose existence the world's history, the world's evolution, made the greatest preparations, evident from the fact that two human bodies were formed, and in one of them up to the twelfth year, and in the other from the twelfth to the thirtieth year, the individuality of Zarathustra dwelt.

Since these two Jesus figures were such significant individualities, Jesus of Nazareth certainly stands high; but not in the same way as an adept does, for the adept goes forward continuously from incarnation to incarnation. And apart from this: in the thirtieth year, when the Christ enters into the body of Jesus of Nazareth, this very Jesus of Nazareth forsakes his body, and from the moment of the Baptism by John—even if we do not now speak of the Christ—we have to do with a human being who must be designated in the truest sense of the word as a 'mere man', save that he is the bearer of the Christ. But we must distinguish between the bearer of the Christ and the Christ Himself. Once the body which was to be the bearer of the Christ had been forsaken by Zarathustra, there dwelt in it no human individuality who had attained any especially high development. The stage of development shown by Jesus of Nazareth sprang from the fact that Zarathustra dwelt in him. As we know, however, this human nature was forsaken by Zarathustra. Thus it was that this human nature, as soon as the Christ had taken possession of it, brought against Him all that otherwise comes forth from human nature—the tempter. That is why the Christ could go through the extremities of despair and sorrow, as shown to us in the happenings on the Mount of Olives.

Anyone who leaves out of account these essential points cannot come to a real knowledge of the Being of the Christ. The Christ-bearer was truly a man—not an adept. Recognition of this fact will open for us a first glimpse into the whole nature of the events of Golgotha, the events of Palestine. If we were to look upon Jesus Christ simply as a high adept, we should have to place Him in a line with other adepts. Some people may perhaps tell us that we do not do this because from the very outset, owing to some preconceived idea, we want to place Jesus Christ beyond all other adepts, as a still higher adept. Those who might say this are not aware of what we have to impart as the results of esoteric research in our time.

The question is not in the very least whether the prestige of other adepts would be impaired. Within the worldview to which we must adhere according to the esoteric results of the present time, we know just as well as others that there existed as a contemporary of Jesus

Christ another significant individuality whom we regard as a true adept. And unless we go into exact details, it is even difficult for us to distinguish inwardly this human being from Jesus Christ, for he really appears quite like Him. When, for instance, we hear that this contemporary of Jesus Christ was announced before his birth by a heavenly vision, it reminds us of the Annunciation of the birth of Jesus, as told in the Gospels. When we hear that he was not designated merely as of human birth, but as a son of the Gods, this reminds us again of the beginning of the Gospels of Matthew and Luke. When we hear that the birth of this individuality took his mother by surprise, so that she was overwhelmed, we are reminded of the birth of Jesus of Nazareth, and of the events in Bethlehem, as told in the Gospels. When we hear that the individuality grew up and surprised all around him by his wise answers to the questions from the priests, it reminds us of the scene of the twelve-year-old Jesus in the Temple. When we are told that this individuality came to Rome and met there the funeral procession of a young girl, that the procession was brought to a halt and that he awakened the dead, we are reminded of an awakening from the dead in the Gospel of Luke. And if we wish to speak of miracles, numberless miracles are recorded in connection with this individuality, who was a contemporary of Jesus Christ. Indeed, the similarity goes so far that after the death of this individuality, he is said to have appeared to humans, as Jesus Christ appeared after His death to the disciples. And when from the Christian side all possible reasons are brought forward either to depreciate this being or to deny altogether his historical existence, this is no less ingenious than what is said against the historical existence of Jesus Christ Himself. The individuality in question is Apollonius of Tyana,[18] and we speak of him rightly as a truly high adept.

If we now ask about the essential difference between the life of Jesus Christ-Event and the life of Apollonius, we must be clear what the important point is in the life of Apollonius.

Apollonius of Tyana is an individuality who went through many incarnations; he won for himself high powers and reached a certain climax in his incarnation at the beginning of our era. Hence, the individual we are considering is he who lived in the body of

Apollonius of Tyana and had therein his earthly field of action. It is with him that we are concerned. Now we know that a human individuality takes part in the building up of his earthly body. Hence, we must say: the body of this individuality was built up by him to a certain form for his own particular use. This we cannot say of Jesus Christ. In the thirtieth year of Jesus of Nazareth, the Christ came into the physical body, etheric body, and astral body of Jesus; hence He had not himself built up this body from childhood. The relationship between the Christ and this body is quite different from that between Apollonius and his body. When in spirit we turn our gaze to Apollonius of Tyana, we say: 'It is a matter of this individuality, and this matter plays itself out as the life of Apollonius of Tyana.' If we want to represent in a diagram a course of life of this kind, we can do it like this:

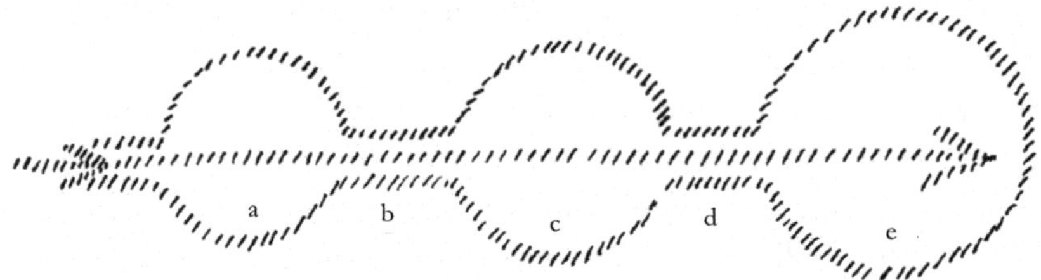

Let the continuous individuality be shown by the horizontal line; then we have in (a) a first incarnation, in (b) a life between death and a new birth, in (c) a second incarnation followed again by (d) a life between death and a new birth, then a third incarnation, (e) and so on. What passes through all these incarnations—the human individuality—is like a thread of human life, independent of the sheaths of the astral body, etheric body, and physical body, and also, between death and a new birth, independent of those parts of the etheric body and astral body which remain behind. Thus the thread of life is always separated from the external cosmos.

If we want to represent the nature of Christ's life, we must draw it otherwise. When we consider the preceding incarnations of Jesus of Nazareth, the life of Christ certainly develops in a certain way. But when we draw the thread of life, we have to show that in the thirtieth year of the life of Jesus of Nazareth the individuality forsakes this body, so that from now onwards we have only the sheaths of physical body, etheric body, and astral body.

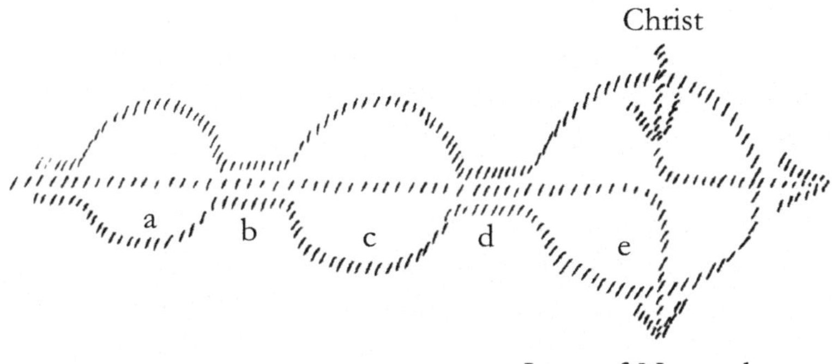

The forces which the individuality develops, however, are not in the external sheaths. They lie in the thread of life of the ego, which goes from incarnation to incarnation. Thus the forces that belonged to the individuality of Zarathustra, and were present in the body of Jesus of Nazareth, preparing that body, pass out with the individuality of Zarathustra. Hence, the sheaths which remain are a normal human organism, not the organism of an adept, but the organism of a simple man, a weak man. And now the objective event occurs: whereas in other cases the thread of life simply goes farther, as in (a) and (b), it now turns along a side path (c); for through the Baptism by John in the Jordan, the Being of Christ entered into the threefold organism. In this organism, the Being of Christ lived from the Baptism until the thirty-third year, until the Event of Golgotha, as we have often described.

Whose concern, then, is the life of Jesus Christ from the thirtieth to the thirty-third year? It is not the concern of the individuality who went from incarnation to incarnation, but rather of that individuality who entered into the body of Jesus of Nazareth from out of the cosmos; the concern of an Individuality, a Being who was never before connected with the Earth, who from out of the cosmos connected Himself with a human body. In this sense, the event that took place between the thirtieth and thirty-third years of the life of Jesus Christ, between the Baptism of John and the Mystery of Golgotha, are those of the Divine Being, Christ, and not of a man. Hence, this event was not a concern of the Earth, but rather a concern of the supra-sensible worlds, for it had nothing to do with a man. As a sign of this—that it had to do with no man—the human being who had dwelt in this body up to the thirtieth year forsook it.

These happenings have originally something to do with events that took place before such a thread of life as our human one had passed into a physical human organization. We must go back to the ancient Lemurian[19] time, into the age wherein human individualities, coming from divine heights, incarnated for the first time in earthly bodies; back to the event that is indicated for us in the Old Testament or Tanakh as the temptation by the serpent. This event is of a very remarkable kind. All humans suffer from its outcome as long as they are subject to incarnation. For if this event had not happened, the whole evolution of humanity on the Earth would have been different, and we would have passed in a much more perfect condition from incarnation to incarnation. Through this event, however, we became more closely entangled in matter, allegorically designated as the 'Fall of Man'. But it was the Fall that first called us to our present individuality; so that, as we go as an individuality from incarnation to incarnation, we are not responsible for the Fall. We know that the luciferic spirits were responsible for the Fall. Hence, we must say that before humans became human in the earthly sense, there occurred the divine, supra-sensible event by which a deeper entanglement in matter was laid upon us. Through this event, humans have indeed attained to the power of love and to freedom, but through it something was laid upon us that we could not lay upon ourselves by our own power. This becoming entangled in matter was not a human act, but a deed of the Gods, which happened before humans could cooperate in their own fate. It is something that the higher powers of progressive evolution arranged with the luciferic powers. We shall have to go into all these events and characterize them more exactly. Today we will place only the chief point before our minds.

What happened at that time needed a counterpoise. The pre-human event—the Fall—needed a counterpoise, but this again was a concern not of human beings, but of the Gods among themselves. And we shall see that this action had to take its course as deeply in matter as the first action had taken place above it. The God had to descend as deeply into matter as He had allowed humans to sink into matter.

Let this fact work upon you with its full weight; then you will understand that this incarnation of the Christ in Jesus of Nazareth was something that concerned Christ Himself. And what part were humans called upon to take in it? First of all, as spectators, to see how the God compensates for the Fall, how He provides the compensating act. It would not have been possible to do this within the personality of an adept, for an adept is one who by his own efforts has worked his way out of the Fall into matter. It was possible only in a personality who was truly human—who, as human, did not surpass other humans. This personality had surpassed them before he was thirty years of age—but then no longer. Through that which then took place, a divine event was accomplished in the evolution of humanity, just as had been done at the beginning of human evolution in the Lemurian time. And humans were partakers in an affair that had taken place among Gods; humans could look upon it, because the Gods had to make use of the world of the physical plane in order to let their transaction play itself out to the end. Hence, it is much better to say: 'Christ offered to the Gods the atonement which He could offer only in a physical human body', than to use any other verbal formula. Humans were spectators of a Divine occasion.

Through this atonement, something had happened for human nature. People simply experienced it in the course of their development. Thereby the third way was opened, besides the two already indicated.

Those who have gone deeply into the nature of Christianity have often pointed out these three ways. From among the large number of those who could be named, I will mention only two who have given eminent testimony to the fact that Christ—who from the twentieth century onwards will be seen through the more highly developed faculties—can be recognized, felt, experienced, through feelings which were not possible in the same form before the Event of Golgotha.

There is, for example, a man who in his whole cast of mind can be looked upon as a sharp opponent of what we have characterized as Jesuitism: Blaise Pascal,[20] a great figure in spiritual history, standing forth as one who has set aside all that had arisen to the detriment of the old Churches, but has also absorbed nothing of modern rationalism.[21] As always with great minds, he really remained alone with his thoughts. But what is the fundamental feature of his thinking at the beginning of the modern period? When we look into the matter, we see from the writings he left behind, particularly from his inspiring *Pensées*—a book easily accessible to anyone—how he perceived and felt what we humans must have become if the Christ-Event had not taken place in the world.

In the secrecy of his soul, Pascal set himself the question: What would have become of humans if Christ had not entered into human evolution? And he replied: We can feel that in our souls, humans approach two dangers. One danger is that we should recognize God as identical with our own being: knowledge of God in knowledge of humans. Where does this lead? When it arises so that we recognize ourselves as God, it leads to pride, haughtiness, arrogance; and we destroy our best powers because we harden them in haughtiness and pride. This is a knowledge of God that would always have been possible, even if no Christ had come, even if the Christ-Event had not worked as an impulse in the hearts of all humans. Human beings would always have been able to recognize God, but they would have become proud through this consciousness in their own breasts. Or there might be human beings who hide themselves from the knowledge of God, who want to know nothing about God. Their gaze falls on something else; it falls on human powerlessness, on human misery, and then of necessity there follows human despair. That would have been the other danger, the danger of those who had put away from them the knowledge of God.

Only these two ways, said Pascal, are possible: pride and arrogance, or despair. Then the Christ-Event entered into human evolution, and worked so that all humans received a power which not only enabled them to experience God, but the very God who had become like unto humans, who had lived with humans. That is the sole remedy for pride: when we turn our gaze upon the God who bowed to the Cross; when the soul looks to Christ bowing to death on the Cross. And that, too, is the only healing for despair. For this is not a humility that makes a human weak, but a humility that gives healing strength that transcends despair. As the mediator between pride and despair, there dawns in the human soul the Helper, the Saviour, as Pascal understood Him. This can be felt by every human being, even without clairvoyance. This is the preparation for the Christ who, from the twentieth century onwards, will be visible for everyone; who as the healer for pride and despair will be resurrected in every human breast, but earlier could not be felt in the same way.

The second witness I would summon from the long line of people who have this feeling, a feeling that every Christian can make his own, is one already mentioned in many other connections, Vladimir Solovyov.[22] Solovyov also points to two powers in human nature, between which the personal Christ must stand as a mediator. There is a duality, he says, for which the human soul longs: immortality, and wisdom or moral perfection; but neither belongs to human nature from the start. Human nature shares the characteristic of all natures, and nature leads not to immortality, but to death. In beautiful meditations, this great thinker of modern times works out how external science shows that death extends over everything. If we look at external nature, our knowledge replies, 'Death is!' But within us lives the longing for immortality. Why? Because of our longing for perfection. We have only to glance into the human soul to see that a longing for perfection lives in us. Just as truly, says Solovyov, as the red rose is endowed with red colour, so truly is the human soul endowed with the longing for perfection. But to strive after perfection without longing for immortality, he continues, is to give the lie to existence. It would be meaningless if the soul were to end with death, as all natural being ends. Yet all natural existence tells us, 'Death is!' Hence the human soul is under the necessity of going beyond natural existence and seeking the answer elsewhere.

Proceeding from this thought, Solovyov says: Look at the natural scientists, what answer do they give when they wish to teach the connection of the human soul with nature? A mechanical natural order, they say, prevails and humanity is part of it. And what do the philosophers answer? That the spiritual, meaning an empty abstract world of thought which pervades all the facts of nature, is to be recognized philosophically. Neither of these statements is an answer for individuals who are conscious of themselves, and ask from out of their consciousness, 'What is perfection?' If they are conscious that they have a longing for perfection, a longing for the life of truth; if they ask what power can satisfy this longing, there opens for them an outlook into a realm, the realm of Grace over and above nature, which at first stands before the soul as a riddle; and unless the answer to it can be found, the soul is constrained to regard itself as a falsehood. No philosophy, no natural science, can connect the realm of Grace with existence, for natural forces work mechanically, and the powers of thought have only as much reality as thoughts. But what is it that is able, with full reality, to unite the soul with nature? He who is the personal Christ working in the world. And only the living Christ, not one that is merely thought of, can give the answer. Anything that works merely in the soul leaves the soul alone, for the soul cannot of itself give birth to the kingdom of Grace. That which transcends nature, which like nature itself stands there as a real fact, the personal historic Christ—He it is who gives not an intellectual answer, but a real answer.

And now Solovyov comes to the most complete, the most fully spiritual answer that can be given at the end of the period now closing, before the doors open to that which has so often been intimated to you: the vision of Christ which will have its beginning in the twentieth century. In the light of these facts, a name can be given to the consciousness which Pascal and Solovyov have so memorably described: we can call it faith. So, too, it has been named by others.

With the concept of faith we can come from two directions into a strange conflict regarding the human soul. Go through the evolution of the concept of faith and see what the critics have said about it. Today, we are so far advanced that we say faith must be guided by knowledge, and a faith not supported by knowledge must be put aside. Faith must be dethroned, as it were, and replaced by knowledge. In the Middle Ages, the things of the higher worlds were apprehended by faith, and faith was held to be justified on its own account.

The fundamental principle of Protestantism, also, is that faith, alongside knowledge, is to be looked upon as justified. Faith is something that goes forth from the human soul, and alongside of it is the knowledge that ought to be common to all. It is interesting to see how Kant,[23] whom many consider a great philosopher, did not get beyond this concept of faith. His idea is that what we should attain concerning such matters as God, immortality, and so forth, ought to shine in from quite other regions, but only through a moral faith, not through knowledge.

The highest development of the concept of faith comes from Solovyov, who stands before the closed door as the most significant thinker of his time, pointing already to the modern world. For Solovyov knows a faith quite different from all previous concepts of it. Whither has the prevailing concept of faith led humanity? It has brought humanity to the atheistic, materialistic demand for mere knowledge of the external world, in line with Lutheran and Kantian ideas, or in the sense of the monistic[24] philosophy of the nineteenth century; to the demand for the knowledge which boasts of knowledge, and considers faith as something that the human soul had framed for itself out of its necessary weakness up to a certain time in the past. The concept of faith has finally come to this, because faith was regarded as merely subjective. In the preceding centuries, faith had been demanded as a necessity. In the nineteenth century, faith is attacked just because it finds itself in opposition to the universally valid knowledge that should stem from the human soul.

And then comes a philosopher who recognizes and prizes the concept faith in order to attain a relationship to Christ that had not previously been possible. He sees this faith, in so far as it relates to

Christ, as an act of necessity, of inner duty. For with Solovyov, the question is not, 'to believe or not to believe'; faith is for him a necessity in itself. His view is that we have a duty to believe in Christ, for otherwise we paralyze ourselves and give the lie to our existence. As the crystal form emerges in a mineral substance, so does faith arise in the human soul as something natural to itself. Hence the soul must say: 'If I recognize the truth, and not a lie about myself, then in my own soul I must realize faith. Faith is a duty laid upon me, but I cannot do otherwise than come to it through my own free act.' And therein Solovyov sees the distinctive mark of Christ's Deed, that faith is both a necessity and at the same time a morally free act. It is as though it were said to the soul: You can do nothing else. If you do not wish to extinguish the self within you, you must acquire faith for yourself; but it must be by your own free act! And, like Pascal, Solovyov brings what the soul experiences, in order not to feel itself a lie, into connection with the historic Jesus Christ as He entered into human evolution through the events in Palestine. Because of this, Solovyov says: If Christ had not entered into human evolution, so that He has to be thought of as the historic Christ; if He had not brought it about that the soul perceives the inwardly free act as much as the lawful necessity of faith, the human soul in our post-Christian times would feel itself duty-bound to extinguish itself and to say, not 'I am', but 'I am not'. That, according to this philosopher, would have been the course of evolution in post-Christian times: an inner consciousness would have permeated the human soul with the 'I am not'. As soon as the soul pulls itself together to the point of attributing real existence to itself, it cannot do otherwise than turn back to the historic Jesus Christ.

Here we have, for exoteric thought also, a step forward along the path of faith in establishing the third way. Through the message of the Gospels, a person not able to look into the spiritual world can come to recognition of Christ. Through what the consciousness of the seer can impart to him, he can likewise come to a recognition of the Christ. But there was also a third way, the way of self-knowledge, and as the witnesses cited, together with thousands and thousands of other human beings, can testify from their own experience, it leads to a recognition that self-knowledge in post-Christian time is impossible without placing Jesus Christ by the side of humanity, and a corresponding recognition that the soul must either deny itself, or, if it wills to affirm itself, it must at the same time affirm Jesus Christ.

Why this was not so in pre-Christian times will be shown in the next few days.

Lecture 4

KARLSRUHE, 8 OCTOBER 1911

WE can perhaps sum up the outcome of the last lecture in the following way. From the Mystery of Golgotha until the coming of the epoch at whose portal we now stand, an individual could attain by various exoteric means to an experience of the Christ-Impulse[25]—an experience preceding any actual initiation. One of these exoteric ways is through the Gospels, through the New Testament. The contents of the Gospels, when they are received into our souls and permitted to work upon us, can in fact bring about for each one of us an inner experience, and this inner experience may indeed be called the Christ-Experience. The second esoteric way was described as that of accepting what an esotericist—he who in a certain sense has been initiated—could make known from the spiritual worlds. By this way also, the individual who as yet was standing before the gate of initiation could come to the Christ-Event, not through the traditional Gospels, but through continuous revelations from the spiritual worlds.

Yesterday, too, we spoke of a third way, that of the inner deepening of heart and soul, and we pointed out that this way must arise in the soul from feelings; but with the proviso that if individuals feel within themselves only the divine spark, they may be driven to pride and arrogance. On the other hand, if they are not conscious of their connection with the divine, they can be driven to despair. We have seen how in fact the swaying between despair on the one hand, and pride and arrogance on the other, if at the same time individuals fix their gaze upon the events in Palestine, can lead on to the birth of the Christ-Event within them.

It was then pointed out that within the next 3,000 years, beginning from our own epoch, everything concerning the evolution of humanity will change. We also indicated the significant event that follows from the Mystery of Golgotha, but will be seen only in the supra-sensible worlds. We pointed out that the capacities of human beings will be enhanced, and that, from our own epoch onwards, a sufficiently large number of persons will grow up able to look on the Christ. What has hitherto had a justified place in the world as faith will be replaced by what may be called the vision of Christ.

Now it will be our task to show further how from the usual way of experiencing Christ, as an experience of the heart, the path opens out quite naturally to what may be called Christian initiation. In the next few days, we shall speak more exactly about the gradual building up of the Christian initiation, and we shall also need to characterize more closely the nature of the Christ-Event. Thus a picture of Christian initiation, and of the Christ-Event, from the Baptism by John to the consummation of the Mystery of Golgotha, should come before our souls.

If you keep this summary in mind, the following quite justified question may arise. What is the relation between external Christianity, Christian evolution as it appears in world history, and the Christ-Event itself? To everyone who stands consciously in the present, who has gone through no special psychic experience of a mystical kind, or has perhaps the preliminary stages of esotericism behind them, it must appear strange that in every human being a quite definite kind of psychic experience should be so dependent upon an historic fact—the events in Palestine, on Golgotha—and that previously for these human souls something was not possible which afterwards, through these events, became possible, namely the inner experience of Christ.

The leaders of the first Christians, and also the first Christians themselves, had a very distinct consciousness of these facts, and in preparation for the coming days it will be well to consider a little how these things appeared to their souls.

One can easily believe—and later this belief turned more and more into an orthodox, very one-sided view—that human beings of the pre-Christian times were radically different from those of the post-Christian period. That this view is one-sided you can gather from the words of Augustine[26]: 'What we now call the Christian religion existed already among the ancients, and was not lacking in the earliest days of the human race. When Christ appeared in the flesh, the true religion, which was already in existence, received the name of Christianity.' In the days of Augustine, it was well known that there was not so radical a difference between pre-Christian and post-Christian times as orthodoxy maintained.

Justin Martyr[27] also makes a quite remarkable statement in his writings. Justin, who is recognized by the Church as one of the Fathers and a martyr, enlarges upon the relation of Socrates[28] and Heraclitus[29] to Christ. With a certain simple clarity he sees in Christ what we set forth yesterday in the relation of Christ to Jesus of Nazareth, and he works out his idea of the Being of Christ accordingly. In his *Apologia* he says, in the context of his own time, something we can repeat today in the same words: Christ, or the Logos, was incarnated in the man, Jesus of Nazareth. Justin then asks: Was the Logos not present in eminent personalities of pre-Christian times? Was man in pre-Christian times quite unacquainted with the Logos? To this question Justin Martyr answers: No. Socrates and Heraclitus were also humans in whom the Logos lived. They did not possess the Logos completely; but through the Christ-Event it became possible for us to experience inwardly the Logos in its complete original form.

From such a passage by a recognized Father of the Church we can gather, first, that the early Christians were acquainted with something which, after having been, as Augustine says, 'always there', had entered into the evolution of the Earth in an enhanced form through the Mystery of Golgotha. Secondly, we have an answer from the earliest Christian centuries to the question we ourselves have raised today. Individuals such as Justin Martyr were still near to the Event of Golgotha, and they knew much more than we can about the nature of those who were but a few centuries removed from them, as Heraclitus and Socrates were. Justin held that in the time of Socrates, although such eminent individuals could experience the Logos themselves, they could not experience it fully in its most intense form. And that is important. As testimony from those early times, it indicates—if we look away from the Event of Golgotha—how it was felt that between the centuries before and after Christ there was something whereby pre-Christian individuals could be distinguished from post-Christian. It can be shown from numerous other historical instances that individuals in earlier centuries consciously said: 'Human nature has indeed changed; it has acquired another quality.' Someone living in the third century after Christ, looking back to individuals who had lived in the third century before Christ, could say that although in their own way they could penetrate deeply into the secrets of existence, yet something that could happen in individuals living after the time of Christ could not have happened previously. The message of John the Baptist, 'Change your outlook on the world, your idea of the world, for the times have become other than they were'—a statement confirmed by esoteric science—continued to be strongly and intensely felt.

We must grasp quite clearly that if we want to understand human evolution, we must give up the completely false idea that humanity has always been as it is today. For—apart from the fact that in the West no meaning could then be attached to the idea of reincarnation—tradition and esoteric science are at one in showing that in early times, human beings really possessed something that now exists only in the subconscious, namely a certain power of clairvoyance; that later they descended from this height of clairvoyance; and that the lowest point in this descending evolution, when those forces developed which obscured the old clairvoyant powers, lies in the time of the Mystery of Golgotha.

We know that in the material sphere a great quantity of fluid can be affected by the infusion of a very small quantity of a given substance. If you put a drop of some substance into a suitable fluid, it spreads through the fluid and colours the whole of it. In the material sphere, everyone understands this. But it is impossible to understand spiritual life if this principle is not understood in a spiritual sense. Our Earth is not merely the material body we see with our eyes; it has a spiritual sheath. As we ourselves have an etheric body and an astral body, so the Earth has such higher bodies. And just as a small quantity of substance spreads through a fluid, so that which rayed forth spiritually from the Act on Golgotha spread throughout the spiritual atmosphere of the Earth, permeated it, and it is still there. Something new has thus been imparted to our Earth. And since souls do not merely live everywhere enclosed by matter, but are like drops in the sea of the earthly-spiritual, even so are human beings embedded in the spiritual atmosphere of our Earth, which is permeated by the Christ-Impulse. That was not so before the Mystery of Golgotha, and it marks the great difference between pre-Christian and post-Christian life. If we cannot imagine such a thing happening in spiritual life, we are not yet far enough advanced to grasp Christianity truly as a mystical fact, the full meaning of which can be recognized and acknowledged only in the spiritual world.

Anyone who looks back over the disedifying disputes concerning the being and personality of Jesus of Nazareth, and the Being and Individuality of the Christ, will be able to feel everywhere in the gnostic[30] and mystical views of the early Christian centuries that the most advanced of those who were concerned to extend Christianity stood with reverent awe before this mystical fact. Even though the words and phrases of Christian teachers are often abstruse, we can see clearly that these teachers stand in reverent awe before all that came to pass for the world's evolution through Christianity. Again and again they declare that weak human understanding, and the feeble powers of human feeling and perception, are inadequate to express truly the immense significance and depth of all that happened through the Mystery of Golgotha. A powerlessness to give real expression to the highest truths that humanity has to grope for—this is something that passes like a magic breath through the first Christian teachings. The reading of such writings is a good lesson for anyone, even in our times. We can learn thereby to exercise a certain modesty with regard to the highest truths. If we have the necessary humility and modesty towards things that are more easily recognized at the portal of a new Christian epoch than they were in the first Christian centuries, we can say: Certainly it is now possible to know more than could be known then, but no one who ventures to speak of the mysteries of Christianity should remain unconscious of the fact that what we are able to say today concerning the deepest truths of human evolution will, in a comparatively short time, be imperfect again. And because we wish to come gradually to a deeper characterization of Christianity, we must pay special attention at this juncture to individuals' inward attitude towards the spiritual world, if they accept or wish to spread abroad the truths which since the nineteenth and the beginning of the twentieth century can stream into us.

Thus, even if we do not speak much about the concept of grace, we must make great use of it in practice. Every esotericist today clearly understands that this concept of grace must belong to his inner practice of life in a quite special degree. What does this mean?

It means that today investigations can be made concerning the deepest truths of Christianity, quite independently of the Gospels and of every tradition. Everything, however, which is connected with a certain thirst for knowledge, with a passion for gaining as quickly as possible a certain number of ideas, will lead, if not into complete error, quite certainly to a distortion of the truth. Individuals who say that since they are esoterically prepared, they must provide an explanation, for example of the Pauline Epistles or the Gospel of Matthew, showing how their content is to be understood—anyone who set out to do that and believed he could complete it within a fixed time would quite certainly deceive himself. In a human way, we can go deeply into these documents, but all that can be known about them cannot be made known today. For there is a golden saying which applies precisely to the esoteric investigator: 'Have patience and wait, until you no longer wish to grasp the fruits by your own efforts, but they come to you'.

Many individuals can approach the Pauline Epistles feeling themselves ready to understand this or that, because in the spiritual world it meets their opened eyes. Should they wish at the same time to understand another passage, perhaps quite close to it, they may not be able to do so. A curbing of this thirst for knowledge is necessary today. One should rather say to oneself: 'Grace has brought me to a certain number of truths. I will wait patiently until further truths flow to me.' Today there is really more need for a certain passive attitude towards these truths than there was perhaps twenty years ago. This attitude is necessary because our minds must first completely ripen in order to allow truths to enter into us in their right form. This is a practical lesson regarding investigation of the spiritual worlds, especially in their relation to the Christ-Event. It is fundamentally wrong when people think they can grasp at that which ought to stream towards them in a certain passive way. For we must be conscious that we can be what we ought to be only in so far as we are judged worthy by the spiritual powers to be this or that. And all that we can do by way of meditation, contemplation, and so forth, is really done only to open our eyes, not in order to seize the truths, but to let them come to us, for we may not run after them.

Those who through this inward passivity have developed feelings of whole-hearted devotion in the sense described—and with no other feelings can one enter the spiritual world—are ripe to understand the fact that we have placed in the forefront of our subject today: the fact that something like a drop of spiritual substance flowed from the Deed on Golgotha. In our time, souls are ripe for this understanding. If it were not so, we would have lacked many things that our modern period has brought forth. I need mention only one example: if the soul of Richard Wagner[31] had not ripened in a certain passive way; if concerning the Mystery of Golgotha he had not in some sense surmised the flowing forth of that which came drop by drop into the spiritual atmosphere of earthly humanity, we could not have had his *Parsifal*. We can discern this in the passages where he refers to the significance of the Blood of Christ. In our day, we can find many such minds that show how the spiritual substance which hovers in the atmosphere is grasped by the souls into which it penetrates.

Anthroposophy is here because many more souls now have the possibility of being able, without realizing it, to gather from the spiritual world the influences described above; but they need to have their difficulties lightened by an understanding of the spiritual world. In fact, no one whose heart is unripe enters into anthroposophy; no one who has not more or less of a sincere longing to know something of what has just been mentioned. It may indeed be that some are impelled into our movement by curiosity or the like, but those who come in with upright hearts feel the longing to be able to open their souls towards what is making ready for the future epoch of human evolution that begins in our time. People need anthroposophy today because their souls are becoming different from what they were a short time ago. Just as souls underwent a great change during the period in which the Event of Golgotha fell, so will they again experience a great change in this millennium and in the succeeding ones. The rise of our movement is connected with the fact that souls, even if they are not clearly conscious of it, have an obscure feeling that something of the kind is going on in our time.

For this reason, it became necessary, on the ground of anthroposophical development, that a certain explanation of the foundations of the Gospels should be undertaken. And if you can convince yourselves through honest inner feeling that there is something true in the Christ-Event, as it was described in the last lecture, you will find you can understand what has happened as regarding the explanation of the Gospels. You will understand that the anthroposophical interpretation of the Gospels differs radically from all previous interpretations. Anyone who takes up our printed cycles of lectures on the Gospels, or recalls them from memory, will see that everywhere a return has been made to true meanings, which can no longer be found simply by reading the present-day Gospel texts. From the existing translations, in fact, we can no longer reach what the Gospels wish to indicate. To a certain extent, as they exist today, they are no longer fully of use. What, then, has been done towards reaching an explanation of the Christ-Event, and what must be done?

To those who approach an understanding of the Christ-Event by the path of anthroposophy, it must be clear that these Gospels were written by individuals who could look upon the Christ-Event spiritually, with spiritual eyes. Hence, they had no wish to write an external biography, but instead followed the old writings on initiation. (This connection is shown in greater detail in my book, *Christianity as Mystical Fact*.)[32] They maintained that what had taken place in the depths of the Mysteries[33] had, in the Christ-Event, occurred on the plane of history through the divine ordering of human evolution. What had happened on a small scale within the Mysteries to the candidates for initiation was carried out by the Being we call the Christ on the great stage of world history, without the preparation that was necessary for human beings, and without the seclusion of the Mysteries. What had previously been seen only by the pupil of the Mysteries, in their innermost sanctuary, was enacted before all eyes. This again is something for which the first Christian teachers felt a reverential awe. When they considered what the Gospels ought to be, there arose in the genuine Christian teachers a feeling of their own unworthiness, of their inability to grasp the true kernel and meaning of the Gospels.

This fact is the cause of something else connected with the necessity of interpreting the Gospels as we do today in our movement. If you have followed the explanations of the Gospels given here, you will have noticed that the traditional books of the Gospels are not, in the first place, taken as the basis, for what they say is regarded as something altogether unreliable. Instead, through the reading of the Akashic Record,[34] we are taken back to the spiritual writing as it is given out by those who can themselves read spiritually. Only when we make explanatory reference to some passage do we take into account the sentence as it stands in the printed books. We then examine whether, or how far, it agrees with the form that can be recovered from the Akashic Record. The Gospels of Matthew, Mark, and Luke must be reconstructed in this way from the Akashic Record. Only a comparison of the tradition with the original form can show how this or that passage must be read. Every tradition that rests only upon the printed text is bound to go astray and fall into error. In the future, the Gospels must be not only explained, but first reconstructed in their true, original form. Then, when we examine what is there set forth, we will no longer be able to say that this may or may not be true, for where agreement is shown, it will be clear why for us it is only the reading in the Akashic Record that can guarantee the right text of the Gospels. And then the Gospels will again be evidence for the correctness of what stands written there. This can be shown in countless passages.

As an example, let us take the following. When at the condemnation of Jesus Christ He was asked whether He was a king sent from God, He replied: 'Thou sayest it!' Now anyone who thinks straightforwardly, and does not wish to explain the Gospels according to the professorial methods of the present day, must admit that with this answer of Jesus Christ no clear sense can be connected in terms either of feeling or of reason. From the side of feeling, we must ask why Jesus Christ speaks so indefinitely that no one can recognize what He means by saying 'Thou sayest it'. If He means 'Thou art right', there is no meaning in it, for the words of the interrogator are not a declaration but a question. How then can this be a meaningful answer? Or, from the side of reason, how can we think that He whom we imagine to be possessed of all-comprehending wisdom should choose such a form for His answer? When, however, these words are given as they stand in the Akashic Record, they have quite another sense. For in the Akashic Record it is not 'Thou sayest it', but, 'This, thou alone mayest give as answer', which means, when we understand it rightly, 'To thy question I should have to give an answer that no one may ever give with reference to himself: it can be given only by someone who stands opposite him. Whether the answer is true or not true, of that I cannot speak; the acknowledgement of this truth lies not with me, but with thee. Thou must say it; then and then only would it have a meaning.'

Now you may say: 'That may be true or may not be true.' As an abstract judgment that would certainly be correct. But if we look at the whole scene and ask ourselves, 'Can we understand it better when we take the version from the Akashic Record?', it will be apparent to everyone that this scene can be understood only in this way. We can say, too, that the last transcriber or translator of this passage did not understand it, because of its difficulty, and so wrote down something inaccurate. Anyone who knows how many things in the world are inexactly written down will not be surprised that here we have to do with an inaccurate version. Have we then no right, when a new epoch of humanity is beginning, to lead the Gospels back to their original form, which can be authenticated from the Akashic Record?

The whole thing comes out clearly—and this can be shown even from external history—if we consider in this connection the Gospel of St Matthew. The best that has been said about the origin of the Gospel of St Matthew may be read in the third volume of Blavatsky's[35] *Secret Doctrine*, a work which must be understood if we are to judge and value it correctly.

There was a certain Father of the Church, Jerome,[36] who wrote towards the end of the fourth century. From what he writes, we learn something that can be fully confirmed by esoteric research: the Gospel of Matthew was originally written in Hebrew. In the copy that Jerome had obtained, or, as we should perhaps say nowadays, in the edition he possessed, he had before him the original language of this Gospel, written in the Hebrew letters still in use, though its language was not the customary Hebrew of that time. Jerome's Bishop had given him the task of translating this version of the Gospel of St Matthew for his Christians. As a translator, Jerome behaved in a most singular way. In the first place, he thought it would be dangerous to translate this Gospel of Matthew as it was, because there were things in it which those who up to then had possessed it as their sacred writing wished to keep from the profane world. He thought that this Gospel, if it were translated complete, would cause destruction rather than edification. So he omitted the things which, according to his own and the ecclesiastical views of that period, might have a destructive effect, and replaced them by others. But we can learn still more from his writings, and this is the most suspect portion of the whole proceeding: Jerome knew that the Gospel of Matthew could be understood only by those who were initiated into certain secrets. He knew, too, that he was not one of those. In other words, he admitted that he did not understand this Gospel! Yet he translated it. Thus the Gospel of St Matthew lies before us today in the dress given to it by a man who did not understand it, but who became so accustomed to this version that he afterwards condemned as heresy anything asserted about this Gospel if it was not in accord with his own rendering. These are all absolute facts.

The next point of interest we must examine is the following. Why, in the very earliest days of Christianity, did those who held especially to the Gospel of Matthew communicate it only to such persons as were initiated into the secret meaning of certain things?

It is possible to understand why this was so only if we are somewhat familiar with the character of initiation. Such things have often been spoken of to you in one connection or another, and in particular you have heard that initiation, when by means of it individuals attain clairvoyant power, leads them to acquire knowledge of certain fundamental truths concerning the world. These fundamental truths are such that to the ordinary consciousness they at first appear absurd. All it can say about them is: That is a paradox. But there is more to it than that. If the highest truths, that is, those accessible to an initiate, were to become known to unprepared individuals—either if they were to guess them, which in a certain case might be possible, or if they were imparted to them when they were in an imperfect condition to receive them—then, even if they were the most elementary truths, they would be in the highest degree dangerous for them. Even if the purest, the highest, truth concerning the world were set before them, it would work destructively on them and on their surroundings.

For this reason, individuals today who are in possession of the highest truths know that it cannot be right merely to call someone to them and impart to them the highest mysteries of the world. The highest truths cannot be so imparted that a mouth simply pronounces them and an ear simply hears them. The way in which the highest truths are imparted is quite different. A person who wishes to become a pupil is slowly and gradually prepared, and this preparation takes place in such a way that the last conclusion, the imparting of the mystery, does not pass from mouth to ear. At a definite point of time, the pupils are so conditioned by preparation that the secret, the mystery, rises up before them. It does not need to be pronounced by a mouth, nor does it need to be heard by an ear; it must be born in the soul through what has passed between teacher and pupil.

There are no means of wringing from an initiate the last things of the Mysteries, for no one can be compelled—by any means available on the physical plane—to betray with his mouth anything of the higher Mysteries. So it is with the higher Mysteries. And if what should be born from the soul, as the higher Mysteries must be, were to be communicated to an unripe person through the mouth of another, it would be full of danger for this other person also. For the individual who had imparted the knowledge would be given completely into the power of the hearer for the rest of their incarnation. This, however, can never happen if the teacher simply prepares the pupil, and the pupil allows the truths to be born from out of his own soul.

When we know this, we understand that the original Gospel of Matthew could not be imparted without further preparation because humanity was not ripe to receive what was in it. For if Jerome, a Father of the Church, was himself not ripe for what it contained, then certainly others were not. Those who were originally in possession of these communications, the Ebionites,[37] did not impart them because, if received by unripe persons, they would have been so distorted that they must have led to what Jerome meant when he said that they would serve not for edification but for destruction. Now Jerome understood this; yet he allowed himself to impart in a certain way the Gospel of Matthew to the world. Hence, we must realize that this Gospel has been imparted in a certain way and has had a corresponding effect upon the world. Now if we look round and see what influence it has had, then in the light of esoteric truths we shall find many things comprehensible. Who, standing on the ground of esotericism, would care to say that all the persecutions and so on in the Christian world could be connected with the principles of Jesus Christ? Who, standing on the ground of esotericism, would not say that into external evolution there must have flowed something not in accordance with Christian evolution? In short, a great misunderstanding must here exist.

We mentioned yesterday how on the ground of Christianity we should speak, for example, of Apollonius of Tyana; we set before us his greatness and significance and even called him an adept. Yet when we go through early Christian literature, we find everywhere accusations against Apollonius, as though everything he did, everything he accomplished, had been achieved only under the influence of the devil. There we have something that must be called a distortion, not only a misunderstanding of the personality and acts of Apollonius of Tyana. This is only one example among many. We understand it only when we see that the Gospels have been handed down in a way that must lead to misunderstandings, and that today, on the ground of esotericism, our task is to go back to the true meaning of Christianity, concerning which the first teachers made many mistakes. It will then appear understandable that the next epoch of Christianity will be experienced differently from the earlier epochs. On the other hand, as already indicated, many things are stated here which can be said only because the listeners have taken part in the development of our anthroposophy during the last few years, or are rightly disposed to enter into it: persons in whose souls there is a corresponding feeling and mood that will allow what is imparted to work upon them. Because souls have gone through at least one period of teaching, one incarnation between the Mystery of Golgotha and the present time, the Gospels can be spoken of today without fear that harm may result.

Thus we have before us the singular fact that the Gospels had to be communicated, but that Christianity could be understood only in its most imperfect form. Hence the Gospels have been subject to a method of research which can no longer determine what is historical and what is not, so that finally everything is denied. In their original form, they must enter our hearts and souls, and this must give rise to a new power whereby the findings that will now be presented to humanity can be accepted by those who have been able worthily to feel the events from the Baptism of John to the Event of Golgotha.

An interpretation of the Christ-Event from the esoteric standpoint is thus a necessary preparation for the souls that in the near future are to experience something new, souls that are to look out on the world with new faculties. The old form of the Gospels will first receive its true value through our learning to read the Gospels with the aid of the Akashic Record; through this alone will their full value be restored. In particular, the true significance of the Event of Golgotha can be fully demonstrated only by esoteric research. Only when the original significance of this Event is understood through esoteric research will the results it can have for human souls be recognized. Our task in the next few days will be to throw light, as far as is possible in one short cycle of lectures, on everything the human soul can experience under the influence of the Christ-Impulse, so that we may come to a deeper knowledge than was previously possible of all that took place in Palestine and on Golgotha.

Lecture 5

KARLSRUHE, 9 OCTOBER 1911

I f you recall that in the course of our lectures we have come to look upon the Christ-Impulse as the most profound event in human evolution, you will doubtless agree that some exertion of our powers of mind and spirit is needed to understand its full meaning and scope of influence. Certainly in the widest circles we find the bad habit of saying that the highest things in the world must be comprehensible in the simplest terms. If what someone is constrained to say about the sources of existence appears complicated, people turn away from it because 'the truth must be simple'. In the last resort, it certainly is simple. But if at a certain stage we wish to learn to know the highest things, it is not hard to see that we must first clear the way to understanding them. And in order to enter into the full greatness, the full significance, of the Christ-Impulse, from a particular point of view, we must bring together many different matters.

We need only turn to the Pauline Epistles and we shall soon see that Paul, who sought specially to bring within range of human minds the supra-sensible nature of the Being of Christ, has drawn into the concept, the idea, of the Christ, the whole of human evolution, so to speak. If we let the Pauline Epistles work upon us, we have finally something that, through its extraordinary simplicity and through the deeply penetrating quality of its words and sentences, makes a most significant impression. But this is so only because Paul, through his own initiation, had worked his way up to that simplicity which is not the starting point of what is true, but the consequence, the goal. If we wish to penetrate into what Paul was able finally to express in wonderful, monumental, simple words concerning the Being of

Christ, we must come nearer to an understanding of human nature, for whose further development on Earth the Christ-Impulse came. Let us therefore consider what we already know concerning human nature, as shown through esoteric sight.

We divide human life into two parts: the period between birth and death, and the period that runs its course between death and a new birth. Let us first of all look at humans and their physical bodies. We know that esoteric sight sees them as fourfold beings, but as a fourfold being in a process of development. Esoteric sight sees the physical body, etheric body, astral body, and the ego. We know that in order to understand human evolution, we must learn the esoteric truth that this ego, of which we become aware in our feelings and perceptions when we simply look away from the external world and try to live within ourselves, proceeds from incarnation to incarnation. But we also know that this ego is, as it were, ensheathed—although 'ensheathed' is not a good expression, we can use it for the present—by three other members of human nature, the astral body, the etheric body, and the physical body.

Of the astral body, we know that in a certain respect it is the companion of the ego through the various incarnations. For though during *Kamaloka* much of the astral body must be shed, it remains as a kind of body of forces that holds together the moral, intellectual, and aesthetic progress we have stored up during an incarnation. Whatever constitutes true progress is maintained by the power of the astral body, is carried from one incarnation to another, and is linked, as it were, with the ego, which passes as the fundamentally eternal in us from incarnation to incarnation. Further, we know that from the etheric body, too, very much is cast off immediately after death, but an extract of this etheric body remains with us, an extract we take with us from one incarnation to another. In the first days directly after death, we have before us a kind of retrospective review, like a great tableau, of our life up to that time, and we take with us a concentrated etheric extract. The rest of the etheric body is dissolved into the general etheric world in one form or another, according to the development of the person concerned.

When, however, we look at the fourth member of the human being, the physical body, it seems at first as if the physical body simply disappears into the physical world. One might say that this can be externally demonstrated, for to external sight the physical body is brought in one way or another to dissolution. The question, however, which everyone who occupies himself with anthroposophy must put to himself is the following: Is not all that external physical cognition can tell us about the fate of our physical body perhaps only *maya*? The answer does not lie very far away for anyone who has begun to understand anthroposophy. When we say to ourselves, 'All that is offered by sense-appearance is *maya*, external illusion', how can we think it really true that the physical body, delivered over to the grave or to the fire, disappears without trace, however crudely the appearance may obtrude on his senses? Perhaps, behind the external *maya* there lies something much deeper.

Let us go further into this. You will realize that in order to understand the evolution of the Earth, we must know the earlier embodiments of our planet; we must study the Saturn, Sun, and Moon embodiments of the Earth.[38] We know that the Earth has gone through its 'incarnations' just as every human being has done. Our physical body was prepared in the course of human evolution from the Saturn period of the Earth. With regard to the ancient Saturn time, we cannot speak at all of etheric body, astral body, and ego in the sense of the present day. But the germ for the physical body was already sown, was embodied, during the Saturn evolution. During the Sun period of Earth's evolution, this germ was transformed, and then in this germ, in its altered form, the etheric was embodied. During the Moon period of the Earth, the physical body was again transformed, and in it, and at the same time in the etheric body, which also came forth in an altered form, the astral body was incorporated. During the Earth period, the ego was incorporated. And is it conceivable that the part of us which was embodied during the Saturn period, our physical body, simply decomposes or is burned up and disappears into the elements, after the most significant endeavours had been made by divine and spiritual beings through millions and millions of years, during the Saturn, Sun and Moon periods, in order to produce this physical body? If this were true, we should have before us the very remarkable fact that through three planetary stages, Saturn, Sun, Moon, a whole host of divine beings worked to produce a cosmic element, such as our physical body is, and that during the Earth period this cosmic element is destined to vanish every time a person dies. It would be a remarkable drama if *maya*—and external observation knows nothing else—were right. So now we ask: Can *maya* be right?

At first, it certainly seems as though esoteric knowledge declares *maya* to be correct, for, strangely enough, esoteric knowledge seems in this case to harmonize with *maya*. When we study the description given by spiritual knowledge of human development after death, we find that scarcely any notice is taken of the physical body. We are told that the physical body is thrown off, is given over to the elements of the Earth. We are told about the etheric body, the astral body, and the ego. The physical body is not further touched upon, and it seems as though the silence of spiritual knowledge were giving tacit assent to knowledge based on *maya*. So it seems, and in a certain way we are justified by anthroposophy in speaking thus, for everything further must be left to a deeper grounding in Christology. Concerning what goes beyond *maya* with regard to the physical body, we cannot speak at all correctly unless the Christ-Impulse and everything connected with it has first been sufficiently explained.

If we first of all observe how this physical body stood before consciousness at some decisive moment in the past, we shall reach a quite remarkable result. Let us enquire into three kinds of folk-consciousness, three different forms of human consciousness concerning all that is connected with our physical body, during decisive periods in human evolution. We will enquire first of all among the Greeks.

We know that the Greeks were that remarkable people who rose to their highest development in the fourth post-Atlantean epoch[39] of civilization. We know that this epoch began about the eighth century before our era, and ended in the thirteenth, fourteenth, and fifteenth centuries after the Event of Palestine. We can easily confirm what is said about this period from external information, traditions, and documents. The first dimly clear accounts concerning Greece hardly go back further than the sixth or seventh century before our era, although legendary accounts come down from still earlier times. We know that the greatness of the historical period of Greece has its source in the preceding period, the third post-Atlantean epoch. The inspired utterances of Homer reach back into the period preceding the fourth post-Atlantean epoch; and Aeschylus,[40] who lived so early that a number of his works have been lost, points back to the drama of the Mysteries, of which he offers us but an echo. The third post-Atlantean epoch[41] extends into the Greek age, but in that age the fourth epoch comes to full expression. The wonderful Greek culture is the purest expression of the fourth post-Atlantean epoch.

Now there falls upon our ear a remarkable saying from this land of Greece, a saying which permits us to see deeply into the soul of the man who felt himself truly a Greek, the saying of the hero [Achilles]: 'Better a beggar in the upper world, then a king in the land of shades'. Here is a saying which betrays the deep susceptibility of the Greek soul. One might say that everything preserved to us of Greek classical beauty and classical greatness, of the gradual formation of the human ideal in the external world—all this resounds to us from that saying.

Let us recall the wonderful training of the human body in Greek gymnastics and in the great games, which are only caricatured in these days by persons who understand nothing of what Greece really was. Every period has its own ideals, and we must keep this in mind if we want to understand how this development of the external physical body, as it stands there in its own form on the physical plane, was a peculiar privilege of the Greek spirit. So, too, was the creation of human ideals in plastic art, the enhancement of the human form in sculpture. And if we then look at the character of the Greek consciousness, as it held sway in a Pericles,[42] for example, when individuals had a feeling for the universally human, and yet could stand firmly on their own feet and feel like lords and kings in the domain of their city—when we let all this work upon us, then we must say that the real love of the Greeks was for the human form as it stood there before them on the physical plane, and that aesthetics, too, were turned to account in the development of this form. Where this human form was so well loved and understood, one could give oneself up to the thought: 'When what gives us this beautiful form on the physical plane is taken away from human nature, one cannot value the remainder as highly as the part destroyed by death'. This supreme love for the external form led unavoidably to a pessimistic view of what remains of humans when they have passed through the gate of death. And we can fully understand that the Greek soul, having looked with so great a love upon the outer form, felt sad when compelled to think: 'This form is taken away from the human individuality. The human individuality lives on without this form!' If for the moment one looks at it solely from the point of view of feeling, then we must say: We have in Greece that branch of the human race which most loved and valued the human body, and underwent the deepest sorrow when the body perished in death.

Now let us consider another consciousness that developed about the same time, the Buddhistic consciousness, which had passed over from Buddha to his followers. There we have almost the opposite of the Greek attitude. We need only remember one thing: the kernel of the four great truths of Buddha is that human individuality is drawn by longing, by desire, into the existence where it is enshrouded by an external form. Into what kind of existence? Into an existence described in Buddha's teaching as 'Birth is sorrow, sickness is sorrow, old age is sorrow, death is sorrow!' The underlying thought in this kernel of Buddhism is that by being enshrouded in an external bodily sheath, our individuality, which at birth comes down from divine, spiritual heights and returns to divine, spiritual heights at death, is exposed to the pain of existence, to the sorrow of existence. Only one way of human salvation is expressed in the four great and holy truths of Buddha: to become free from external existence, to throw off the external sheath. This means transforming the individuality so that it comes as soon as possible into a condition that will permit this casting off. We note that the active feeling here is the reverse of the feeling dominant among the Greeks. Just as strongly as the Greek loved and valued the external bodily sheath, and felt the sadness of casting it aside, just as little did the adherent of Buddhism value it, regarding it as something to be cast aside as quickly as possible. And linked with this attitude was the struggle to overcome the craving for existence, an existence enshrouded by a bodily sheath.

Let us go a little more deeply into these Buddhist thoughts. A kind of theoretical view meets us in Buddhism concerning successive human incarnations. It is not so much a question of what the individual thinks about the theory, as of what has penetrated into the consciousness of the adherents of Buddhism. I have often described this. I have said that we have perhaps no better opportunity of feeling what an adherent of Buddhism must have felt in regard to continual human incarnations, than by immersing ourselves in the traditional conversation between King Milinda and a Buddhist sage. 'Thou hast come in thy carriage: then reflect, O great King,' said the sage Nagasena,[43] 'that all thou hast in the carriage is nothing but the wheels, the shaft, the body of the carriage and the seat, and beyond these nothing else exists except a word which covers wheels, shaft, body of carriage, seat, and so on. Thus thou canst not speak of a special individuality of the carriage, but thou must clearly understand that "carriage" is an empty word if thou thinkest of anything else than its parts, its members.' And another simile was chosen by Nagasena for King Milinda. 'Consider the almond-fruit which grows on the tree, and reflect that out of another fruit a seed was taken and laid in the earth and has decayed; out of that seed the tree has grown, and the almond-fruit upon it. Canst thou say that the fruit on the tree has anything else in common other than name and external form with the fruit from which the seed was taken and laid in the earth, where it decayed?' Nagasena meant to say that a human has just as much in common with the human of his preceding incarnation as the almond-fruit on the tree has with the almond-fruit which, as seed, was laid in the earth. Anyone who believes that the human form which stands before us, and is wafted away by death, is anything else than name and form, believes something as false as he who thinks that in the carriage—in the name 'carriage'—something else is contained than the parts of the carriage—the wheels, shaft, and so on. From the preceding incarnation nothing of what we call our ego passes over into the new incarnation.

That is important! And we must repeatedly emphasize that it is not to the point how this or that person chooses to interpret this or that saying of the Buddha, but rather how Buddhism worked in the consciousness of the people, what it gave to their souls. And what it gave to their souls is indeed expressed with intense clearness and significance in this parable of King Milinda and the Buddhist sage. Of what we call the 'ego', and of which we say that it is first felt and perceived by individuals when they reflect upon their inner being, the Buddhists say that fundamentally it is something that flows into them, and belongs to *maya* as much as everything else that does not proceed from incarnation to incarnation.

I have elsewhere mentioned that if Christian sages were to be compared with Buddhist ones, they would have spoken differently to King Milinda. The Buddhist said to the King: 'Consider the carriage, wheels, shaft, and so on; they are parts of the carriage, and beyond these parts, "carriage" is only a name and form. With the word carriage thou hast named nothing real in the carriage. If thou wilt speak of what is real, thou must name the parts.' In the same case, the Christian sage would have said:

> O wise King Milinda, thou hast come in thy carriage; look at it! In it thou canst see only the wheels, the shaft, the body of the carriage and so on, but I ask thee now: Canst thou travel hither with the wheels only? Or with the shaft only, or with the seat only? Thou canst not travel hither on any of the separate parts. So far as they are parts they make the carriage, but on the parts thou canst not come hither. In order that the assembled parts can make the carriage, something else is necessary than their being merely parts. There must first be the quite definite thought of the carriage, for it is this that brings together wheels, shaft, and so on. And the thought of the carriage is something very necessary: thou canst indeed not see the thought, but thou must recognize it!

The Christian sage would then turn to us and say: 'Of the individual person thou canst see only the external body, the external acts, and the external psychic experiences; thou seest in the human being just as little of our ego as in the name carriage thou seest its separate parts. Something quite different is established within the parts, namely what enables thee to travel hither. So also in humans: within all their parts something quite different is established, namely that which constitutes the ego. The ego is something real that as a supra-sensible entity goes from one incarnation to another.'

How can we make a schema of the Buddhist teaching of reincarnation, so that it will represent the corresponding Buddhist theory?

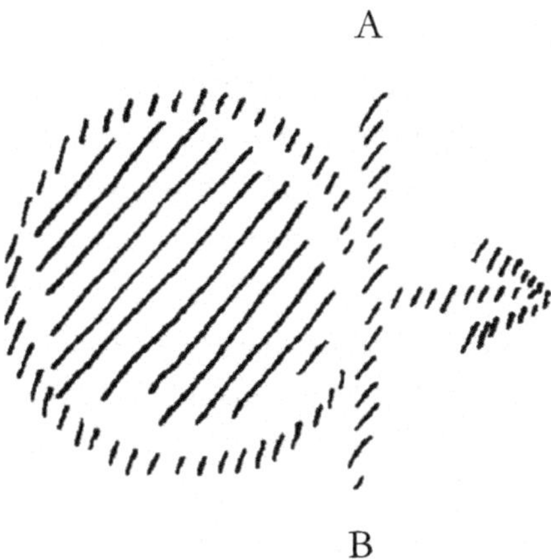

With the circle, we indicate humans between birth and death. The humans die. The time when they die is marked by the point where the circle touches the line *AB*. Now what remains of all that has been spellbound within his existence between birth and death?

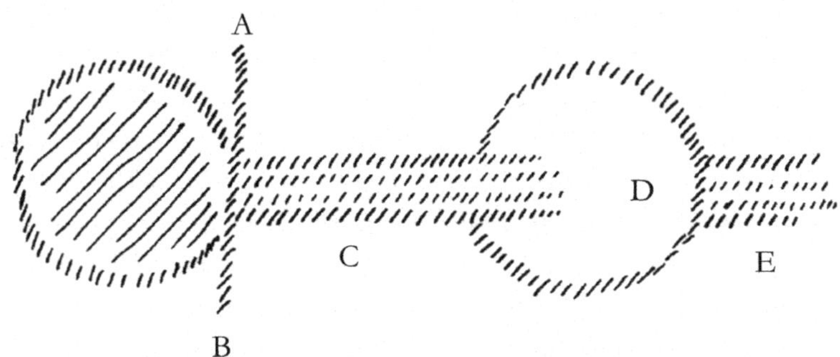

A summation of causes: the results of acts, of everything a human has done, good or bad, beautiful or ugly, clever or stupid. All that remains over in this way works on as a set of causes, and so forms the causal nucleus C for the next incarnation. Round this causal nucleus new body-sheaths D are woven for the next incarnation. These bodily sheaths go through new experiences, as did the bodily sheaths around the earlier causal nucleus. From these experiences, there remains again a causal nucleus E for the following incarnations. It can include experiences that have towered over into it from earlier incarnations, together with something quite independent that is added to it during the preceding incarnation. Hence, it serves as the causal nucleus for the next incarnation, and so on. This means that what goes through the incarnations consists of nothing but causes and effects. There is no continuing ego to connect the incarnations; nothing but causes and effects working over from one incarnation into the next. So when in this incarnation I call myself an 'ego', this is not because the same ego was there in the preceding incarnation. What I call my ego is only a *maya* of the present incarnation.

Anyone who really knows Buddhism must picture it in this way, and he must clearly understand that what we call the ego has no place in Buddhism. Now let us proceed to what we know through anthroposophical cognition.

How have we ever been able to develop our ego? Through the evolution of the Earth. Only in the course of the evolution of the Earth have we reached the stage of developing our egos. It was added to our physical body, etheric body, and astral body on the Earth. Now, if we remember all we had to say concerning the evolutionary phases of humans during the Saturn, Sun, and Moon periods, we know that during the Moon period, the human physical body had not yet acquired a quite definite form; it received this first on Earth. Hence, we speak of earthly existence as the epoch in which the Spirits of Form first took part, and metamorphosed the human physical body so that it has its present form. This forming of the human physical body was necessary if the ego were to find a place in humanity. The physical earthly body, set down on the physical Earth, provided the foundation for the dawn of the ego as we know it. If we keep this in mind, what follows will no longer seem incomprehensible.

With regard to the valuation of the ego among the Greeks, we saw that for them it was expressed externally in the human form. Let us now recall that Buddhism, according to its knowledge, sets out to overcome and cast off as quickly as possible the external form of the human physical body. Can we then wonder that in Buddhism we find no value attached to anything connected with this bodily form? It is the essence of Buddhism to value the external form of the physical body as little as it values the external form that the ego needs in order to come into being: indeed, all this is completely set aside. Buddhism lost the form of the ego through the way in which it undervalued the physical body.

Thus we see how these two spiritual currents are polarically opposed: the Greek current, which set the highest value on the external form of the physical body as the external form of the ego, and Buddhism, which requires that the external form of the physical body, with all craving after existence, shall be overcome as soon as possible, so that in its theory it has completely lost the ego.

Between these two opposite worldviews stands ancient Hebraism. Ancient Hebraism is far from thinking so poorly of the ego as Buddhism does. In Buddhism, it is heresy to recognize a continuous ego, going on from one incarnation to the next. But ancient Hebraism held very strongly to this so-called heresy, and it would never have entered the mind of an adherent of that religion to suppose that his personal divine spark, with which he connected his concept of the ego, is lost when he goes through the gate of death. If we want to make clear how the ancient Hebrews regarded the matter, we must say that they felt themselves connected in their inner being with the Godhead, intimately connected; they knew that through the finest threads of their life of soul, as it were, they were dependent on the Being of this Godhead.

With regard to the concept of the ego, the ancient Hebrews were quite different from the Buddhists, but in another respect, they were also very different from the Greeks. When we survey those ancient times as a whole, we find that the estimation of human personality, and hence that valuation of the external human form which was peculiar to the Greeks, is not present in ancient Hebraism. For the Greek it would have been absolute nonsense to say: 'Thou shalt not make to thyself any image of thy God.' They would not have understood if someone had said to them: 'Thou shalt not make to thyself any image of thy Zeus, or thy Apollo.' For they felt that the highest thing was the external form, and that the highest tribute someone could offer to the Gods was to clothe them with this human form that they themselves valued so much. Nothing would have seemed more absurd to him than the commandment: 'Thou shalt make to thyself no image of God'. As artists, the Greeks gave their human form to their gods. They thought of themselves as made in the likeness of the divine, and they carried out their contests, their wrestling, their gymnastics and so on, in order to become a real copy of the god.

But the ancient Hebrews had the commandment, 'Thou shalt make to thyself no image of God!' This was because they did not value the external form as the Greeks had done; they regarded it as unworthy in relation to the divine. The ancient Hebrews were as far removed on the one side from the disciples of Buddhism, who would have much preferred to cast off the human form entirely on passing through death, as they were on the other side from the Greeks. They were mindful of the fact that it was this form that gave expression to the commands, the laws, of the Divine Being, and they clearly understood that 'righteous individuals' handed down through the following generations what they, as righteous individuals, had gathered together. Not the extinguishing of the form, but the handing on of the form through the generations was what concerned the ancient Hebrews. Their point of view stood midway between that of the Buddhists, who had lost the value of the ego, and that of the Greeks, who saw in the form of the body the very highest, and felt sorrow when the bodily form had to disappear with death.

So these three views stand over against one another. And for a closer understanding of ancient Hebraism, we must make it clear that what the Hebrews valued as their egos was in a certain sense also the Divine Ego. The God lived on in humanity, lived within humans. In their union with the God, the Hebrews felt at the same time their own egos, and felt them to be coincident with the Divine Ego. The Divine Ego sustained them; the Divine Ego was active within them. The Greeks said: 'I value my ego so greatly that I look with horror on what will happen to it after death.' The Buddhists said: 'That which is the cause of the external human form must fall away from humans as soon as possible.' The Hebrews said: 'I am united with God; that is my fate, and as long as I am united with Him, I bear my fate. I know nothing else than the identification of my ego with the Divine Ego.'

This old, Judaic mode of thought, standing midway between Greek thought and Buddhism, does not involve, as Greek thought does from the outset, a predisposition to tragedy in face of the phenomenon of death, but a tragic feeling is indirectly present in it. It is truly Greek for the hero to say: 'Better a beggar in the upper world'—i.e. with the human bodily form—'than a king in the realm of shades', but a Hebrew could not have said it without something more. For the Hebrews know that when in death their bodily form falls away, they remain united with God. They cannot fall into a tragic mood simply through the fact of death. Still, the predisposition to tragedy is present indirectly in ancient Hebraism, and is expressed in the most wonderfully dramatic story ever written in ancient times, the story of Job.

We see there how Job's ego feels bound up with his God, how it comes into conflict with his God, but differently from the way in which the Greek ego comes into conflict. We are shown how misfortune after misfortune falls upon Job, although he is conscious that he is a righteous man, and has done all he can to maintain the connection of his ego with the Divine Ego. And while it seems that his existence is blessed and ought to be blessed, a tragic fate breaks over him.

Job is not aware of any sin; he is conscious that he has acted as a righteous man must act towards his God. Word is brought to him that all his possessions have been destroyed, all his family slain. Then his external body, this divine form, is stricken with grievous disease. There he stands, the man who can consciously say to himself: 'Through the inward connection I feel with my God, I have striven to be righteous before my God. My fate, decreed to me by this God, has placed me in the world. It is the acts of this God which have fallen so heavily upon me.' And his wife stands there beside him, and calls upon him in strange words to deny his God. These words are handed down correctly. They are one of the sayings that correspond exactly with the Akashic Record: 'Renounce thy God, since thou hast to suffer so much, since He has brought these sufferings upon thee, and die!' What endless depth lies in these words: Lose the consciousness of the connection with thy God; then thou wilt fall out of the Divine connection, like a leaf from the tree, and thy God can no longer punish thee! But loss of the connection with God is at the same time death! For as long as the ego feels itself connected with God, death cannot touch it. The ego must first tear itself away from connection with God; then only can death touch it.

According to outward appearance, everything is against righteous Job; his wife sees his suffering and advises him to renounce God and die; his friends come and say: 'You must have done this or that, for God never punishes a righteous man.' But he is aware, as far as his personal consciousness is concerned, that he has done nothing unrighteous. Through the events he encounters in the external world, he stands before an immense tragedy: the tragedy of not being able to understand human existence, of feeling himself bound up with God, and not understanding how what he is experiencing can have its source in God.

Let us think of all this lying with its full weight upon a human soul. Let us think of this soul breaking forth into the words that have come down to us from the traditional story of Job: 'I know that my Redeemer liveth! I know that one day I shall again be clothed with my bones, with my skin, and that I shall look upon God with whom I am united.' This consciousness of the indestructibility of the human individuality breaks forth from the soul of Job in spite of all the pain and suffering. So powerful is the consciousness of the ego as the inner content of the ancient Hebrew belief! But here we meet with something in the highest degree remarkable. 'I know that my Redeemer liveth,' says Job. 'I know that one day I shall again be covered with my skin, and that with mine eyes I shall behold the glory of my God.' Job brings into connection with the thought of the Redeemer the external body, skin and bones, eyes which see physically. Strange! Suddenly, in this consciousness that stands midway between Greek thought and Buddhism—this ancient Hebrew consciousness—we meet a consciousness of the significance of the physical bodily form in connection with the thought of the Redeemer, which then becomes the foundation, the basis, for the thought of Christ. And when we take the answer of Job's wife, still more light falls on everything Job says. 'Renounce thy God and die'. This signifies that he who does not renounce his God does not die. That is implied in these words.

But then, what does 'die' mean? To die means to throw off the physical body. External *maya* seems to say that the physical body passes over into the elements of the earth, and, so to speak, disappears. Thus in the answer of Job's wife there lies the following: 'Do what is necessary that thy physical body may disappear!' It could not mean anything else, or the words of Job that follow would make no sense. For we can understand anything only if we can understand the means whereby God has placed us in the world; if, that is, we can understand the significance of the physical body. And Job himself says, for this too lies in his words: 'O, I know full well that I need not do anything that would bring about the complete disappearance of my physical body, for that would be only an external appearance. There is a possibility that my body may be saved, because my Redeemer liveth. This I cannot express otherwise than in the words: My skin, my bones, will one day be recreated. With my eyes I shall behold the Glory of my God. I can lawfully keep my physical body, but for this I must have the consciousness that my Redeemer liveth.'

So in this story of Job there comes before us for the first time a connection between the form of the physical body, which the Buddhist would strip off, which sadly the Greek sees pass away, and the consciousness of the ego. We meet for the first time with something like a prospect of deliverance for what the host of Gods from Ancient Saturn, Sun, and Moon, down to the Earth itself, have brought forth as the form of the physical body. And if the form is to be preserved, if we are to say of it that what has been given us of bones, skin and sensory organs is to have an outcome, then we must add: 'I know that my Redeemer liveth.'

This is strange, someone might now say. Does it really follow from the story of Job that Christ awakens the dead and rescues the bodily form which the Greeks believed would disappear? And is there perhaps anything in the story to indicate that for the general evolution of humanity it is not right, in the full sense of the word, that the external bodily form should disappear completely? May it not be interwoven with the whole human evolutionary process? Has this connection a part to play in the future? Does it depend upon the Being of Christ?

These questions are set before us. And they mean that we shall have to widen in a certain connection what we have so far learnt from anthroposophy. We know that when we pass through the gate of death we retain at least the etheric body, but we strip off the physical body entirely; we see it delivered up to the elements. But its form, which has been worked upon through millions and millions of years—is that lost in nothingness, or is it in some way retained?

We will consider this question in the light of the explanations you have heard today, and tomorrow we will approach it by asking: How is the impulse given to human evolution by the Christ related to the significance of the external physical body—that body that throughout Earth evolution is consigned to the grave, the fire or the air, although the preservation of its form is necessary for the future of humanity?

By taking our start from what was said yesterday, we shall be able to come nearer to the fundamental questions of Christianity and to penetrate into its essential nature. We shall see that only by this means can we look into the heart of what the Christ-Impulse has become for the evolution of humanity, and what it will become in the future.

People are always insisting that the answers to the highest questions must not be complicated; the truth must be brought directly to each person in the simplest way. In support of this they argue, for example, that the Apostle John in his last years expressed the quintessence of Christianity in the maxim: 'Children, love one another'. No one, however, should conclude that a person who simply pronounces the words, 'Children, love one another', knows the essence of Christianity and of all truth for humanity. Before the Apostle John was entitled to pronounce these words, he had fulfilled various preconditions. We know it was at the end of a long life, in his ninety-fifth year, that he came to this utterance; only then, in that particular incarnation, had he earned the right to use such words. Indeed, he stands there as a witness that this saying, if it came from any chance individual, would not have the power it had from him. For he had achieved something else, also. Although the critics dispute it, he was the author of the Gospel of St John, the Apocalypse, and the Epistles of John. Throughout his life he had not always said, 'Children, love one another!' He had written a work which belongs to the most difficult human creations, the Apocalypse, and the Gospel of St John, which penetrates most intimately and deeply into the human soul. He had gained the right to pronounce such a saying only through a long life and through what he had accomplished. If anyone lives a life such as his, and does what he did, and then says, as he did, 'Children, love one another!', there are no grounds for objecting to it. We must, however, be quite clear that although some things can be compressed into a few words, so that these few words signify very much, the same few words may also say nothing. Many a person who pronounces a word of wisdom, which with appropriate preparation would perhaps signify something very deep, believes that by merely uttering it he has said a very great deal.

That recalls a story about a ruler who once visited a prison, and was brought before a resident of this prison, a thief. The ruler asked the thief why he had stolen, and the thief said, because he was hungry. Now, the question of how hunger is to be alleviated is one with which many people have occupied themselves. The ruler, however, said to the thief that he had never heard that one should steal when hungry; rather, one should eat! Without doubt, that is a correct answer. But one asks whether this answer is appropriate for the corresponding situation. For saying that the answer is true does not say anything about its appropriateness to the matter at hand.

The writer of the Apocalypse and of the Gospel of St John, at his advanced age, could speak the words 'Children, love one another!' out of the essence of Christianity, but the same words from the mouth of another person may be a mere phrase. We must gather matters for the understanding of Christianity from far afield, so that we may apply them to the simplest truths of daily life.

Yesterday we had to approach the question, so fateful for modern thought: What are we to make of the physical body in relation to the fourfold being of humanity?

We shall see how the points brought out yesterday in looking at the differing views of the Greeks, the ancient Hebrews, and the Buddhists will lead us further towards understanding the nature of Christianity. But if we are to learn more concerning the fate of the physical body, we must first take up a question which is actually central to the whole Christian worldview; a question which lies at the very core of Christianity when we learn something about the question of the destiny of the physical body. We are led to nothing less than to the essential question of Christianity: How it is with the Resurrection of Christ? Must we not assume that for the understanding of Christianity it is essential to reach an understanding of the Resurrection?

To see how important this is, we need only recall a passage in the first Epistle of Paul to the Corinthians, I Corinthians 15:13–20:

> But if there be no resurrection of the dead, then is Christ not risen: and if Christ be not risen, then is our preaching vain, and your faith is also vain. Yes, and we are found false witnesses of God; because we have testified of God that he raised up Christ: whom he raised not up, if so be that the dead rise not. For if the dead rise not, then is not Christ raised: and if Christ be not raised, your faith is vain; ye are set in your sins. Then they also which are fallen asleep in Christ are perished. If in this life only we have hope in Christ, we are of all men most miserable.
>
> But now is Christ risen from the dead, and become the first fruits of them that slept.

We must remember that Christianity, in so far as it has extended over the world, began with Paul. And if we are disposed to take these important words seriously, we cannot simply pass them over by saying that we must leave the question of the Resurrection unexplained. For what is it that Paul says? That the whole of Christianity has no justification, and the whole Christian Faith no meaning, if the Resurrection is not true! That is what is said by Paul, with whom Christianity as a fact of history had its starting point. And it means that anyone who is willing to give up the Resurrection must give up Christianity as Paul understood it.

And now let us pass over almost two thousand years and ask people of the present day how, according to the requirements of modern culture, they stand with regard to the question of the Resurrection. I shall not now take note of those who simply deny Jesus entirely; it is naturally quite easy for them to be clear regarding the question of the Resurrection. If Jesus never lived, one need not trouble about the Resurrection. Leaving such persons aside, we will turn to those who about the middle or in the last third of the nineteenth century had accepted the current ideas of our time—the time in which we are still living. We will ask them what they think, in conformity with the whole culture of our day, concerning the question of the Resurrection.

We will take a man who has gained great influence over the way of thinking of those who consider themselves best informed—David Friedrich Strauß.[44] In his work on Reimarus, a thinker of the eighteenth century, we read: 'The Resurrection of Jesus is really a shibboleth, concerning which not only the various conceptions of Christianity, but the various worldviews and stages of spiritual evolution, are at variance.' And in a Swiss journal almost of the same date we read: 'As soon as I can convince myself of the reality of the Resurrection of Christ, this absolute miracle, I tear down the modern conception of the world. This breach in what I believe to be the inviolable order of nature would make an irreparable rent in my system, in my whole world of thought.'

Let us ask how many persons of our present time who, according to the modern standpoint, must and do subscribe to these words, would say, 'If I were obliged to recognize the Resurrection as historical fact, I would tear down my whole system of thought, philosophical or otherwise.' Let us ask how should the Resurrection, as historical fact, fit in with our modern outlook on the world?

Let us recall something indicated in my first public lecture on this subject, that the Gospels are to be taken first and foremost as writings of initiation. The leading events depicted in the Gospels are fundamentally initiatory—events which had formerly taken place within the secret places of the temples of the Mysteries, when this or that person, who had been deemed worthy, was initiated by the hierophants. Such a person, after he had been prepared for a long time, went through a kind of death and a kind of resurrection. He had also to go through certain situations in life which reappear for us in the Gospels—in the story of the Temptation, the story set on the Mount of Olives, and other similar ones. That is why the accounts of ancient initiates, which do not aim to be biographies in the usual sense, show such resemblance to the Gospel stories of Jesus Christ. And when we read the history of the greatest initiates, of Apollonius of Tyana, or indeed even of Buddha or Zarathustra, or the life of Osiris or of Orpheus, it often seems that important characteristics of their lives are the same as those narrated of Jesus Christ in the Gospels. But although we must grant that we have to seek in the initiatory ceremonies of the old Mysteries for the prototypes of important events narrated in the Gospels, on the other hand we see palpably that the great teachings of the life of Jesus Christ are saturated throughout with individual details which are not intended as a mere repetition of initiatory ceremonies, but make it very plain that what is described is actual fact. Must we not say that we receive a remarkably factual impression when the following is pictured for us in the Gospel of John 20:1–17:

> The first day of the week cometh Mary Magdalene early, when it was yet dark, unto the sepulchre, and seeth the stone taken away from the sepulchre. Then she runneth, and cometh to Simon Peter, and to the other disciple, whom Jesus loved, and saith unto them, They have taken away the Lord out of the sepulchre, and we know not where they have laid him. Peter therefore went forth, and that other disciple, and came to the sepulchre. So they ran both together: and the other disciple did outrun Peter, and came first to the sepulchre. And he stooping down, and looking in, saw the linen clothes lying; yet went he not in. Then cometh Simon Peter following him, and went into the sepulchre, and seeth the linen clothes lie, and the napkin, that was about his head, not lying with the linen clothes, but wrapped together in a place by itself. Then went in also that other disciple, which came first to the sepulchre, and he saw, and believed. For as yet they knew not the scripture, that he must rise again from the dead. Then the disciples went away again unto their own home.
>
> But Mary stood without at the sepulchre weeping: and as she wept, she stooped down and looked into the sepulchre, and seeth two angels in white sitting, the one at the head, and the other at the feet, where the body of Jesus had lain. And they say unto her, Woman, why weepest thou? She saith unto them, Because they have taken away my Lord, and I know not where they have laid him. And when she had thus said, she turned herself back, and saw Jesus standing, and knew not that it was Jesus. Jesus saith unto her, Woman why weepest thou? She, supposing him to be the gardener, saith unto him, Sir, if thou have

> borne him hence, tell me where thou hast laid him, and I will take him
> away. Jesus saith unto her, Mary. She turned herself, and saith unto
> him, Rabbani; which is to say, Master. Jesus saith unto her, Touch me
> not; for I am not yet ascended to my Father: but go to my brethren,
> and say unto them, I ascend unto my Father, and to your Father; and
> to my God, and your God.

Here is a situation described in such detail that if we wish to picture it
in imagination there is hardly anything lacking—when, for example, it
is said that the one disciple runs faster than the other, or that the nap-
kin which had covered the head was laid aside in another place, and
so on. In every detail something is described which would have no
meaning if it did not refer to a fact. Attention was drawn on a former
occasion to one detail, that Mary did not recognize Jesus Christ, and
we asked how was it possible that after three days anyone could fail
to recognize in the same form a person previously known. Hence, we
had to note that Christ appeared to Mary in a changed form, or these
words would have no meaning.

Here, therefore, a distinction must be kept in mind. First, we
have to understand the Resurrection as a translation into historic
fact of the awakening that took place in the holy Mysteries of all
times, only with the difference that he who in the Mysteries raised
up the individual pupil was the hierophant; while the Gospels indicate that He who raised up Christ is the Being whom we designate
as the Father—that the Father Himself raised up the Christ. Here
we are shown that what had formerly been carried out on a small
scale in the depths of the Mysteries was now and once and for all
enacted for humanity by divine spirits, and that the Being who is
designated as the Father acted as hierophant in the awakening to life
of Jesus Christ. Thus we have here, enhanced to the highest degree,
something which formerly had taken place on a small scale in the
Mysteries.

That is the first point. The other is that, interwoven with matters which carry us back to the Mysteries, there are descriptions so
detailed that even today we can reconstruct from the Gospels the
situations even to their minute particulars, as we have just seen in
the passage read to you. But this passage includes one detail that

calls for particular attention. There must be a meaning in the words, 'For they did not as yet know the Scripture, that He must rise from the dead. Then the disciples went back to their homes.' Let us ask: Of what had the disciples been able so far to convince themselves? It is described as clearly as anything can be that the linen wrappings are there, but the body is not there, is no longer in the grave. The disciples had not been able to convince themselves of anything else, and they understood nothing else when they now went home. Otherwise the words have no meaning. The more deeply you enter into the text, the more you must say that the disciples who were standing by the grave were convinced that the linen wrappings were there, but that the body was no longer in the grave. They went home with the thought: 'Where has the body gone? Who has taken it out of the grave?'

And now, from the conviction that the body is not there, the Gospels lead us slowly to the events through which the disciples were finally convinced of the Resurrection. How were they convinced? Through the fact that, as the Gospels relate, Christ appeared to them by degrees, so that they could say, 'He is there!', and this went so far that Thomas, called the Doubter, could lay his finger in the stigma. In short, we can see from the Gospels that the disciples became convinced of the Resurrection through Christ having come to them after it as the Risen One. The proof for the disciples was that He was there. And if these disciples, who had gradually come to the conviction that Christ was alive, although He had died, had been asked what they actually believed, they would have said: 'We have proofs that Christ lives.' But they certainly would not have spoken as Paul spoke later, after he had gone through his experience on the road to Damascus.

Anyone who allows the Gospels and the Pauline Epistles to work upon him will notice the deep underlying difference between the fundamental tone of the Gospels as regards the understanding of the Resurrection, and the Pauline conception of it. Paul, indeed, draws a parallel between his conviction of the Resurrection and that of the Gospels, for in saying 'Christ is risen', he indicates that Christ, after He had been crucified, appeared as a living

Being to Cephas [Peter], to the Twelve, then to five hundred brethren at one time; and last of all to himself, Paul, as to one born out of due time, Christ had appeared from out of the fiery glory of the spiritual. Christ had appeared to the disciples also; Paul refers to that, and the events lived through with the Risen One were the same for Paul as they had been for the disciples. But what Paul immediately joins to these, as the outcome for him of the event of Damascus, is his wonderful and easily comprehensible theory of the Being of Christ.

From the event of Damascus onwards, what was the Being of Christ for Paul? The Being of Christ was for him the 'Second Adam'; and he immediately differentiates between the first Adam and the second Adam, the Christ. He calls the first Adam the progenitor of humans on Earth. But how? We do not have to go far in order to obtain the answer to this question. Paul calls him the progenitor of all humans on Earth because he sees in him the first human, from whom all other humans are descended. For Paul, it is Adam who has bequeathed to human beings the body that they carry about with them as a physical body. All individuals have inherited their physical bodies from Adam. This is the body that meets us in external *maya*, and is mortal; it is the body inherited from Adam, the corruptible body, the human, physical body that decays in death. With this body, individuals are 'clothed'. The second Adam, Christ, is regarded by Paul as possessing, in contrast to the first, the incorruptible, the immortal body. Paul then presumes that through Christian evolution, human beings are gradually made ready to put on the second Adam in place of the first Adam; the incorruptible body of the second Adam, Christ, in place of the corruptible body of the first Adam.

What Paul seems to require of all who call themselves true Christians is no less than something that violates all the old conceptions of the world. As the first corruptible body is descended from Adam, so must the incorruptible body originate from the second Adam, from Christ. Every Christian could say: 'Because I am descended from Adam, I have a corruptible body as Adam had; but in that I set myself in the right relationship to Christ, I receive from Him, the second Adam, an incorruptible body.' For Paul, this view shines out directly from the experience of Damascus.

What does Paul intend to say, in other words? We can perhaps express what Paul wishes to say by means of a simple diagram:

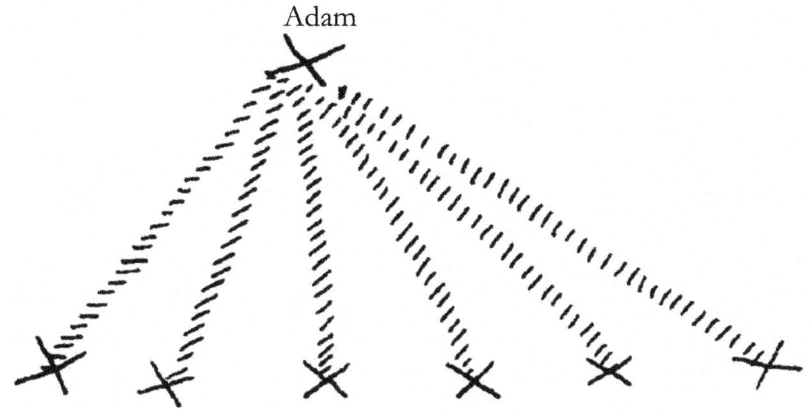

Here [x, x ...] we have a number of people at some given time. Paul would trace them all back genealogically to the first Adam, from whom they are all descended and by whom they are given the corruptible body.

According to Paul's conception, however, something else is possible. Just as humans can say to themselves with regard to their humanity: we are related because we are all descended from the first human, from Adam, so also they must say in the sense of Paul: because without our doing we can trace these lines back to Adam through the relationships that are given in the physical reproduction of humanity, it must be possible for us to allow something to arise within us that makes something different possible. Just as the natural lines lead back to Adam, so it must be possible to represent lines which lead, not to the corruptible body of the fleshly Adam, but to the body that is incorruptible. Through our relationship to Christ, we can—according to the Pauline view—bear this incorruptible body within us, just as through Adam we bear the corruptible body.

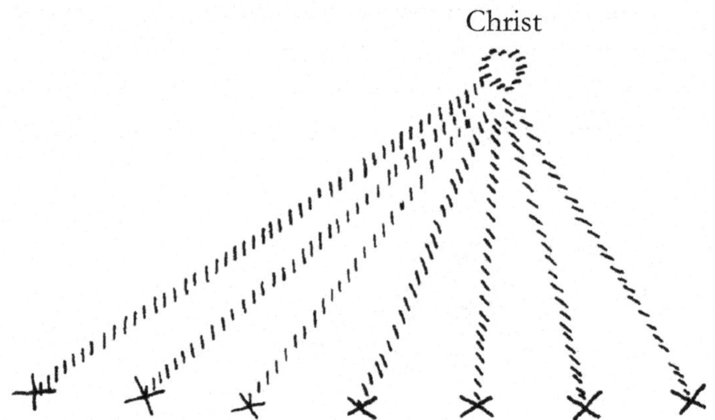

There is nothing more uncomfortable for modern consciousness than this idea. For looking at the matter quite soberly, what does it demand from us? It demands something that, for modern thought, is really monstrous. Modern thought has long disputed whether all human beings are descended from one primeval human being, but it may be allowed that all are descended from a single human being who was the first on Earth as regards physical consciousness. Paul, however, demands the following. He says: 'If you desire to be a Christian in the true sense, you must conceive that within you something can arise which can live in you, and from which you can draw spiritual lines to a second Adam, to Christ, to that very Christ who on the third day rose from the grave, just as all humans can trace lines back to the physical body of the first Adam.' So Paul demands that all who call themselves Christians should cause something within them to arise that is a reality in them, and which leads, just as the corruptible body can be traced, back to Adam; something leading to that Entity which on the third day rose out of the grave in which the body of Jesus Christ had been laid. Anyone who does not grant this cannot come into any relationship with Paul; he cannot say he understands Paul. If humans, as regards their corruptible bodies, are descended from the first Adam, then, by receiving the Being of Christ into their own being, they have the possibility of having a second ancestor. This ancestor, however, is He who, on the third day after His body had been laid in the Earth, rose out of the grave.

Let us clearly understand that Paul makes this demand, however displeasing it may be to modern thinkers. From this Pauline statement we will indeed approach the modern thinker; only one ought not to have any other opinion concerning what confronts us so clearly in the Pauline writings; one ought not to twist the meaning of something so clearly expressed by Paul. Certainly, it is comfortable to interpret something allegorically and to say it was meant in such and such a way; but all these interpretations make no sense. If we wish to connect a meaning with the Pauline statement, we are bound to say—even if modern consciousness regards it as superstition—that, according to Paul, Christ rose from the dead after three days.

Let us go further. An assertion such as this, made by Paul after he had reached the summit of his initiation through the event of Damascus—the assertion concerning the second Adam and His rising from the grave—could be made only by someone whose whole mode of thought and outlook had been derived from Greek thought; by one whose roots were in Greece, even if he were also a Hebrew; by one who in a certain respect had brought all his Hebraism as an offering to the Greek mind. For, if we come closer to all this, what is it that Paul really declares? Looking with inner vision on what the Greeks loved and valued, the external form of the human body, concerning which they had the tragic feeling that it comes to an end when the individual passes through the gate of death, Paul says out of his worldview: 'With the Resurrection of Christ, the body has been raised in triumph from the grave'! If we are to build a bridge between these two worldviews, we can best do it in the following way.

The Greek hero said from his Greek feeling: 'Better a beggar in the upper world than a king in the land of shades.' He said this because he was convinced that the external form of the physical body, so highly cherished by the Greeks, was lost forever in passing through the gate of death. On this same soil, out of which this tragic mood of intoxication with beauty had grown, Paul appeared, he who first proclaimed the Gospel to the Greeks. We do not deviate from his words if we translate them as follows: 'That which you value above all, the human bodily form, will no longer be destroyed.

Christ is risen as the first of those who are raised from the dead! The form of the physical body is not lost, but is given back to humanity through the Resurrection of Christ!' What the Greeks valued most highly was given back to them with the Resurrection by Paul the Jew, who had been steeped in Greek culture. Only a Greek would so think and speak, but only someone who had become a Greek with all the preconceptions derived from his Jewish ancestry. Only a Jew who had become a Greek could speak in this way; no one else.

But how can we approach these things from the standpoint of anthroposophy? For we have reached the point of knowing that Paul demands something which thoroughly upsets the calculations of the modern thinker. Let us endeavour from the standpoint of anthroposophy to get nearer to what Paul demands. Let us collect what we know from anthroposophy, so as to bring an idea to meet Paul's statement.

When we review the very simplest anthroposophical truths in order to get an idea of Paul's assertions, we know that the human being consists of physical body, etheric body, astral body, and ego. If now you ask someone who has studied anthroposophy a little, but not very thoroughly, whether they know the human physical body, they will be sure to answer: 'I know it quite well, for I see it when a person stands before me. The other members are supra-sensible, invisible, and one cannot see them, but the physical human body I know very well.' But is it really the human physical body that appears before our eyes when we meet someone with our ordinary, physical vision and our physical understanding? I ask you, who without clairvoyant vision has ever seen a physical human body? What is it that people have before them if they see only with physical eyes and physical understanding? A human body, but one consisting of physical body, etheric body, astral body, and ego. And when someone stands before us, it is as an organized assembly of physical body, etheric body, astral body, and ego. It would make as little sense to say that a physical body stood before us as it would if, when giving someone a glass of water, we were to say, 'There is hydrogen in that glass.' Water consists of hydrogen and oxygen, just as the human being consists of physical, etheric and astral bodies, and ego. Their assemblage is visible, just as water is, but the hydrogen and oxygen are not. Anyone who said he saw hydrogen in the water would be seriously mistaken.

So are individuals who think they see the physical body when they see a human being in the external world. What he normally sees is not a physical human body, but a four-membered being. He sees the physical body only in so far as it is permeated by the other members of the human being. And it is then changed in the same way that hydrogen is changed when it is permeated with oxygen in water. For hydrogen is a gas, and oxygen also; from the two gases united we get a liquid. Why should it be incomprehensible that the individuals who meet us in the physical world are quite unlike their single members, the physical, etheric and astral bodies and the ego, just as water is quite unlike hydrogen? And so he is! Hence, we cannot rely upon the *maya* which appears to us as the physical body. We must think of the physical body in a quite different way if we want to draw nearer to its nature.

The observation of the physical human body, in itself, belongs to the most difficult clairvoyant problems, the hardest of all! Suppose we allow the external world to perform upon us the experiment which is similar to the disintegration of water into hydrogen and oxygen. In death, this experiment is performed by the great world. We then see how the human being lays aside his physical body. But do humans really lay aside their physical bodies? The question seems absurd, for what could be clearer than the apparent fact that at death we lay aside our physical bodies? But what is it that he lays aside? It is something no longer imbued with the physical body's most important possession during life: its form. Directly after death, the form begins to withdraw from the dead body. We are left with decaying substances, no longer characterized by the form. The body laid aside is composed of substances and elements that we can trace also in nature; in the natural order of things they would not produce a human form. Yet this form belongs quite essentially to the physical human body. To ordinary clairvoyance, it seems evident that at death, a person simply discards these material substances, which are then handed over to decay or burning, and that nothing of the physical body is left. The clairvoyant then observes how after death the ego, astral body, and etheric body remain connected during the person's review of his past life. Then the clairvoyant sees as the experiment progresses how the etheric body separates itself, how an extract of it remains, while the main portion dissolves in one way or another into the universal cosmic ether. It does indeed seem that the person has laid aside his physical body, with its substances and forces, and then, after a few days, the etheric body. When the clairvoyant follows the person further through the *Kamaloka* period, he sees how an extract of the astral body goes with him during the life between death and a new birth, while the rest of the astral body is given over to the cosmic astrality.

So we see that physical, etheric, and astral bodies are laid aside, and that the physical body seems to drain away completely into materials and forces which, through decay or burning or some other form of dissolution, are returned to the elements. But the more clairvoyance is developed in our time, the clearer will it be that the physical forces and substances laid aside are not the whole physical body, for its complete configuration could never derive from them alone.

Rather, to these substances and forces there belongs something else, best called the human 'phantom'. This phantom is the supra-sensible form that as a spiritual texture works up the physical substances and forces so that they fill out the form that we encounter as an individual on the physical plane.

The sculptor cannot bring a statue into existence if he merely takes marble or something else, and strikes away wildly so that single pieces spring off just as the substance permits. As the sculptor must have the idea that he impresses on the substance, so is an idea present for the human body: not in the same way as the thought of the artist, for the material of the human body is not marble or plaster, but as a real thought, the phantom, in the external world. Just as the sculptors' thought is stamped upon their material, so the phantom of the physical body is stamped upon the substances of the Earth which we see given over after death to the grave or the fire. The phantom belongs to the physical body as its enduring part, a more important part than the external substances. The external substances are merely loaded into the network of the human form, as one might load apples into a cart. The phantom is something important! The substances that fall asunder after death are essentially those we meet externally in nature. They are merely caught up by the human form.

If you think more deeply, can you believe that all the work of the great divine Spirits through the Saturn, Sun, and Moon periods has merely created something that is handed over at death to the elements of the Earth? No! What has evolved during the Saturn, Sun, and Moon phases is not at all the physical body that is laid aside at death. It is the phantom, the form, of the physical body! We must be quite clear that to understand the physical body is not an easy thing. Above all, this understanding must not be sought in the world of illusion, the world of *maya*. We know that the foundation stone, the germ, of this phantom of the physical body was laid down by the Thrones during the Saturn period;[45] during the Sun period the Spirits of Wisdom worked further upon it; the Spirits of Movement during the Moon period; and the Spirits of Form during the Earth period. And it is only in this last phase that the physical body received the phantom. Thus we call these Spirits the Spirits of Form, because they actually live in the phantom of the physical body. So in order to understand the physical body, we must go back to the phantom of the same.

If we look back to the beginning of our earthly existence, we can say that the hosts from the ranks of the higher Hierarchies who had prepared the physical human body in its own proper form during the periods of Saturn, Sun, and Moon, up to the Earth, had from the outset placed this phantom within the evolution of Earth. In fact, the phantom, which cannot be seen with the physical eye, was what was first there of the human physical body. It is a transparent body of forces. What the physical eye sees are the physical substances that a person eats and takes into himself, and they fill out the invisible phantom. If the physical eye looks upon a physical body, what it sees is the mineral part that fills the physical body, not the physical body itself. But how has this mineral part found its way into the phantom of the human physical body? To answer this question, let us picture once more the genesis, the first becoming, of humans on Earth.

From Saturn, Sun, and Moon there derived that network of forces which in its true form meets us as the invisible phantom of the physical body. For a higher clairvoyance, it appears as phantom only when we look away from all the external substance that fills it out. Thus it is the phantom that stands at the starting point of human existence on Earth, when we were invisible as a physical body. Let us suppose that to this phantom of the physical body the etheric body is added; will the phantom then become visible? Certainly not; for the etheric body is invisible for ordinary sight. Thus the physical body as phantom, plus etheric body, is still invisible to the external physical senses. And the astral body even more so; hence the combination of physical body as phantom with the etheric and astral bodies is still invisible. And when the ego is added it would certainly become perceptible inwardly, but not externally visible. Thus, as humans evolved out of the Saturn, Sun, and Moon periods, they were still visible only to a clairvoyant. How did they become visible? But for the occurrence described in the Bible symbolically, and factually in esoteric science, as the entry of the luciferic influence,[46] we would not have become visible. What happened through that influence?

Read what is said in my book *An Outline of Esoteric Science*.[47] Out of that path of evolution in which our physical, etheric, and astral bodies were still invisible, humans were thrown down into denser matter, and they were compelled under the influence of Lucifer to take this denser matter into themselves. If the luciferic force had not been introduced into our astral body and ego, this dense materiality would not have become as visible as it has become. Hence, we have to represent ourselves as an invisible being, made visible in matter only through forces which entered into us under the influence of Lucifer. Through this influence, external substances and forces are drawn into the domain of the phantom and permeate it. As when we pour a coloured fluid into a transparent glass, so that the glass looks coloured even though it is otherwise transparent to our eye, so we can imagine that the luciferic influence poured forces into the form of the human phantom, with the result that humans were adapted for taking in on Earth the requisite substances and forces that make our form visible. Otherwise, our physical bodies would have remained always invisible.

What makes human beings visible? The luciferic forces within make humans as visible as they appear on the physical plane. Otherwise their physical bodies would have remained invisible. Thus the alchemists always insisted that the human body really consists of the same substance that constitutes the perfectly transparent, crystalline 'Philosopher's Stone'. The physical body is itself entirely transparent, and it is the luciferic forces within us that have brought us to a non-transparent state so that we are opaque and tangible. Hence you will understand that humans have become beings who take up external substances and forces of the Earth, which are released again at death, only because Lucifer tempted us, and certain forces were poured into our astral body. It follows that because the ego was drawn into connection with the physical, etheric, and astral bodies under the influence of Lucifer, humans became what they are on Earth and otherwise would not have been—the bearer of a visible, earthly organism.

Now let us suppose that at a certain point of time in life, the ego were to go out from a human organism, so that there stood before us the physical, etheric, and astral bodies, but not the ego. This is what happened in the case of Jesus of Nazareth in the thirtieth year of His life. The human ego then left this cohesion of physical, etheric, and astral bodies. And into this cohesion, the Being of Christ entered at the Baptism in the Jordan. We now have the physical, etheric, and astral bodies of a man, and the Being of Christ. The Being of Christ had now taken up His abode in a human organism, as otherwise the ego would have done. What now differentiates this Jesus Christ from all other humans on Earth? It is this: that all other humans bear within themselves an ego that once was overcome by Lucifer's temptation, but Jesus no longer bears an ego within Him; instead, He bears the Being of Christ. So that from this time, beginning with the Baptism in Jordan, Jesus bears within Himself the residual effects that had come from Lucifer, but with no human ego to allow any further luciferic influences to enter the human body. A physical body, an etheric body, and astral body—in which the residue of the earlier luciferic influences was present, but into which no more luciferic influence could enter during the next three years—and the Being of Christ: thus was Jesus Christ constituted.

Let us set before us exactly what the Christ is from the Baptism in the Jordan until the Mystery of Golgotha: a physical body, an etheric body, and an astral body that make this physical body together with the etheric body visible because it still contains the residue of the luciferic influence. Because the Being of Christ had the astral body that Jesus of Nazareth had possessed from birth to his thirtieth year, the physical body was visible as the bearer of the Christ. Thus from the time of the Baptism in the Jordan, we have before us a physical body that as such would not be visible on the physical plane; an etheric body that would not have been perceptible as such; the remnants of the astral body that makes the other two bodies visible and so makes the body of Jesus of Nazareth into a visible body; and, within this organism, the Being of Christ.

We will inscribe firmly in our souls this fourfold nature of Jesus Christ, saying to ourselves: Every person who stands before us on the physical plane consists of a physical body, an etheric body, an astral body, and an ego; and this ego is such that it always works into the astral body up to the hour of death. The Being of Jesus Christ, however, stands before us as One who had a physical body, an etheric body, and an astral body, but no human ego, so that during the three years up to his death He was not subject to the influences that normally work upon human beings. The only influence came from the Being of Christ.

We want to present that clearly to our souls, and consider the matter further from this point onwards.

Lecture 7

Yesterday we saw that in a certain respect the question of Christianity is the question of the Resurrection of Jesus Christ. In particular, we spoke of Paul, the proclaimer of Christianity, who from his knowledge of the essential nature of the Christ-Impulse recognized immediately that after and since the Event of Golgotha, Christ lives. We saw that for Paul, after his experience on the road to Damascus, a powerful, magnificent picture of human evolution opened up.

From this point, we went on to build up a picture of what Jesus Christ was directly after the Baptism in the Jordan by John. Our next task will be to inquire into the course of events from the Baptism to the Mystery of Golgotha. But if we are to rise to an understanding of the Mystery of Golgotha, we must clear away certain hindrances. From all that has been said concerning the Gospels in the course of years, and also from what has been said already in these few lectures, you will have been able to gather that certain theosophical ideas, which in some quarters are esteemed sufficient, are really not sufficient to answer the question with which we are here concerned.

Before everything else, we must take quite seriously what has been said about the three streams of human thought: the stream which has its source in ancient Greece; the stream which comes down from ancient Hebraism, and lastly the stream which found expression in Gautama Buddha half a millennium before our era. We have seen that this Buddha stream, especially as it developed among his followers, is least of all adapted to an understanding of the Mystery of Golgotha. To the modern individual, whose consciousness is filled with the intellectual culture of the present day, the stream of thought that finds expression in Buddhism certainly offers something very pleasant. Hardly any other form of thought suits so well the concepts of the present day, in so far as they prefer to remain silent in face of the greatest question that humanity has to grasp—the question of the Resurrection. For with this question the whole evolutionary history of humanity is connected. Now in Buddhist teaching, the real being of the ego, which in the true sense we can call the fourth member of human nature, has been lost. Certainly, in these matters one can employ all kinds of interpretations; one can twist them in all sorts of ways, and plenty of people will find fault with what has been said here about Buddhist teaching, but that is not the point. For such things as I have quoted from the heart of Buddhism—for example, the conversation between King Milinda and the Buddhist sage Nagasena—testify clearly that the nature of the ego cannot be spoken of in Buddhism as we must speak of it. For a genuine follower of Buddhism, it would indeed be heretical to speak of the nature of the ego as we must represent it. On this very account, we must ourselves be clear regarding the nature of the ego.

The human ego, which in the case of every human being, even of the highest adept, passes from incarnation to incarnation, is a term which (as we saw yesterday) can be applied to Jesus of Nazareth only from his birth to the Baptism in Jordan. After the Baptism, we still have before us the physical body, the etheric body, and the astral body of Jesus of Nazareth; but now there dwells in the external human sheaths not a human ego, but rather a Cosmic Being, the Being of Christ. Through years of endeavour we have tried by means of words to bring the Being of Christ nearer to our understanding. As soon as one comprehends the whole nature of Jesus Christ, it is obvious that for Him one must rule out any kind of physical or bodily reincarnation. The expression employed in my Mystery Drama, *The Soul's Probation*, about Christ having been present only once in a body of flesh, must be taken seriously and quite literally. Accordingly, we must first concern ourselves with the being, the nature, of the ordinary human ego. The Being of Jesus Christ was completely independent of the human ego from the Baptism to the Mystery of Golgotha.

In earlier lectures, it was shown that the evolution of the Earth was preceded by the existences of Saturn, of the Sun, and of the Moon, and these three planetary embodiments were followed by the fourth, the embodiment of Earth. You know from those lectures that only during the embodiment as Earth proper, the fourth of the planetary conditions which were necessary to bring into existence our Earth with all its creatures, could the human ego enter into connection with human nature. Just as in the Ancient Saturn period we speak of the beginning of the physical body, so in the period of the Ancient Sun we speak of the first development of the etheric body, in the Moon of the first development of the astral body, and only in the Earth embodiment of the unfolding of the ego. In this way, the whole matter is brought cosmically and historically into view. But how is it when we look at the history of peoples?

Through our former studies, we know that although the germ of the ego was laid down in human beings during the Lemurian time, the possibility of attaining ego-consciousness arose only towards the end of the Atlantean period,[48] and that even then this ego-consciousness was very dim and vague. Indeed, after the Atlantean epoch, through the various periods of civilization that preceded the Mystery of Golgotha, the ego-consciousness was still dull, dreamlike, and dim. But if you turn your attention to the development of the Hebrew people, it will be clear to you that here the ego-consciousness found expression in a very unusual way. A kind of folk-ego[49] lived in each single member of the Ancient Hebrew people; in fact, all of these people traced their egos back to their ancestor in the flesh, to Abraham. The ego of the Ancient Hebrew people was still such that we can designate it as a group-ego, a folk-group-ego.[50] Consciousness had not yet penetrated as far as the separate individuality in each person. Why was this so?

Each part of the four-membered human being we now regard as normal developed gradually in the course of the Earth's evolution. It was only towards the end of the Atlantean period that part of the etheric body, which until then had been external to the physical body, was gradually drawn into the body. This led towards the condition now recognized by clairvoyant consciousness as normal, namely that the physical body and the etheric body approximately coincide. Only then was it possible for humans to develop their ego-consciousness. Let us slowly and gradually form an impression of the very peculiar way in which this ego-consciousness meets us in the human being.

I described yesterday how people speak of the Resurrection when they approach it with all the intellectual preconceptions of the present day. If, they say, 'I had to assent to the real Pauline teaching about the Resurrection, I would have to tear up my whole conception of the world.' That is what they say, these up-to-date people who have at their command all the resources of modern intellectualism. To people who speak thus, what must now be said will seem very strange.

But is it not possible that such a person might reflect: 'Yes, if I am to accept the Resurrection, I shall have to tear up all my intellectual concepts. But is that a reason for setting this question aside? Because we cannot understand the Resurrection and have to regard it as a miracle, must we assume that the only way out of this difficulty is to pass it by? Is there no other way?'

The other way is far from easy for modern individuals, for they would have to admit to themselves: 'Perhaps it is not the fault of the Resurrection that I am unable to comprehend it. Perhaps the reason is that my intellect is unfitted to understand it.'

So little is this matter taken seriously in our day that we may say: Modern individuals are prevented by their pride—and just because they do not suspect that pride could come into it—from admitting that their intellects may be incompetent to fathom this question. For which is more reasonable: to say that I am setting aside something that shatters my intellectual outlook, or to admit that it may be beyond my understanding? Pride, however, forbids this admission.

Of course, anthroposophists must have trained themselves to rise above this kind of pride. It should not be far from the heart of true anthroposophists to say: 'Perhaps my intellect is not competent to form an opinion about the Resurrection.' But then they have to face another difficulty: they now have to answer the question why the human mind is not adapted to comprehend the greatest fact in human evolution. To answer this question, we must go somewhat more closely into the real nature of human understanding. Here

I should like to remind you of my Munich lectures, *Wonders of the World*,[51] of which I will now give a résumé as far as we need one.

The elements that go to make up our soul life, our thoughts, feelings and perceptions, are not to be found in our present-day physical body; they penetrate only as far as the etheric body. In order to be clear about this, let us imagine our human nature, in so far as it consists of ego, astral body, and etheric body, enclosed in an ellipse:

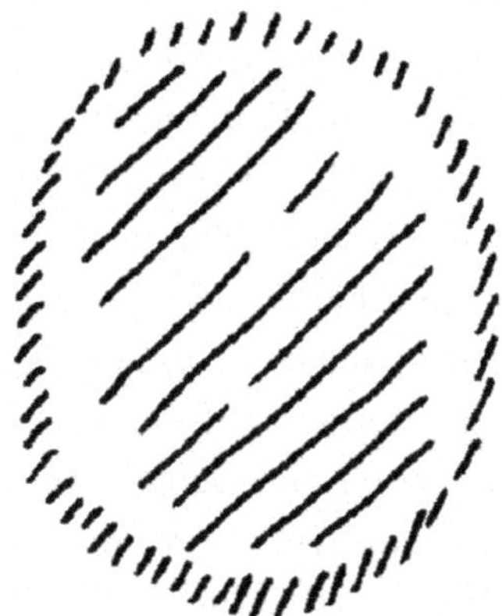

We will take this diagram to represent schematically what we call our inner life and can experience in our souls; the diagram shows it coming to expression only in the streams and forces of the etheric body. If we experience a thought or perception, it has three lines of action in our psychic nature, as indicated in the following diagram.

Soul - experiences

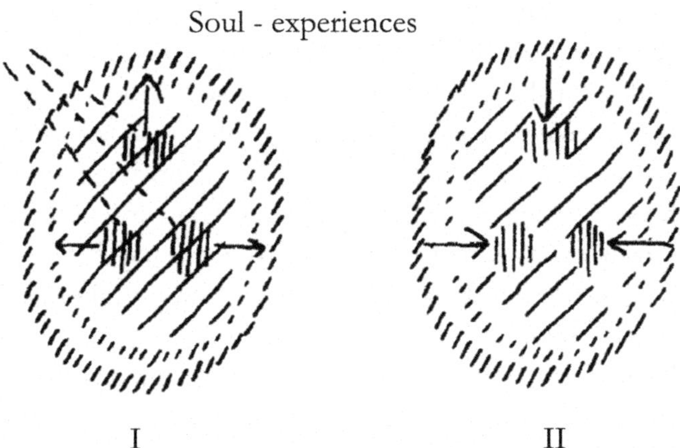

I   II

Within our psychic nature there is nothing that is not present in this way. Now if individuals' ordinary earthly consciousness were restricted to psychic experiences within the confines of the diagram, the experiences would occur, but they would not be conscious of them; they would remain unconscious. Our psychic experiences become conscious only through a process which an analogy will help us to understand. Imagine you are going in a certain direction, looking straight ahead. Your name is Smith. While you are going straight ahead you do not see Smith, yet you are he, you experience him, you are the person 'Smith'. Imagine that someone puts a mirror in front of you. Now 'Smith' stands before you. What you had previously experienced, you now see; it meets you in the mirror.

So it is with human psychic life. People have an experience, but they do not become conscious of it without a mirror. The mirror is the physical body. The perceptions, the thoughts, are thrown back by the sheath of the physical body. Thereby we become conscious of them. Hence, in the diagram we can represent the physical body as the enclosing sheath. For us, as earthly individuals, the physical body is in truth a reflecting apparatus.

If in this way you go more and more deeply into the nature of the human soul and of human consciousness, it will be impossible for you to consider as in any way dangerous or significant all those things which are brought forward again and again by materialism in opposition to the spiritual conception of the world. If through any damage to the reflecting apparatus, the psychic experience is no longer perceived by the consciousness, it is absolute nonsense to conclude that the psychic experience itself is bound up with the mirror. If someone breaks a mirror in which you see yourself, they do not break you. You merely disappear from your own field of vision. So it is when the reflecting apparatus for the psychic life, the brain, is destroyed. Perception ceases, but the psychic life itself, in so far as it goes on in the etheric body and the astral body, is not in the least disturbed.

But have we not come to a point when we must consider closely the nature of the physical body? You will agree that without consciousness, we could not be conscious of the ego. In order to make ego-consciousness our own during life on Earth, our physical body, with its brain organization, has to be a reflecting apparatus. We learn to become conscious of ourselves through our own mirrored reflection. If we had no mirror apparatus, we could not be conscious of our own selves. What is this mirror?

We are shown by esoteric investigations, which reach back through reading the Akashic Record as far as the origin of our earthly existence, that in the beginning of the Earth epoch this reflecting apparatus, the external physical body, came under luciferic influence and was changed. Yesterday we saw what this physical body has become for earthly humanity. It has become something that falls to pieces when we pass through the gate of death. We have said that the body that falls to pieces is not the body which Divine Spirits had prepared through four planetary evolutions so that it should become the physical body on Earth. What the Divine Spirits prepared, which yesterday we called the phantom, belongs to the physical body as a form-body[52] that permeates, and at the same time holds together, the material parts that are woven into our physical body. If no luciferic influence had intervened, then, at the beginning of our earthly existence, we humans would have received this phantom in full strength together with our physical body. But into the human organization, in so far as it consists of physical body, etheric body, and astral body, the luciferic influence penetrated, and the consequence was the destruction of the phantom of the physical body. As we shall see, this is symbolically expressed in the Bible as the Fall, together with the fact, related in the Tanakh or Old Testament, that death followed the Fall.

Death was indeed the destruction of the phantom of the physical body. The outcome is that, when we go through the gate of death, we have to see the dissolution of our physical body. This crumbling physical body, lacking the strength of the phantom, is indeed borne by us throughout the whole of our earthly lives, from birth to death. The crumbling away goes on all the time, and the decomposition, the death of the physical body, is only the final stage of a continuous evolution, a continuous process. For if the disintegration of the body—preceded by the disorganization of the phantom—is not countered in the same way by processes of reconstruction, what we call death finally ensues.

If no luciferic influence had intervened, the destructive and reconstructive forces in the physical body would have remained in balance. But then everything in earthly human nature would have been different; there would, for example, have been no mind incapable of comprehending the Resurrection. For what kind of understanding is it that cannot grasp the Resurrection? It is the kind that is bound up with the decadence of the physical body, and is what it is because the individual has incurred, through the luciferic influence, the progressive destruction of the phantom of the physical body. In consequence, the human understanding, the human intellect, has become so thin, so threadbare, that it cannot take in the great processes of cosmic evolution. It looks on them as miracles, or says it cannot comprehend them. If the luciferic influence had not intervened, and the anabolic forces in the human body had held the destructive forces in balance, then the human understanding, equipped with all that was intended for it, would have seen into the anabolic forces, rather as one follows a laboratory experiment. But our understanding is now such that it remains on the surface of things and has no insight into the cosmic depths.

Anyone, therefore, who wishes to characterize these conditions correctly must say: In the beginning of our earthly existence, the physical body was prevented by the luciferic influence from becoming what it should have become according to the will of the Powers who worked through Saturn, Sun, and Moon. Instead, it took into itself a destructive process. Since the beginning of the earthly phase of evolution, we have lived in a physical body that is subject to destruction; a body which cannot adequately counter the destructive forces with anabolic forces.

So there is truth in something that appears to the modern individual as such folly: that a hidden connection exists between what has come to pass through the working of Lucifer, and death! And now let us look at this working. What was the effect of this destruction of the physical body? If we had the physical body completely, as was intended at the beginning of earthly existence, our psychic powers would reflect themselves in quite another way: we should then know in truth what we are. As things stand, we do not know what we are because the physical body is not given us in its completeness. We do certainly speak of the nature and being of the human ego—but how far do humans know the ego? So dubious is the ego that Buddhism can even deny that it goes from one incarnation to another. So dubious is it that Greece could fall into the tragic mood that found expression in those words of the Greek hero: 'Better a beggar in the upper world than a king in the realm of shades.' Nothing less was said then that when the Greeks saw the treasured physical body—the body shaped by the phantom—given over to destruction, they felt a sadness in face of the darkening, the fading away, of the ego, for they felt that it could exist only together with the ego-consciousness. And when they saw the form of the physical body falling into decadence, they shuddered at the thought that the ego would grow dark and dim, this ego which is reflected by the form of the physical body.

And when we follow human evolution from the beginning of the Earth to the Mystery of Golgotha, we find that the process we have just indicated shows itself in an ever-increasing degree. In earlier times, for example, no one would have preached the annihilation of the physical body in so radical a fashion as did Gautama Buddha. For such teaching to be given, it was necessary that the decadence of the physical body, its complete annihilation as regards its form, should have become more and more nearly complete, so that the human mind no longer had any idea that the entity which becomes conscious through the physical body—that is, through the form—can pass over from one incarnation to another. The truth is that humans, in the course of the evolution of the Earth, lost the form of the physical body, so that they no longer have what the Divine beings had intended for them from the beginning of the Earth.

This is something they must regain; but it had first to be imparted to them once more. And we cannot comprehend Christianity unless we understand that at the time when the events of Palestine took place, the human race on Earth had reached a stage where the decadence of the physical body was at its peak, and where, because of this, the whole evolution of humanity was threatened with the danger that ego-consciousness—the specific achievement of earthly evolution—would be lost. If this process had continued unchanged, the destructive element would have penetrated ever more deeply into the human bodily organism, and humans born after the time when the events of Palestine were due would have had to live with an ever-duller feeling of the ego. Everything that depends on perfect reflection from the physical body would have become increasingly worn out.

Then came the Mystery of Golgotha; it came as we have characterized it, and through it something happened which is so hard to grasp for an intellect bound up with the physical body only, a body in which the destructive forces preponderate. It came to pass that one man, who was the bearer of the Christ, had gone through such a death that after three days the specifically mortal part of the physical body had to disappear, and out of the grave there rose the body which is the bearer of forces of the physical, material parts. The body that was really intended for humanity by the rulers of Saturn, Sun, and Moon—the pure phantom of the physical body with all the attributes of the physical body—this it was that rose out of the grave. So the possibility of that spiritual genealogy was given of which we have spoken.

Let us think of the body of Christ that rose out of the grave. Just as from the body of Adam the bodies of earthly humans are descended, in so far as these humans have bodies that crumble away, even so are the spiritual bodies, the phantoms, descended from that which rose out of the grave. And it is possible to establish a relationship with Christ through which earthly human beings can bring into their otherwise decaying physical bodies this phantom which rose out of the grave of Golgotha. It is possible for humans to receive into their organisms those forces which then rose from the grave, just as through their physical organisms at the beginning of Earth evolution, as a consequence of the luciferic forces, they received the organism of Adam.

It is this that Paul wishes to say. Just as humans, through their place in the stream of physical evolution, inherit the physical body in which the destruction of the phantom, the force-bearer, is gradually taking place, so from the pure phantom that rose out of the grave they can inherit what they have lost. They can inherit it; they can clothe themselves with it, as they clothed themselves with the first Adam; they can become one with it. Thereby they can go through a development by means of which they can climb upwards again, even as before the Mystery of Golgotha they had descended in evolution. In other words, what had been taken from them through the luciferic influence can be given back to them through its presence as the Risen Body of Christ. That is what Paul wishes to say.

Now, just as it is very easy, from the standpoint of modern anatomy or physiology, to refute what has been said in this lecture— apparently to refute it—so is it childishly easy to raise another objection. Some such question as this might be asked: If indeed Paul really believed that a spiritual body had risen, what has this spiritual body which had risen out of the grave to do with what we all now bear in ourselves? This is not hard to understand: we need only consider the analogy offered by the coming into existence of human individuals. It could be asked: Whence proceeds the individual human being? As physical human beings, they begin from a single cell; a physical body consists entirely of cells that are all children of the original cell; all cells that compose a human body are traceable to the original cell. Now imagine that, through what we may call a mystical Christological process, we humans acquire a body quite other than the one we have gradually acquired in our downward evolution. Then think of each of these new bodies as having an intimate connection with the pure phantom that rose from the grave, somewhat as the human cells of the physical body are connected with the original cell. That is, we must think of the phantom as multiplying itself, as does the cell that gives rise to the physical body. So, in the evolution that follows the Event of Golgotha, all humans can inwardly acquire something that is spiritually descended from the phantom that rose from the grave, just as—to echo Paul—the ordinary body that falls into dissolution is descended from Adam.

Of course it is an insult to the human intellect, which thinks so arrogantly of itself at the present time, to say that a process similar to the multiplication of the cell, which if need be can be seen, takes place in the invisible. This outcome of the Mystery of Golgotha, however, is an esoteric fact. To someone who contemplates evolution with esoteric sight, it is apparent that the spiritual cell, the body which overcame death, the body of Jesus Christ, has risen from the grave and in the course of time imparts itself to anyone who enters into the corresponding relationship with the Christ. To anyone resolved to deny supra-sensible happenings altogether, this statement will naturally seem absurd. But to anyone who grants the supra-sensible, the event with which we are here concerned must be presented in the way described. The phantom which rose from the grave communicates itself to those who make themselves fitted for it. This, then, is a fact that everyone who grants the supra-sensible can understand.

If we can inscribe upon our souls what is in very truth the Pauline teaching, we come to regard the Mystery of Golgotha as a reality that took place and had to take place in the evolution of the Earth; for it signifies literally the rescue of the human ego. We have seen that if the process of evolution had continued along the path it had followed up to the time of the events of Palestine, ego-consciousness could not have been developed; it would not only have failed to advance, but would have gone down ever further into darkness. But the path turned upwards, and will continue to ascend in proportion as humans find their relation to the Being of Christ.

Now we can understand Buddhism very well. About five hundred years before the events of Palestine, a truth was proclaimed—but not taking into account the event of Golgotha in the direction of its development: 'Everything that envelops us as our physical body and makes us into a being incarnated in the flesh—all this must be looked upon as worthless; it is fundamentally a left-over from the past and must be cast off.' Certainly up to that time, conditions were such that humanity would have had to set its course towards this philosophy of life if nothing else had intervened. But there came the Event of Golgotha, an Event which completely restored the lost principles of human evolution. As far as humans take into themselves the incorruptible body we spoke of yesterday, and have brought before our souls in closer detail today, if they clothe themselves with this incorruptible body, they will become more and more clearly aware of their ego-consciousness, and of that part of their nature which journeys on from one incarnation to another.

What came into the world with Christianity must therefore not be regarded merely as a new teaching—this must be expressly emphasized—and not as a new theory, but as something real, something factual. Hence, when people insist that everything Christ taught had been known previously, this signifies nothing for a real understanding of Christianity. The important thing is not what Christ taught, but what He gave: His Body! For the Body that rose from the grave of Golgotha had never before entered into human evolution. Never before had there been present on Earth, through someone's death, what came to be present as the Risen Body of Jesus Christ. Previously, after humans had passed through the gate of death, and had gone through the period between death and a new birth, they had brought to Earth with them the defective phantom, given over to deterioration. No one had ever caused a perfect phantom to arise.

Here we can refer to the initiates and adepts. They always had to receive initiation outside their physical bodies, by overcoming their physical bodies, but this overcoming never went as far as a resuscitation of the physical phantom. No pre-Christian initiations went further than the outermost limits of the physical body; they did not touch the forces of the physical body, except in so far as the inner organism impinges in a general way on the outer. No one, having gone through death, had ever overcome death as a human phantom. Similar things had certainly occurred, but never this—that someone had gone through a complete human death and that the complete phantom had then gained victory over death. Just as it is true that only this phantom can give rise to complete humanity in the course of human evolution, so is it true that this phantom took its beginning from the grave of Golgotha.

That is the important fact in Christian evolution. Hence the commentators are not at fault when they say again and again that the teaching of Jesus Christ has been transformed into a teaching about Jesus Christ. It had to be so. For the important thing is not what

Jesus Christ taught, but what He gave to humanity. His Resurrection is the coming to birth of a new member of human nature—an incorruptible body. But for this to happen, this rescue of the human phantom through death, two things were necessary. It was necessary, first, that the Being of Jesus Christ should be such as we have described it—constituted of physical body, etheric body, and astral body, and—instead of a human ego—the Being of Christ.

Secondly, it was necessary that the Being of Christ should have resolved to descend into a human body, to incarnate in a human body of flesh. For if we are to contemplate the Being of Christ in the right light, we must seek Him in the time before the beginning of humans on Earth. The Being of Christ was of course existent at that time. He did not enter into the circulation of human evolution; He dwelt in the spiritual world. Humanity continued along its ever-descending path. At a point in time when the crisis of human evolution had been reached, the Being of Christ incorporated Himself into the body of a man. That is the greatest sacrifice that could have been brought to the earthly evolution by the Being of Christ! And the second thing we must learn to understand is wherein this sacrifice consisted. Yesterday we dealt with one part of the question concerning the nature of Christ, confining our study to the time after the Baptism by John in Jordan. We must now go on to ask: What is the significance of the fact that at the Baptism the Being of Christ descended into a body of flesh, and how did death come about in the Mystery of Golgotha?

That will occupy us in the following days.

LECTURE 8

KARLSRUHE, 12 OCTOBER 1911

YESTERDAY we indicated that it was now necessary to answer the question: What really happened to that Being whom we designate as Jesus Christ from the Baptism by John in the Jordan to the Mystery of Golgotha? To answer this question as far as possible, we must recall briefly what we know from former lectures concerning the life of Jesus of Nazareth, who in his thirtieth year became the bearer of the Christ. The essential points are given in my recently published book, *The Spiritual Guidance of the Individual and Humanity*.[53]

We know that in Palestine, at the time that concerns us, not one but two Jesus-children were born, one of them from the Solomon line of the House of David. This is the Jesus child of whom the Gospel of St Matthew speaks. The peculiar contradiction between the beginnings of the Gospels of St Matthew and St Luke derives from the fact that the writer of the Gospel of St Matthew was concerned with one of the Jesus-children, the one born from the Solomon line. Then, at almost but not quite the same time, another Jesus-child was born, from the Nathan line of the House of David.

The important thing is to understand clearly what kind of beings these two children were. Esoteric investigation shows that the individuality who was in the Solomon Jesus-child was none other than Zarathustra. After Zarathustra's most important mission, of which we have spoken in connection with the Ancient Persian civilization, he had been incarnated again and again; lastly during the Babylonian-Chaldaic civilization, and now as the Solomon Jesus-child. This individuality of Zarathustra, with all the great and powerful inner forces which in the nature of things he had brought over from earlier incarnations, had to incarnate in a body descended from the Solomon side of the House of David; a body adapted for working up and further developing the great faculties of Zarathustra, in the way that human faculties, when they are already at a very high level, can be brought further on, in so far as they belong to the being who is going from incarnation to incarnation. We are concerned therefore with a human body which did not wait until later years to work on these faculties, but could do so in a youthful, child-like and yet powerful organism. Hence, we see Zarathustra growing up in such a way that the faculties of the child developed comparatively early. The child soon showed an extent of knowledge that would normally have been impossible at his age.

One fact, however, we must keep firmly in mind: the Solomon Jesus-child, although the incarnation of so lofty an individuality, was only a highly developed man. Hence, he was encumbered—as even the most highly developed individual must be—with certain liabilities to error and moral difficulties, though not exactly vices or sins. Then we know that in his twelfth year the individuality of Zarathustra, by an esoteric process known to everyone who has made himself conversant with such facts, forsook the body of the Solomon Jesus-child and went over into the body of the Nathan Jesus-child. Now the body of this Nathan Jesus-child—or, better, his threefold bodily organization of physical body, etheric body, and astral body—was formed in quite a special manner. In fact, this body was such that the child showed capacities exactly contrary to those of the Solomon Jesus-child. Whereas the latter was remarkable because of his great gifts in relation to things one can learn externally, it might almost be said that in this respect the Nathan Jesus-child was untalented. You will understand that saying this implies not the slightest deprecation.

The Nathan Jesus-child was not in a position to familiarize himself with the products of human culture on Earth. By contrast, the remarkable fact is that he could speak as soon as he was born. A faculty which belongs more to the physical body was thus present in him from his birth. But—according to a good tradition which can be esoterically confirmed—the language he spoke could be understood by his mother only. The child's most strongly marked characteristics were qualities of the heart. He had an immense capacity for love and a disposition capable of immense self-sacrifice. And the remarkable thing is that from the first days of his life, his mere presence, or his touch, had beneficent effects—magnetic effects, one might perhaps call them nowadays. Thus all the qualities of heart were manifest in this child, enhanced to such a degree that they could have a beneficent, magnetic influence on his environment.

We know also that active in the astral body of this child were the forces which had once been acquired by that Bodhisattva who became Gautama Buddha. We know indeed—and in this respect the Oriental tradition is absolutely correct, for it can be confirmed by esoteric science—that the Bodhisattva, who on becoming Buddha five centuries before our era no longer needed to incarnate further on Earth, worked from the spiritual world upon all those who devoted themselves to his teachings. It is characteristic of such an individuality, who rises to heights from which he need no longer incarnate in a body of flesh, that he can then take part in the affairs and destiny of our earthly existence from out of the spiritual worlds. This can happen in the most manifold ways. In fact, the Bodhisattva who went through his last incarnation on the Earth as Gautama Buddha has taken an essential part in the further evolution of humanity.

Our human spiritual world stands continually in connection with all the rest of the spiritual world. The human being not only eats and drinks, and so takes into himself the substance of the physical earth; he continually receives psychic and spiritual nourishment from the spiritual world. In the most varied ways, forces continually flow into physical, earthly existence from out of the spiritual world. Such an inflow of the forces which Buddha had gained for himself came into the wider stream of humanity through the fact that the Buddha forces permeated the astral body of the Nathan Jesus-child. We know, too, from earlier lectures, that the words we still have today as a Christmas message—'The Divine reveals itself from the heights, and on earth peace will spread in the hearts of men of good will!'—originate in essence from the influence that flowed down into human evolution through the immersion of the powers of Buddha in the astral body of the Nathan Jesus-child.

Thus we see the forces of the Buddha working further in the stream of earthly existence that took its start from the events of Palestine. These forces of the Buddha then continue to work. And it is interesting that precisely the researches made by Western esotericism in quite recent years have led to the recognition of a very important connection between European civilization and the Buddha forces. For a long time, these Buddha forces have been working from the spiritual worlds, particularly upon everything in Western civilization that is unthinkable without the specific influence of Christianity. All those philosophical streams that have developed during recent centuries up to the nineteenth century, in so far as they are Western spiritual currents, are permeated by the Christ-Impulse, but the Buddha has always been working into them from out of the spiritual worlds. Hence the most important thing that European humanity can receive from Buddha today does not depend on the handing down of the teaching that Buddha gave to humans about 500 years before the Christian era, but on what he has become since that time. For he has not remained at a standstill; he has progressed; and it is through this progress, as a spiritual being in the spiritual worlds, that he has in the most eminent sense been able to take part in the further evolution of Western civilization. The outcome of our own esoteric investigation harmonizes in a wonderful way with much that had been known previously, before this important influence could be investigated again. For we know that the same individuality who appeared as Gautama Buddha in the East had previously worked in the West, and that certain legends and traditions connected with the name of Buddha or Wotan have to do with this same individuality, just as Buddhism has with Gautama Buddha in the East; hence the same field of action in human evolution which had been prepared earlier by the same individuality has again been occupied in a certain sense. Thus are interlaced the ways taken by the spiritual currents within the evolution of humanity.

Today the most important thing for us is to establish that in the astral body of the Jesus-child described by Luke, we have the Buddha forces at work. And when this Nathan Jesus-child was twelve years old, the Zarathustra individuality passed over into his threefold being.

Why is it, then, that this Jesus-child had the remarkable qualities we have just characterized? It was because he was not a human individuality like every other, but in a certain respect quite different, and in order to understand him we must go back to the ancient Lemurian time in which, strictly speaking, the earthly evolution of humans took its start. We must clearly understand that everything before the Lemurian time was really only a repetition of the Saturn, Sun, and Moon periods. Only in the Lemurian time was the first germ-condition laid down in human beings as a potentiality, so that during earthly evolution he could receive the fourth member of his being, the ego. We can say the expansion of humanity over the Earth—a subject dealt with more precisely in my *Outline of Esoteric Science*—is to be traced to certain human ancestors in the Lemurian period, the period with which our present Earth took its start.

It is only after a certain point of time in this Lemurian period that we can speak correctly, in a modern sense, of the human race. Before this, those egos who have since continued to incarnate were not present in humans on Earth. That was not the case. They were not yet separate from the substance of that Hierarchy which had first brought the human Ego into being: the Hierarchy of the Spirits of Form. We can now picture to ourselves—esoteric research shows this—that part of the substance of the Spirits of Form entered into human incarnations for the building up of the human ego. But when in due time humans were given over to their physical incarnations on the Earth, something was held back. A certain ego-substance was not brought into the stream of physical incarnations. If we were to represent the stream of physical human incarnations, beginning with the one whom the Bible calls 'Adam', the progenitor of the human race, we should have to draw a genealogical tree with wide-spreading branches. Instead, let us simply imagine that the substance poured down from the Spirits of Form now flows onward, but that something was held back: a sort of ego that was now protected from entering into physical incarnations. Instead, this ego, which did not appear again as an ego, preserved the form, the substantiality, that humans had possessed before proceeding to their first earthly incarnation. This ego lived on *collaterally* with the rest of humanity, and at the time of which we are now speaking, when the event of Palestine was to take place, it was still in the same condition, if we wish to speak according to the Bible, as was the ego of Adam before his first embodiment in flesh. Such an ego was always present.

In touching a bit on what esoteric science knows about this ego— which naturally for us moderns is something extremely foolish— we see that this ego, which was, as it were, held back 'in reserve', was given into the care of the holy Mysteries through Atlantean and post-Atlantean times. It was preserved in an important Mystery centre, as in a tabernacle, and because of this it had quite special characteristics; it was untouched by everything that a human ego could have learnt on Earth. It was therefore untouched by any luciferic and ahrimanic influences; it was indeed something we can think of, in contrast to other human egos, as an empty sphere, still completely virginal with regard to all earthly experiences—a nothing, a negative, in this respect. Hence it seemed as though the Nathan-child, described in the Luke Gospel, really had no human ego; as though he consisted only of physical, etheric, and astral body. And it is quite adequate if at first, we say that an ego, developed as egos had developed in Atlantean and post-Atlantean times, was not there at all in the Luke Jesus-child.

We speak in the true sense of the word when we say that in the Matthew Jesus-child we have to do with a completely developed human being; whereas in the Nathan Jesus-child of the Gospel of St Luke we have to do with a physical, an etheric, and an astral body which are interrelated in the harmonious unity that belonged to humans when they emerged from the Saturn, Sun, and Moon evolutions. Hence this Jesus-child, as the Akashic Record tells us, was untalented for all that human culture had developed. He could not receive culture because he had never experienced it. External abilities and adaptations to existence are the outcome of certain experiences in earlier incarnations. Anyone who had never shared in such experiences would show himself without talent for all that humans have accomplished during the evolution of Earth. If the Nathan Jesus-child had been born in our time, he would have been totally ungifted for learning to write, since in Adamic times writing was unknown. Thus, for everything that was such that it was gradually acquired in the course of earthly existence, the Luke Jesus-child exhibited no talent. By contrast, the Luke Jesus-child revealed in a high degree the qualities he had brought with him—qualities that had not fallen into decadence through the luciferic influence. Even more interesting is the remarkable language he spoke.

Here we must bring to mind something I mentioned in *The Spiritual Guidance of the Individual and of Humanity*: that the languages which are now spread over the Earth took their rise comparatively late in evolution. They were preceded by what can truly be called a primal human language. It is the divisive spirits of the luciferic and ahrimanic world who have made many languages out of the primal language. The primal language is lost, and can be spoken today by nobody with an ego that has passed from incarnation to incarnation in the course of earthly evolution. This Jesus-child, who had not gone through human incarnations, acquired from the beginning of human evolution the faculty of speaking, not this or that language, but a language of which we can rightly say that it was not comprehensible to those around him. But, because of the inner qualities of heart that lived in it, it was understood by his mother's heart. This points to a phenomenon of immense significance in the case of the Luke Jesus-child.

We have seen that when this Luke Jesus-child was born, he was provided with everything that had not been influenced by the luciferic and ahrimanic forces. He did not possess an ego that had been through a series of incarnations; therefore, nothing had to be discarded when, in his twelfth year, the individuality of Zarathustra passed over from the Solomon Jesus-child into the Nathan Jesus-child. I have already said that the human element that had remained behind, and up to this time had developed in the Mysteries by the side of the rest of humanity, was born for the first time in the

Palestine period as the Nathan Jesus-child. There was a transference from a Mystery centre in western Asia, where this human kernel had been preserved, into the body of the Nathan Jesus-child. This child grew on apace, and in his twelfth year the individuality of Zarathustra overcame him. We know also that this overcoming is intimated in the scene of the twelve-year-old Jesus in the Temple. It was quite natural that the parents of the Nathan Jesus-child, who were accustomed to regard him in the light we have described, should find a remarkable change when they discovered him in the Temple after he had been lost. For that was the moment when Zarathustra passed over into this twelve-year-old child. From the twelfth to the thirtieth year, therefore, we have to do with the individuality of Zarathustra in the Luke Jesus-child.

Now in the Luke Gospel we have a remarkable expression which indicates something that can be made clear only by esoteric investigation. You know that in the Luke Gospel, after the description of the scene with the twelve-year-old Jesus in the Temple, there is a passage: 'And Jesus increased in wisdom and stature, and in favour with God and man' [Luke 2:52]. ...[54] In truth, this passage stands as follows when we restore the text of the Gospels from the Akashic Record: The twelve-year-old child increased in everything wherein an astral body can increase, namely, in wisdom; in everything wherein an etheric body can increase, namely, in all the qualities of kindliness, goodness, etc.; and in everything wherein a physical body can increase, that is, in all that pours itself into external beauty of form. In this passage, therefore, a special indication is given that the Jesus-child, not having gone from incarnation to incarnation, had up to his twelfth year remained untouched, and could not be touched in his individuality by the luciferic and ahrimanic forces. The Luke Gospel intimates this again by tracing the sequence of generations back through Adam to God, thus indicating that the substance in question was uninfluenced by all that had taken place in human evolution.

So this Jesus-child lived on, increasing in all that was possible for a threefold organism not touched by the contamination which has affected the threefold bodies of other humans. And this enabled the individuality of Zarathustra, from the twelfth to the thirtieth year of life, to pour into this threefold human being all that could come from the heights to which he himself had previously attained. The individuality of Zarathustra was not led astray, but rather could develop everything that an ideal physical body, an ideal etheric body, and an ideal astral body could develop from the external world. That is what is indicated by the sentence from the Gospel of St Luke that was just adduced. Thereby the possibility was given of which we can say: in the thirtieth year of life, Zarathustra was in a position to pour everything that can come from such a highly developed being into this threefold, human bodily nature. Hence, we form a correct idea of Jesus of Nazareth, up to the thirtieth year of his life, when we think of him as a lofty human individuality, for whose coming into existence the greatest possible preparations had been made.

But we must now be clear about one thing if we want to understand how the fruits of a development we go through in our bodies are of benefit to the individuality. Our bodies enable our individuality to absorb the fruits of our life for its future evolution. When in death we forsake our bodies, we do not usually leave in them what we have achieved and gained for ourselves as individuals. Later on we shall see under what special conditions something may remain in the bodies; but it is not the rule that the individualities should leave behind in their bodies whatever they have won for themselves. When Zarathustra forsook the threefold bodily being of Jesus of Nazareth in the thirtieth year, he left behind the three bodies, physical, etheric, and astral. But all that he had been able to gain through these instruments went into the individuality of Zarathustra, who now exists in these three bodies, and lived on further with him, to his benefit. Something however, was gained by the threefold bodily organism of Jesus of Nazareth. His human nature, still free, as it always had been, from luciferic and ahrimanic influences, was conjoined for a period with the individuality who had unequalled insight into the spirituality of the cosmos.

Think what this Zarathustra had experienced! While he was founding the Ancient Persian civilization and looking up to the great Sun Spirit, he was even then gazing out into the cosmic realms of the spiritual. Through successive incarnations, his development went on. When the innermost part of human nature, together with the most intensive powers of sympathy and love, had become manifest through the unsullied human substance which had been preserved until the birth of the Nathan Jesus, and when the astral body had permeated itself with the forces of Gautama Buddha, there was present in this child what we may call the most intimate human inwardness. And then into this bodily nature there entered the individuality who above all others had seen most clearly and deeply into the spirituality of the Macrocosm. By this means, the bodily instrument, the entire organism of the Nathan Jesus was so transformed that it could be the vehicle capable of receiving into itself the Christ-extract of the Macrocosm. If this bodily nature had not been permeated by the individuality of Zarathustra up to the thirtieth year, the eyes would not have been able to endure the substance of the Christ from the thirtieth year up to the Mystery of Golgotha; the hands would not have been capable of being permeated with the substance of the Christ in the thirtieth year. To be able to receive the Christ, this bodily nature had to be prepared, expanded, through the individuality of Zarathustra. Thus in Jesus of Nazareth, as he was at the moment when Zarathustra took leave of him and the Christ entered into him, we have to do neither with an adept, nor with anything like a higher human being. For an adept is an adept because he has a highly developed individuality, and it was just this that had passed out of the threefold bodily nature of Jesus of Nazareth. We have simply the bodily nature so prepared through the indwelling of Zarathustra that it could take into itself the Christ. But now, through the union of the Christ with this bodily nature, by necessity the following consequence came about.

During these three years, from the Baptism by John in the Jordan onwards to the actual Mystery of Golgotha, the development of the physical body, the etheric body, and the astral body was quite different from the bodily development of other human beings. Since the Nathan Jesus had received no influence from the luciferic and ahrimanic powers, the possibility was given that, from the Baptism in Jordan onwards—now that there was in Jesus of Nazareth no human ego, but solely the Christ—everything which is normally at work in a human organism was not developed.

We said yesterday that the human phantom, the primal form that draws into itself the material elements that fill out the physical body and are laid aside at death, had degenerated in the course of time up to the Mystery of Golgotha. At the beginning of human evolution, it was intended that the phantom should remain untouched by the material elements that we take for our nutrition from the animal, plant, and mineral kingdoms. It was supposed to remain untouched. But it did not remain untouched. For the luciferic influence brought about a close connection between the phantom and the forces which we absorb through our earthly evolution; a connection particularly with the ashy constituents. The result was that the phantom, while continuing to accompany us during our further evolution, was strongly drawn to these ashy constituents, and instead of adhering to the etheric body, it attached itself to these products of disintegration. Those were all consequences of luciferic influence. But where the luciferic influences had been kept away, as they were from the Nathan Jesus, where there was no human ego, but rather the cosmic Being of Christ was present from the Baptism in the Jordan onwards, no force of attraction arose between the phantom and the material elements that had been taken into the bodily organism. Throughout the three years from the Baptism up to the Mystery of Golgotha, the phantom remained untouched by these elements.

In esoteric terms, we can say: The human phantom, according to its intended development through the Saturn, Sun, and Moon epochs, should not have been attracted to the ashy constituents, but only to the dissolving salt constituents, so that it would have taken the path of volatilization in so far as the salt constituents dissolved. In an esoteric sense, one can say that it would have dissolved and passed over, not into the Earth, but rather into its volatile constituents. The remarkable fact is that with the Baptism in Jordan and the entry of the Christ into the body of the Nathan Jesus, all connection of the phantom with the ashy constituents was wiped out; only the connection with the salt constituents remained.

This is alluded to in the passage where Jesus Christ wishes to explain to his first-chosen disciples: 'Through the way in which you feel yourselves united with the Christ Being, a certain possibility for the future evolution of humanity will come about. It will be possible for the one body risen from the grave—the spiritual body—to pass over into humans.' That is what Christ wished to say when he used the phrase, 'You are the salt of the Earth'. All these words we find in the Gospels, reminding us of the terminology and craft language of the later alchemists, of later esotericism, have the deepest imaginable significance. And in fact this significance was well known to the medieval and later alchemists—not to the charlatans mentioned in the history books—and not one of them spoke of these connections without feeling in his heart a connection with Christ.

Thus it followed that when Jesus Christ was crucified, when His Body was nailed to the Cross—you will notice that here I use the exact words of the Gospel, for they are confirmed by true esoteric research—when this Body of Jesus of Nazareth was fastened to the Cross, the phantom was perfectly intact; it existed in a spiritual bodily form, visible only to supra-sensible sight, and was much more loosely connected with the body's material content of earthly elements than has ever happened with any other human being. In every other human being, a connection of the phantom with these elements has occurred, and it is this that holds them together.

In the case of Jesus Christ, it was quite different. The ordinary law of inertia sees to it that certain material portions of a human body hold together after death in the form we have given them, until after some time they crumble away, so that hardly anything of them is visible. So it was with the material portions of the Body of Jesus Christ. When the Body was taken down from the Cross, the parts were still coherent, but they had no connection with the phantom; the phantom was completely free of them. When the Body became permeated with certain substances, which in this case worked quite differently from the way in which they affect any other body that is embalmed, it came to pass that after the burial, the material parts quickly volatilized and passed over into the elements. Hence the disciples who looked into the grave found the linen cloths in which the

Body had been wrapped, but the phantom, on which the evolution of the ego depends, had risen from the grave. It is not surprising that Mary Magdalene, who had known only the earlier phantom when it was permeated by earthly elements, did not recognize the same form in the phantom, now freed from terrestrial gravity, when she saw it clairvoyantly. It seemed to her different.

Moreover, we must clearly understand that it was only through the power of the companionship of the disciples with the Christ that all the disciples, and all those persons of whom the same is told, could see the Risen One, for He appeared to them in the spiritual Body, the Body of which Paul says that it increases as a grain of seed and passes over into all people. Paul himself is convinced that it was not a Body permeated by the earthly elements that had appeared to the other Apostles, but that the same which had appeared to him had also appeared to them, as he says in the following passage:

> For I have delivered unto you as of first importance what I also received, that Christ died for our sins in accordance with the scriptures, that he was buried, that he was raised on the third day in accordance with the scriptures; and that he appeared to Cephas, then to the twelve. Then he appeared to more than five hundred brethren at one time, most of whom are still alive, though some have fallen asleep. Then He appeared to James, then to all the apostles. Last of all, as to one untimely born, he appeared also to me. [I Corinthians 15:3–8.]

Christ appeared to Paul through the Event at Damascus. And that the manner in which He appeared to Paul is equated with His appearance to the Apostles, shows that Christ appeared to Paul in the same form as to the others. But what was it that convinced Paul?

In a certain sense, Paul was an initiate before the Event of Damascus. His initiation had combined the ancient Hebrew principle and the Greek principle. He knew that an initiate became, in his etheric body, independent of the physical body, and could appear in the purest form of his etheric body to those who were capable of seeing it. If Paul had had the vision only of a pure etheric body, independent of a physical body, he would have spoken differently. He would have said that he had seen someone who had been initiated and would be living on further in the course of earthly evolution, independently of the physical body. He would not have found this particularly surprising. What Paul experienced on the road to Damascus could not have been that. He had experienced something that he knew could be experienced only when the Scriptures were fulfilled; when a perfect human phantom, a human body risen from the grave in a supra-sensible form, would appear in the spiritual atmosphere of the Earth. And that is what he saw! That is what appeared to him on the road to Damascus and left him with the conviction: 'He was there—He is risen! For what is there could come only from Him: it is the phantom which can be seen by all human individualities who seek to relate themselves to the Christ.' This is what convinced him that Christ was already there; that He would not come first in the future, but was actually present there in a physical body, and that this physical body had rescued the primal form of the human physical body for the salvation of all humanity.

That this Deed could be accomplished only through the greatest unfolding of divine love, and in what sense it was an act of love, and then in what sense the word 'salvation' is to be understood in the further evolution of humanity—this will be our subject tomorrow.

LECTURE 9

KARLSRUHE, 13 OCTOBER 1911

THE lectures given so far have led essentially to two questions. One relates to the objective event connected with the name, Jesus Christ; to the nature of that impulse which as the Christ-Impulse entered into human evolution. The other question is: How can individuals establish their connection with the Christ-Impulse? In other words, how can the Christ-Impulse become effective for the individual? The answers to these two questions are of course interrelated. For we have seen that the Christ-Event is an objective fact of human earthly evolution, and that something real, something actual, comes forth to meet us in the Resurrection. With Christ, there rose out of the grave a kind of seed-kernel for the restoration of our human phantom. And it is possible for this seed-kernel to incorporate itself into those individuals who find a connection with the Christ-Impulse.

That is the objective side of the relationship of the individual to the Christ-Impulse. Today we wish to add the subjective side. We will try to find an answer to the question: 'How do individuals now find it possible gradually to take into themselves what comes forth through the Resurrection of Christ?'

To answer this question, we must first distinguish between two things. When Christianity entered into the world as a religion, it was not merely a religion for those who wished to approach Christ by one or other of the spiritual paths. Rather, it was to be a religion that all humans could accept and make their own. A special esoteric development was not necessary for finding the way to Christ. We must therefore fix our attention first on that path to Christ, the exoteric path, which every soul, every heart, can find in the course of time. We must then distinguish this path from the esoteric path which right up to our own time has revealed itself to the soul who desired to seek the Christ by gaining access to esoteric powers. We must distinguish between the path of the physical plane and the path of the supra-sensible worlds.

In hardly any other century has there been such obscurity concerning the outward, exoteric way to Christ as in the nineteenth. And this obscurity increased during the second half of the century. More and more people came to lose knowledge of the way to Christ. Those imbued with the thought of today no longer form the right concepts, such concepts for example as souls even in the eighteenth century formed on their way to the Christ-Impulse. Even the first half of the nineteenth century was illumined by a certain possibility of finding the Christ-Impulse as something real. But for the most part in the nineteenth century, this path to Christ was lost to humanity. And we can understand this when we realize that we are standing at the beginning of a new path to Christ. We have often spoken of the new way now opening for souls through a renewal of the Christ-Event. In human evolution, it always happens that a kind of low point must be reached in any trend before a new light comes in once more. The turning away from the spiritual worlds during the nineteenth century was only natural in face of the fact that in the twentieth century quite a new epoch for the spiritual life of humanity must begin, in the special sense we have often mentioned.

Even to those who have come to know something of anthroposophy, our movement often appears to be something quite new. If, however, we look away from the enrichment that spiritual endeavours in the West have experienced recently through the inflow of the concepts of reincarnation and karma, bound up with the whole teaching of repeated earthly lives and its significance for human evolution, we must say that, in other respects, ways into the spiritual world, similar to our theosophical way, are by no means new in Western history. Anyone, however, who tries to rise into the spiritual world along the present path of theosophy will find themselves somewhat estranged from the manner in which theosophy was cultivated in the eighteenth century. At that time, in this neighbourhood [Baden], and especially in Württemberg, much theosophy was studied, but everywhere an illuminated view of the teaching concerning repeated earthly lives was lacking, and thereby a cloud was cast over the whole field of theosophical work. For those who could look deeply into esoteric connections, and particularly into the connection of the world with the Christ-Impulse, what they saw was overshadowed for this reason. But within the whole horizon of Christian philosophy and Christian life, something like theosophical endeavours arose continually. This striving towards theosophy was active everywhere, even in the outward, exoteric paths of individuals who could go no further than sharing externally in the life of some congregation, Christian or otherwise.

How theosophical endeavours penetrated Christian endeavours is shown by figures such as Bengel[55] and Oetinger,[56] who worked in Württemberg, men who in their whole way of thinking—if we remember that they lacked the idea of reincarnation—reached all that one can reach of higher views concerning evolution, in so far as they had made the Christ-Impulse their own. The roots of theosophical life have always existed. Hence there is much that is correct in a treatise on theosophical subjects written by Oetinger in the eighteenth century. In the Preface to a book on Oetinger's work, published in 1847, Rothe,[57] who taught at Heidelberg University, wrote:

> What theosophy really wants is often difficult to recognize in the case of the older theosophists ... but it is none the less clear that theosophy, as far as it has gone today, can claim no scientific status and therefore cannot extend its influence more widely. It would be very hasty to conclude that theosophy is only an ephemeral phenomenon, and entirely unjustifiable from a scientific standpoint. History already testifies loudly enough to the contrary. It tells us how this enigmatic phenomenon has never been able to accomplish anything, and yet, unnoticed, it is continually breaking through afresh, held together in its most varied forms by the chain of a never-dying tradition.

Now we must remember that the man who wrote this learnt about theosophy only in the forties of the nineteenth century, as it had been transmitted from many theosophists of the eighteenth. What came over was certainly not clothed in the forms of our scientific thought.

It was therefore difficult to believe that the theosophy of that time could affect wider circles. Apart from this, such a voice, coming to us out of the forties of the nineteenth century, must appear significant when it says:

> The main thing is that once theosophy has become a real science, and has thus clearly yielded definite results, these will gradually become matters of general and even popular conviction, and will be regarded as accepted truths by people who could not follow the paths by which they were discovered and by which alone they could be discovered.

After this there comes a pessimistic paragraph with which, in its bearing on theosophy, we cannot now agree. For anyone familiar with the present form of spiritual-scientific endeavours will be convinced that this theosophy, in the form in which it desires to work, can become popular in the widest circles. Even such a paragraph may therefore inspire us with courage when we read further:

> Still, this rests in the lap of the future, and there we will not encroach: for the present we will gratefully rejoice in what our valued Oetinger has so beautifully set forth, and which may certainly count upon a sympathetic reception in a wide circle.

Thus we see that theosophy was a pious hope of those who came to know something of the old theosophy that was handed down from the eighteenth century.

After that time, the stream of theosophical life was buried under the materialistic trends of the nineteenth century. Only through what we may now accept as the dawn of a new age do we again approach the true spiritual life, and now in a form which can be so scientific that in principle every heart and every soul can understand it. During the nineteenth century, there was a complete loss of understanding for something that the theosophists of the eighteenth century still fully possessed; they called it *Zentralsinn* [inner light]. Oetinger, who worked in Murrhard, near Karlsruhe, was for a time the pupil of a quite simple man in Thuringia, named Voelker, whose pupils knew that he possessed what was called 'inner light'. What in those days was this 'inner light'? It was none other than what now arises in everyone who earnestly and with iron energy works through the content of my book, *How to Know Higher Worlds*. It was fundamentally nothing else that this simple man of Thuringia possessed. What he brought into existence—for his time a very interesting theosophy— was the teaching that influenced Oetinger. It is difficult for us to reconcile ourselves today to the knowledge that a deepening of theosophy occurred so recently, and gave rise to a rich literature, buried though this is in libraries and among antiquarians.

Something else is equally difficult for someone today: to accept the Christ-Event as first of all an objective fact. How much discussion of this matter there was in the nineteenth century! It is impossible in a short course to indicate even in outline how many and diverse are the views of the nineteenth century concerning Jesus Christ. And anyone who takes the trouble to inquire further into opinions concerning Jesus Christ, whether those of theologians or of laymen, will encounter some very real difficulties, if the views of the nineteenth century on this question are considered in relation to the times in which better traditions still prevailed. In the nineteenth century, it even became possible for persons to be regarded as great theologians when they were far removed from any acceptance of an objective Christ who entered into and worked in the history of the world. And here we come to the question: What relationship to the Christ can be found by an individual who takes no esoteric path, but remains entirely in the field of the exoteric?

So long as we keep to the standpoint of those nineteenth-century theologians who held that human evolution can take its course purely in human inwardness, and has nothing to do with the external world of the Macrocosm, we cannot reach an objective appreciation of Jesus Christ; we come to all kinds of grotesque ideas, but never to a relationship with the Christ-Event. For anyone who believes that he can reach the highest human ideal compatible with earthly evolution merely by an inner path of soul, through a kind of self-redemption, a relationship with the objective Christ is impossible. We may also say that wherever human redemption is thought of as a matter for psychology to deal with, there is no relationship to the Christ. Anyone who penetrates further into cosmic mysteries soon finds that when someone believes that he can attain his highest ideal of earthly existence solely through himself, only through his own inner development, he cuts off altogether their connection with the Macrocosm. Such people believe that they have the Macrocosm before them as a kind of nature, and that their inner development of soul, side by side with the Macrocosm, is something running parallel with it. But a connection between the two cannot be found. This is just what is so terribly grotesque in the evolution of the nineteenth century. The connection that should exist between Microcosm and Macrocosm has been torn asunder. If this had not happened, we should not have seen all those misunderstandings that have arisen over the terms 'theoretical materialism' on the one hand and 'abstract idealism' on the other. Just consider: the sundering of Microcosm and Macrocosm has led those who care little for the inner life of the soul to assign it, as well as the external life of the body, to the Macrocosm, thus making everything subject to material processes. Others, aware that there is nevertheless an inner life, have fallen gradually into abstractions concerning everything of significance to the human soul.

To be clear regarding this difficult matter, let us recall something very significant that was learnt in the Mysteries. How many people today believe in their innermost consciousness: 'If I think something—for instance, if I entertain a bad thought about my neighbour—it has no significance for the outer world; the thought is only in myself. It has a quite different significance if I give him a box on the ears. This is something that happens on the physical plane; the other is a mere feeling or a mere thought.' Or again, how many people are there who say, when they fall into a sin or a lie or an error: 'This is something that happens in the human soul'? And, by contrast, if a stone falls from the roof: 'This is something that takes place externally.' And they will readily explain, using crude sensory concepts, that when a stone falls, perhaps accidentally, into water, it sets up ripples that spread out far and wide, so that everything produces effects that continue unobserved; but anything that has occurred in the soul is shut off from the world outside. People could therefore come to believe that to sin, to err, and then to put it right again, is entirely a concern of the individual soul. To anyone with an outlook of this kind, something many of us have witnessed in the last two years must seem grotesque.

Let me recall to you the scene in my Rosicrucian drama, *The Portal of Initiation*, where Capesius and Strader enter the astral world, and it is shown that what they think, speak, and feel is not without significance for the objective world, the Macrocosm, but actually releases storms in the elements. For us moderns it seems absurd to suppose that destructive forces can strike at the Macrocosm through somebody having had wrong thoughts. In the Mysteries, it was made very clear to the pupil that when, for example, anyone tells a lie or falls into error, this is a real process that does not concern himself only. The Germans say 'Thoughts are duty free', because they see no customs barrier when thoughts arise. Thoughts belong to the objective world; they are not merely experiences of the soul. The pupil of the Mysteries saw: 'When you tell a lie, it signifies in the supra-sensible world the darkening of a certain light; when you perpetrate a loveless action, something in the spiritual world is burnt up in the fire of lovelessness; with errors you extinguish light in the Macrocosm.' The effect was shown to the pupil through objective experience: how, through an error, something is extinguished on the astral plane, and darkness follows; or how through a loveless action, something acts like a burning and destroying fire.

In exoteric life, we do not know what is going on around us. We are like ostriches with their heads in the sand; we do not see effects that nevertheless are there. The effects of feeling are there, and they would be visible to supra-sensible sight if we were led into the Mysteries. It was not until the nineteenth century that anyone could say: 'Everything in which individuals have sinned, everything in which they are weak, is their personal affair only. Redemption must come about through an experience in the soul, and so Christ also can be only an experience in the soul.' What is necessary for us not only to find our way to Christ, but that we may not sunder our connection with the Macrocosm, is the knowledge: 'If you incur error and sin, these are objective, not subjective events, and because of them, something happens outside in the cosmos.' And in the moment when we become conscious that with our sin, with our error, something objective happens; when we know that what we have done, what we have given out from ourselves, is not connected merely with our self, but rather with the whole objective course of cosmic development, then we will no longer be able to say to ourselves that compensation for what we have brought about is only an inner concern of the soul. There is indeed a good and significant possibility that someone who sees that thoughts and feelings are objective may also see that what has brought and brings people into mistakes through successive earthly lives is not an inward affair related to a single life, but rather the consequence of karma.

Now an event that was outside history and outside human responsibility, as was the luciferic influence in the old Lemurian period, could not possibly be expunged from the world by a human event. Through the luciferic event, humans gained a great benefit: they became free beings. But they also incurred a liability: the propensity to deviate from the path of the good and the right, and from the path of the true. What has happened in the course of incarnations is a matter of karma. But all that has crept down from the Macrocosm into the Microcosm, all that the luciferic forces have given to us, is something that humans cannot deal with by themselves. To compensate for the objective luciferic event, another objective act was needed. In short, we must feel that what we incur as error and sin is not merely subjective, and that an experience in the soul that is merely subjective is not sufficient to bring about Redemption.

Anyone who is convinced of the objectivity of error will thus understand also the objectivity of the act of redemption. One cannot by any means treat the luciferic influence as an objective act without treating in the same manner the compensating act, the Event of Golgotha. A theosophist can only choose between two things. Everything may be set on the foundation of karma; of course that is quite right as regards everything that we ourselves have brought about. But then we come to the necessity of stretching out the repeated lives forward and backward as far as we like, with no end to it in either direction. It always goes round and round like a wheel.

The other thing—the alternative choice—is the concrete idea of evolution we must hold: that there was a Saturn, a Sun, and a Moon existence which were quite different from the Earth existence; that in the Earth existence the kind of repeated earthly lives as we know them first occurred; that the luciferic intervention was a single, unrepeated event—all this alone gives real content to our theosophical outlook. All this, however, is inconceivable without the objectivity of the Event of Golgotha.

In pre-Christian times, humans were—as you know—different in various ways. One particular difference was that when they came down from spiritual worlds into earthly incarnations, they brought with them, as substance, some of the divine element. For this reason, when individuals reflected on their own weaknesses, they always felt that the best part of them had originated in the divine sphere from which they had descended. But the Divine element gradually became exhausted in the course of further incarnations, and it was quite exhausted when the events of Palestine drew near. Thus people of pre-Christian times, when they reflected on their own weakness, always felt: the best things that humans have originate in the divine sphere, from which we humans have descended.

The last, lingering after-effects continued to be felt, but none of it was left when John the Baptist declared: 'Change your conception of the world, for the times have changed. Now you will no longer be able to rise up into the spiritual as in the past, for the vision that could see into the old spirituality is lost. Change your thinking, and accept the Divine Being who is to give anew to humans what they have had to lose through their descent to Earth!' Consequently—you may deny this if you think in the abstract, but not if you look at history in concrete terms—human feelings and perceptions changed altogether at the turning point of the old and new epochs, a point marked by the events of Palestine.

After these events, humans began to feel forsaken. They felt forsaken when they approached the hardest questions, those which concerned most directly the innermost part of the soul; when, for example, they asked themselves: 'What will become of me when I go through the gate of death with a number of deeds that have not been made good?' Then there came to meet them a thought that certainly might be born from the longing of the soul, but could be allayed only when the soul could say to itself: 'Yes, a Being has lived who entered into the evolution of humanity and to whom you can hold fast. He is working in the outer cosmos, where you cannot go. He is working to bring about compensation for your deeds. He will help you to make good the evil results of the luciferic influence!' Through this feeling forsaken, and then feeling rescued by an objective power, there enters into humanity an intuitive feeling that sin is a real power, an objective fact, and that the act of redemption is also objective. It is an act that cannot be accomplished by individuals, for they have not invoked the luciferic influence, but only by One who works in the worlds where Lucifer is consciously active.

All that I have thus set before you, in words drawn from anthroposophy, was not grasped intellectually, as knowledge. It resided in feelings and intuitive perceptions, and from this came the need to turn to Christ. For those who felt this need, there was of course the possibility of finding in Christian communities ways by which they could deepen all such perceptions and feelings.

After humans had lost their primal connection with the Gods, what did they find when they looked out at the material world? Through their descent into the material realm, their perception of the spiritual, of the physical manifestation of the divine in the cosmos, steadily declined. The remnants of the old clairvoyance that were still there faded by degrees, and nature, for them, was in a certain sense deprived of the divine. A merely material world was spread out before us. And in face of this material universe, they could in no way maintain a belief that the principle of Christ was at work there. The nineteenth-century Kant-Laplace hypothesis,[58] whereby our solar system developed out of a cosmic nebula, and eventually life arose on individual planets, has led finally to the universe being regarded as a collaboration of atoms. If we try to think of Christ in this setting, as conceived by materialistic scientists, it would be madness. There is no place for the Being of Christ in this cosmogony, indeed no place for anything spiritual. You remember someone saying—I read you the passage—that he would have to tear up his whole conception of the universe if he had to believe in the Resurrection. This shows that in contemplating nature, or in thinking about nature, all possibility of penetrating into the living essence of natural facts has disappeared.

When I speak like this, it is not by way of disapproval. The time had to come when nature would be deprived of the divine, deprived of the spirit, so that man could formulate the totality of abstract thoughts required to comprehend external nature, as the outlook of Copernicus,[59] Kepler,[60] and Galileo[61] enabled him to do. The web of thoughts that has led to our age of machinery had to take hold of humanity. On the other hand, it was necessary that this age should have a compensation for the fact that it had become impossible in exoteric life to find a direct path from the Earth to the spiritual. For if we had been able to find this path, we would have been able to find the path to Christ, as we will find it in the coming centuries. There had to be a compensation.

The question now is: What had become necessary as an exoteric path for humanity leading to Christ during the centuries in which an atomistic conception of the universe became gradually accepted, a conception that alienated nature more and more from the divine, and in the nineteenth century grew into the study of nature emptied of the divine?

A twofold remedy was required. A spiritual vision of the Christ could be found exoterically in two ways. One way was to show that all matter is completely foreign to humans' inner spiritual being. We could be shown that it is untrue to say that everywhere in space where matter appears, only matter is present. How could this come about? In no other way than by something being given to humanity which is at one and the same time spirit and matter; something which we know is spirit, and yet seems to be matter. Therefore the transformation, the eternally valid transformation, of spirit into matter, of matter into spirit, had to continue as a vital fact. And this came to pass because the Holy Communion has been celebrated, has been maintained through the centuries as a Christian ritual. And the further we trace back the institution of the Holy Communion through the centuries, the more can we understand how in the older times, not yet so materialistic, it was better understood.

In regard to higher things, when people begin to discuss something, it is a proof, as a rule, that they no longer understand it. Even simple matters, as long as they are understood, are not much discussed. Discussions are a proof that the point at issue is not understood by a majority of the people involved. Thus it was with the Holy Communion. As long as it was known that the Holy Communion furnished a living proof that matter is not merely matter, but that there are ceremonial acts through which the spirit can be united with matter—as long as people knew that this interpenetration of matter with spirit, as it finds expression in the Holy Communion, is a union with the Being of Christ, so long was the Holy Communion accepted without argument. But then came the time when materialism arose, when people no longer understood what lies at the foundation of the Holy Communion. Then they disputed whether the bread and wine are merely symbols of the divine, or whether divine power actually flows into them. For anyone who can see more deeply, all the disputes that arose on this account at the beginning of the new epoch signify that the original understanding of the ritual had been lost. For those who desired to come to Christ, the Holy Communion was a complete equivalent of the esoteric path, if they could not take that path, and thus in the Holy Communion they could find a real union with Christ. For all things have their time.

Certainly, just as it is true in regard to the spiritual life that a quite new age is dawning, so is it true that the way to Christ which for centuries was the right one for many people will remain for centuries more the right one for many. Things pass over gradually into one another, and what was formerly right will gradually pass over into something else when people are ready for it.

The aim of theosophy is to work in such a way that we shall grasp in the spirit itself something concrete, something real. By means of meditation, concentration, and all that we learn as the knowledge of higher worlds, humans become ripe in their inner being not merely to experience realms of thought, or worlds of abstract feelings and perceptions, but to permeate themselves inwardly with the element of the spirit; thereby they will experience the Communion in the Spirit; thereby thoughts, meditative thoughts, will be able to live in us; they will even be the very same, only from within outwards, as the symbol of the Holy Communion, the consecrated Bread, has been from without inwards.

And as undeveloped Christians can seek their way to Christ through the Holy Communion, so developed Christians who, through progressive knowledge of the Spirit, have learnt to know the Form of the Christ, can raise themselves in spirit to what will indeed be in the future an exoteric path for humans. That will be the force that is to bring to humans a widening of the Christ-Impulse. But then all ceremonies will change, and what formerly came to pass through the attributes of bread and wine will come about in the future through a spiritual communion. The thought of the Sacrament, the Holy Communion, will remain. Only it must be made possible that certain thoughts that flow to us through what is imparted within our movement, certain inner thoughts and feelings, shall permeate and spiritualize our inner being—thoughts and feelings as fully consecrated as in the best sense of inner Christian development the Holy Communion has spiritualized the human soul and filled it with the Christ.

When this becomes possible—and it will be possible—we shall have progressed a stage further in evolution. And then we shall see the real proof that Christianity is greater than its external form. For a poor opinion of Christianity is held by anyone who thinks it will be obliterated when the external forms of the Christianity of a certain period are swept away. A true opinion will be permeated with the conviction that all Churches which have cherished the Christ-Thought, all external thoughts, all external forms, are temporal and therefore transitory, while the thought of Christ will live in ever-new forms in human hearts and souls in the future, little as these new forms are evident today. Thus we are first taught by anthroposophy how, along one exoteric path, the Holy Communion had its significance in earlier times.

The other exoteric path was through the Gospels. And here again we must realize what in earlier times the Gospels still were for humans. It is not very long since the Gospels were not read as they were in the nineteenth century. In those days, they were read as a life-giving fountain whence something substantial passed over into the soul. They were not read in the way described in the first lecture of this course, when we were speaking of a false path, but so that a person saw approaching from outside something for which our souls were panting with thirst; they were so read that their souls found pictured therein the real Redeemer, of whom the soul knew that He must be there, in the wide universe.

Those who understood how to read the Gospels in this way never thought of asking the endless questions which first became questions for the intelligent, clever people of the nineteenth century. You need only recall how many times in speaking of these questions, in one form or another, we have had to say that for quite clever people, who have all science and learning at their fingertips, the thought of Jesus Christ and the events of Palestine are truly not compatible with the modern worldview. In an apparently enlightened way, they say that when humans were not aware that the Earth is a quite small heavenly body, they could believe that with the Cross of Golgotha a special new event took place on Earth. But since Copernicus taught that the Earth is a planet like others, can one still believe that Christ came to us from another planet? Why should we believe that the Earth is so exceptionally situated as was formerly thought? A simile is then brought in: 'Since our conception of the universe has been so much enlarged, it seems as though one of the most important artistic presentations had taken place, not on the great stage of a capital city, but on the small stage of some provincial theatre.' So that is how it looks to these people: the Earth is such an insignificant little cosmic body that the events of Palestine appear like the performance of a great cosmic drama on the stage of a small provincial theatre. We can no longer imagine such a thing, because the Earth is so small in comparison with the great universe!

It seems so clever when something like that is said, but after all there is not much cleverness in it, for Christianity never asserted what is here apparently contradicted. Christianity has never placed the beginning of the Christ-Impulse in the magnificent places of the

Earth. It has always seen a certain deep seriousness in the fact that the bearer of the Christ was born in a stable among poor shepherds. Not only the little Earth, but a very obscure place on Earth, was sought out in Christian tradition wherein to place the Christ. Christianity from the very first answered the questions of the clever people. But they have not understood the answers which Christianity itself has given, because they could no longer let the living force of the great majestic pictures work upon the soul.

Nevertheless, through the pictures of the Gospel alone, without the Holy Communion and all that is connected with it—for the Holy Communion stands at the centre of all Christian cults—an exoteric path to Christ could not have been found. For the Gospels could not then have been popularized widely enough for a finding of the way to Christ to depend on them alone. And when the Gospels were popularized, we can see that it was not an unmixed blessing. For at the same time arose the great misunderstanding of the Gospels: they were taken superficially, and then all that the nineteenth century made of them came about; and indeed—speaking quite objectively—it was bad enough. I think anthroposophists will understand what is meant here by 'bad enough'. No censure is intended, for we cannot but acknowledge the diligence that the nineteenth century brought to the task of scientific investigation, including all the work in natural science. The tragedy is that this very science—and anyone familiar with it will grant this—owing to its deep seriousness and its tremendous, devoted industry, which one can only admire, has led to a complete splitting up and destruction of what it wished to teach. When in the future course of evolution people look back at our time, they will feel it to be particularly tragic that people sought to conquer the Bible by means of a science worthy of endless admiration—and succeeded only in losing the Bible.

Thus we can see that as regards these two aspects of the exoteric we are living in a transitional period, and in so far as we have grasped the spirit of theosophy, the old paths must lead over into others. And having now considered the exoteric paths of the past to the Christ-Impulse, we shall see tomorrow how this relationship to Christ takes form in the realm of the esoteric. We will then conclude our study by showing how we can come to grasp the Christ-Event not only for the whole evolution of humanity, but also for each individual. We shall be able to review the esoteric path more briefly, because we have assembled building-stones for it during past years. We will crown our endeavours by fixing our gaze upon the relationship of the Christ-Impulse to every individual human soul.

LECTURE 10

KARLSRUHE, 14 OCTOBER 1911

YESTERDAY we tried to characterize the path to Christ that can still be taken today, as it could especially in earlier times, by exoteric means. We will now touch briefly on the esoteric path—the path which leads to Christ in such a way that He can be found within the supra-sensible worlds.

First of all we must note that this esoteric path to Jesus Christ was also the way of the Evangelists, of those who wrote the Gospels. For although the writer of the Gospel of St John had himself witnessed many of the events he describes—as you can see from the lecture cycle on this Gospel[62]—his chief object was not merely to relate what he remembered, for this applies only to those minute, exact details which surprise us in his Gospel. The great, majestic, crowning features of the work of redemption, of the Mystery of Golgotha, were drawn by the writer of this Gospel from his clairvoyant consciousness also. Consequently, although the Gospels are really revived Mystery rituals—this is shown in my *Christianity as Mystical Fact* — they are so because the writers of the Gospels, following their esoteric path, could procure for themselves out of the supra-sensible world a picture of the events in Palestine which led to the Mystery of Golgotha. Ever since the Mystery of Golgotha, up to our own times, a person who desired to come to a supra-sensible experience of the Christ-Event had to go through the stages which you will find described in earlier lecture cycles as the seven stages of our Christian initiation: the washing of the feet; the scourging; the crowning with thorns; the mystic death; the burial; the Resurrection; and the Ascension. Today we will make clear to ourselves what the pupil can attain by going through this Christian initiation.

First of all, one essential point. As you can convince yourselves by reading the lectures on this subject, Christian initiation is very different from the inappropriate method of initiation described in the first lecture of this course. In Christian initiation, certain feelings that belong to humanity in general are first invoked, and they lead to an Imagination of the washing of the feet. Thus the picture of this in the Gospel of St John is not the first thing to be imagined; rather, the aspirant begins by trying to live for a long time with certain feelings and perceptions. I have often characterized this by saying that the person concerned should gaze upon the plant, which grows out of the mineral ground, takes into itself the materials of the mineral kingdom, and yet raises itself above this kingdom as a higher being than the mineral. If the plant could speak and feel, it would bow down to the mineral kingdom and say: 'Certainly I was destined within the lawfulness of the cosmos to attain a higher stage than you, mineral, but you give me the possibility of existence. In the order of beings you are certainly a lower being than myself, but I have to thank you for my existence, and I bow myself in humility before you.' In the same way, the animal would have to bow down to the plant, although the plant is a lower being than the animal, and say: 'I thank you for my existence; I acknowledge it in humility, and I bow myself before you.' And so would each being that climbs upwards have to bow down to the other standing below, and also he who has risen by way of a spiritual ladder to a higher level must bow down to the beings who alone have made this possible for him.

Persons who permeate themselves with the feeling of humility in regard to the lower, who thoroughly incorporate this feeling into their own being and let it live there for months, perhaps even for years, will see that it spreads itself out in their organism, and so pervades them that they experience a transformation of this feeling into an Imagination. And this Imagination corresponds exactly to the scene represented in the Gospel of St John as the washing of the feet, where Jesus Christ, who is the head of the twelve, stoops to those who stand here below Him in the order of the physical world, and in humility acknowledges that He thanks those who are below Him for the possibility of His higher ascent. He acknowledges before the twelve: 'As the animal thanks the plant, so do I thank you for what I was able to become in the physical world!' Individuals who permeate themselves with this feeling come not only to an Imagination of the washing of the feet, but also to a quite pronounced feeling, as though water were washing over their feet. This can be felt for weeks: it shows how deeply imbued our human nature is with such universal human feelings, which nevertheless can raise us above ourselves.

Further, we have seen that we can go through the experience which leads to the Imagination of the scourging when we place the following vividly before us: 'Much suffering and pain will meet me in the world; yes, from all sides suffering and pain may come; no one escapes them. But I will so steel my will that suffering and pain, the scourgings that come from the world, may do their worst; I will stand upright and bear my fate resignedly, as it comes to pass. For had it not come to pass as it has done, as I have experienced it, I should not have been able to reach the height I have attained.' When the individuals in question make this into feeling, and live within it, they actually feel something like sharp pains and woundings, like strokes of a scourge against their own skin, and the Imagination arises as if they were outside themselves, and were watching themselves scourged according to the example of Jesus Christ. In line with this example, one can experience the crowning of thorns, the mystic death, and so on. This has often been described.

What is attained by individuals who thus seek within themselves to experience first the four stages, and then, when their karma is favourable, the others also, making in all seven stages of Christian initiation? From the foregoing description, you can gather that the whole scale of feelings we go through ought to strengthen us and give us power, and ought to make us into quite another nature, so that in the world we feel ourselves standing strong, powerful, and free, and also capable of every act of devoted love. In Christian initiation, this ought in a deep sense to become a second nature to us. For what has to happen?

Perhaps it has not yet occurred to all those of you who have read the earlier elementary cycles, and so have met with Christian initiation in its seven stages, that owing to the intensity of the experiences that must be undergone, the effects go right into the physical body. For through the strength and power with which we go through these feelings, it really is at first as if water were washing over our feet, and then as if we were transfixed with wounds. We actually feel as if thorns were pressing into our head; we feel all the pain and suffering of the Crucifixion. We have to feel this before we can experience the mystical death, the burial, and the Resurrection, as these also have been described. Even if we have not gone through these feelings with sufficient intensity, they will certainly have the effect that we become strong and full of love in the right sense of the word. But what we then incorporate can go only as far as the etheric body.

When, however, we begin to feel that our feet are as though washed with water, our body as if covered with wounds, then we have succeeded in driving these feelings so deeply into our nature that they have penetrated as far as the physical body. They do indeed penetrate the physical body, and then the stigmata, the marks of the bleeding wounds of Jesus Christ, may appear. We drive the feelings inwards into the physical body and know that they develop their strength in the physical body itself. We consciously feel ourselves more in the grip of our whole being than if the impressions were merely in the astral body and etheric body. The essential thing is that through a process of mystical feeling, we work right into our physical body; and when we do this, we are doing nothing less than making ourselves ready in our physical body to receive the phantom that went forth from the grave on Golgotha. Hence, we work into our physical body in order to make it so living that it feels a relationship with, an attractive force towards, the phantom that rose out of the grave on Golgotha.

And here I would make an incidental remark. In anthroposophy, one must accustom oneself to becoming acquainted with cosmic secrets and cosmic truths gradually. Anyone who is not prepared to wait for the relevant truths will not make good progress.

Of course, people would like to have anthroposophy all at once, preferably in one book or in one course of lectures. But that cannot be so, as you will see from an example. How long is it since in earlier lectures Christian initiation was first described? You heard that such and such takes place, and that individuals, through the feelings that affect their souls, work right into their physical body. Everything said in those earlier lectures was intended to provide some elements for understanding the Mystery of Golgotha, and now for the first time it is possible to describe how an individual, through the requisite exercises of feeling in the course of Christian initiation, makes himself ripe to receive the phantom which rose from the grave of Golgotha. We had to wait until the union of the subjective with the objective could be found; and for this, many preparatory lectures were necessary. Even today there are many things that can be indicated only as 'half-truths'. Individuals who have patience to continue with us—whether in this or in another incarnation, each according to his karma—will have seen how they could advance from the description of the mystical path in the Christian sense to the description of the objective fact, and so to the real meaning of this Christian initiation, and they will see also that still higher truths will be brought to light from out of anthroposophy in the course of the coming years or the next age. Thus we see the aim, the goal, of Christian initiation.

Through what has been characterized as Rosicrucian initiation, that is, what an individual can have of it as initiation today, the same thing in a certain sense is also attained, only by somewhat different means. A bond of attraction is formed between the individual, in so far as he is incorporated in a physical body, and what arose as the real prototype of the physical body from the grave of Golgotha. Now we know from previous lectures that we are at the starting point of an epoch in which we must expect an event that will not take place on the physical plane, as did the Event of Golgotha, but in the supra-sensible world; an event which nevertheless stands in a close and true connection with the Event of Golgotha. The latter was designed to give back to human beings their real physical body of forces, the phantom that had degenerated from the beginning of the earthly evolution, and for the giving back of it a series of events on the physical plane had to occur; but for what is now to happen, an event on the physical plane is not necessary. An incarnation of the Being of Christ in a human body of flesh could take place only once in the course of earthly evolution. When people announce a repetition of the incarnation of this Being, it simply means that the Being of Christ is not understood.

The event now to come, which can be observed only in a supra-sensible world, has been characterized in the words: 'Christ becomes for humans the Lord of Karma.' This means that in future the ordering of karmic transactions will come about through Christ. Ever more and more will we come to feel in the future: 'I am going through the gate of death with my karmic account. On one side stand my good, clever, and beautiful deeds, my clever, beautiful, good, and intelligent thoughts; on the other side stands everything evil, wicked, stupid, foolish, and loathsome. But He who in the future will have the office of judge for the incarnations that will follow in human evolution, in order to bring order into this karmic account of humans, is the Christ!' And truly we have to picture this in the following way.

After we have gone through the gate of death, we shall be incarnated again in a later period. We shall then have to encounter events through which our karma can be balanced, for we must all reap what we have sown. Karma is a just law. But what the karmic law has to fulfil is not there only for individual human beings. Karma not only balances the accounts of each ego, but in every case the balancing must be arranged so as to be in the best possible accord with the concerns of the whole world. It must enable us to give all possible help to the advancement of humanity on Earth. For this we need enlightenment, not merely the knowledge that the karmic fulfilment of our deed must come about. The fulfilment can take a form that will be either less or more useful for the general progress of humanity. Hence, we must choose those thoughts, feelings, or perceptions which will pay off our karma, and at the same time serve the collective progress of humanity. In the future, it will fall to

Christ to bring the balance of our karma into line with the general earthly karma and the general progress of humanity. And this happens principally in the time between death and a new birth. But it will also be prepared for in the epoch of time we are now approaching, before whose door we stand, because humans will more and more acquire the capacity for a special experience. Very few are capable of it now, but from the middle of this century onwards, through the next 1,000 years, more and more people will have the following experience.

Individuals have done this or that. They will feel constrained to reflect on their actions, and something like a dream-picture, arising in their minds, will make a quite remarkable impression on them. They will say to themselves: 'I cannot identify this as a recollection of something I have done, yet it feels like an experience of my own.' Like a dream-picture it will stand before them, closely concerned with them; but they will not be able to recall that they have experienced or done it in the past. If they are anthroposophists, they will understand the matter; otherwise they will have to wait until they come to anthroposophy and learn to understand it. The anthroposophist will know: 'What you see as an apparent consequence of your actions is a picture that will be fulfilled in the future; the balancing of your actions is shown to you in advance'! We are at the beginning of an epoch in which individuals, directly after they have committed a deed, will have a premonition, a feeling, perhaps even a significant picture, of how this deed will be karmically balanced.

Thus, in closest connection with human experience, enhanced capabilities for humanity will arise during the coming epoch. These capabilities will give a powerful stimulus to human morality, and this will signify something quite different from the voice of conscience, which has been a preparation for it. The individual will no longer believe: 'What I have done will die with me.' He will know quite exactly: 'My action will not die when I die; it will have a consequence which will live on with me.' And there is much else that the individual will know. The time during which the doors of the spiritual world have been closed to humanity is nearly over. Humans must again climb up into the spiritual world. Their awakening capacities will enable them to participate in the spiritual world. Clairvoyance will always be different from this participation. Just as there was an ancient dreamlike clairvoyance, so will there be a future clairvoyance that is not dreamlike, the clairvoyance of people who know what they are doing and what it signifies.

Something else, too, will come about. The individual will know: 'I am not alone. Everywhere there are spiritual beings who stand in a relationship to me.' We will learn to communicate with these beings and to live with them. And in the next three thousand years the truth that Christ is acting as karmic judge will become apparent to a sufficiently large number of people. Christ Himself will be experienced by humans in an etheric form. Like Paul on the road to Damascus, they will know quite intimately that Christ lives, and is the source for the reawakening of the physical prototype we received at the beginning of our evolution, and need if the ego is to attain full development.

If through the Mystery of Golgotha something happened which gave the greatest impetus to human evolution, on the other hand it came at the time when the human sensibility, the human soul, were in their darkest condition. There were indeed ancient periods of evolution when humans could know with certainty, because they had an ancestral memory, that the human individuality goes through repeated earthly lives. In the Gospels, the teaching of repeated earthly lives is apparent only when we understand the Gospels and can discern traces of it there. That was the time when humans were least fitted to comprehend this teaching. In the later times, when humans sought for Christ along the path indicated yesterday, everything had to take the form of a childlike preparation. Humans could not then be made acquainted with experiences concerning reincarnation; they were not ripe for it, and it would only have led them into error. Christianity had to develop for nearly 2,000 years without being able to indicate the teaching of reincarnation.

We have shown in these lectures how different it was in Buddhism, and how in Western consciousness the thought of repeated earthly lives arises as something self-evident. Certainly, many mis-understandings still prevail; but whether we take this idea from Lessing or from the psychologist Droßbach, we become aware that for the European consciousness, the teaching of reincarnation concerns humanity at large, whereas in Buddhism, individuals regard the question of how they go from life to life, how they can free themselves from the thirst for existence, as concerning only their personal, inner life. The Oriental makes what is given to him as teaching about reincarnation into a path of individual redemption, whereas for Lessing the essential question was: 'How can the whole of humanity move forward?' According to Lessing, we must distinguish successive periods of time within the progressive development of humanity. Something new is given to humanity in each epoch. We see from history that new civilizing actions keep on emerging in the course of human development. How could one speak of the evolution of the whole of humanity, says Lessing, if a soul lived in only one epoch? Whence could the fruits of civilization come if human beings were not born again, if what they had learnt in one epoch were not carried over into the next, and its fruits into the following epoch and so on?

Thus for Lessing the idea of repeated earthly lives is not only a concern of the individual soul. It concerns the whole course of earthly civilization. And in order that an advanced civilization may arise, a soul which lives in the nineteenth century must carry over into its present existence whatever it had previously gained. For the sake of the Earth and its civilization, human beings must be born again! That is Lessing's thought.

But in this thought of reincarnation as concerning all humanity, the Christ-Impulse has been at work. We are thrown into it. For the Christ-Impulse makes everything someone does or can do into an action of universal relevance, rather than something that touches him only as an individual. Only they can be Christ's disciples who say: 'I do it for the least of the brethren, because I know Thou feelest as though I had done it for Thee.' As the whole of humanity is bound up with Christ, so do they who confess Christ feel that they belong to all humanity. This thought has worked into the thinking, feeling, and sensation of the whole human race. And when the idea of reincarnation reappeared in the eighteenth century, it appeared as a Christian thought. And although Widenmann treated reincarnation clumsily, in an embryonic way, yet in his prize essay of 1851 his thought of reincarnation is permeated by the Christian impulse. He devotes a special chapter to showing the connection between Christianity and the teaching of reincarnation.

It was necessary in human evolution that souls should first accept the other Christian impulses, so that the thought of reincarnation might come to our consciousness in a ripe form. And indeed, this thought of reincarnation will so connect itself with Christianity that it will be felt as something that leads a person on through successive incarnations. We shall understand how individuality, which is completely lost according to the Buddhist view—as we saw from the conversation of King Milinda with the sage Nagasena—first receives its true content by becoming permeated with Christ. We can now understand why the Buddhist view, about 500 years before the appearance of Christ, lost the human ego, while retaining the teaching of successive incarnations. We have reached a time in which the human organism must understand, accept, permeate itself with the thought of reincarnation. For the progress of human evolution does not depend on what teachings are promulgated or find a new foothold. Other laws come into consideration, and they do not depend upon ourselves.

In the future, human nature will develop certain powers that will have the effect that individuals, as soon as they have reached a certain age and have become properly conscious of themselves, will have the feeling: 'There is something in me which I must understand.' This feeling will take hold of humans more and more. In past times, even when human beings were fully aware of themselves, the consciousness that is now to come did not exist. It will express itself somewhat as follows: 'I feel something within me which is connected with my personal ego. Strangely, it will not fit in with all that I have come to know since birth.' Some will understand what is at work here; others will not. Individuals will understand it if they have carried the teachings of anthroposophy into their lives. Then they will know: 'What I am now feeling is foreign to me, because it is the ego that has come over from earlier lives.' This will oppress the heart, will cause fear and anxiety in those who cannot explain it by repeated earthly lives. These feelings, which are not merely a theoretical uncertainty but a starving, a cramping, of life, will disappear through the perceptions given to us by anthroposophy, which tell us: 'You must think of your life as extended over earlier earthly lives.' Then we will see what it means for us to experience a connection with the Christ-Impulse. For it is the Christ-Impulse that will give life to the whole retrospective view, the whole perspective of the past. Individuals will feel: 'Here was this incarnation; there, that one.' Then they will come to a time beyond which they will be unable to go without clearly understanding: 'The Christ-Impulse was then on Earth!' Incarnations will be followed further back to a time when the Christ-Event was not yet there. This illumination of the retrospective view through the Christ-Impulse will be needed by humans for their assurance in the future, as a necessity and a help which can flow into later incarnations.

This transformation of the human soul will derive from the event which begins in the twentieth century and may be called the second Christ-Event, so that those persons in whom higher faculties have awakened will look upon the Lord of Karma. Some of you may say that when the Christ-Event of the twentieth century takes place, many of those now living will be with those who have passed away, will be in the time between death and a new birth. But whether a person is living in a physical body, or in the time between death and a new birth, if he has prepared himself for the Christ-Event, he will experience it. The vision of the Christ-Event does not depend on whether we are incarnated in a physical body, but the preparation for the Christ-Event does so depend. Just as it was necessary that the first Christ-Event should take place on the physical plane in order that the salvation of humanity could be accomplished, so must the preparation be made here in the physical world, the preparation to look with full understanding, with full illumination, upon the Christ-Event of the twentieth century. For a person who looks upon it unprepared, when his powers have been awakened, will not be able to understand it. The Lord of Karma will then appear to him as a fearful judgment. In order to have an illuminated understanding of this event, the individual must be prepared. The spreading abroad of the anthroposophical worldview has taken place in our time for this purpose, so that we can be prepared on the physical plane to perceive the Christ-Event either on the physical plane or on the higher planes. Those who are not sufficiently prepared on the physical plane, and then go unprepared through the life between death and a new birth, will have to wait until, in the next incarnation, they can be further prepared through anthroposophy for the understanding of Christ. During the next 3,000 years, the opportunity will be given to humans of going through this preparation, and the purpose of all anthroposophical development will be to render us more and more capable of participating in what is to come.

Thus we understand how the past flows over into the future. When, for example, we recall how the Buddha permeated the astral body of the Nathan Jesus-child, we see how the activity of the Buddha forces continued after he himself no longer needed to incarnate again on Earth. And when we remember how influences not directly connected with the Buddha worked on in the West, we see how the spiritual world penetrates the physical.

All this preparation is connected with the fact that humans are always drawing nearer to an ideal which dawned in Ancient Greece, an ideal formulated by Socrates: that when we grasp the idea of the good, the moral, the ethical, we feel this idea as so magical an impulse that we become capable of living in accordance with it as an ideal. Today we are not so far advanced that this ideal can be realized; we are only so far on that in certain circumstances, individuals may very well form a concept of the good; they may be very clever and wise, and yet they need not be morally good. The direction of inner evolution, however, is such that the ideas we hold of the good will immediately become moral impulses. That is the intent of the evolution we shall experience in the approaching times. And the teachings given on Earth will increasingly be such that in the course of future centuries and millennia, human speech will come to have an effect unimaginably greater than it has now or ever had in the past.

Today in the higher worlds, anyone can see clearly the connection between intellect and morality; but as yet there is no human speech which works so magically that when a moral principle is stated, it sinks down into us as a new idea, so that we perceive it as directly moral, and cannot do otherwise than act upon it as a moral impulse. After the next 3,000 years, it will be possible to use a form of speech that could not now be entrusted to our heads. It will be such that everything intellectual will at the same time be moral, and this moral element will penetrate into human hearts. During the next 3,000 years, the human race must become as though permeated with magical morality. Otherwise, we would not be able to bear such an evolution; we would only misuse it.

For the special preparation of an evolution of this kind, we must look at a much slandered individuality who lived about a century before our era. He is mentioned, though certainly in a distorted form, in Hebrew writings as Jeshu ben Pandira—Jesus the son of Pandira. From lectures once given in Berne,[63] some of you will know that this Jeshu ben Pandira worked in preparation for the Christ-Event by training pupils, among whom was one who became the teacher of the writer of the Gospel of Matthew. Jeshu ben Pandira, a noble Essene figure, preceded Jesus of Nazareth by a century. Jesus of Nazareth Himself only went among the Essenes, whereas Jeshu ben Pandira was altogether an Essene.

Who was Jeshu ben Pandira?

The successor of that Bodhisattva who in his final earthly incarnation had risen in his twenty-ninth year to be Gautama Buddha was incorporated in the physical body of Jeshu ben Pandira. Every Bodhisattva who rises to the rank of a Buddha has a successor. This Oriental tradition corresponds exactly to esoteric research. The Bodhisattva who worked at that time in preparation for the

Christ-Event was re-embodied again and again. One of his re-embodiments is fixed for the twentieth century. It is impossible to speak here more exactly concerning the re-embodiment of this Bodhisattva; something, however, can be said about the way in which such a Bodhisattva may be recognized.

Through a law which will be demonstrated and explained in future lectures, it is a peculiarity of this Bodhisattva that when they reappear in a new embodiment—and they always reappear thus in the course of the centuries—they are quite dissimilar in their youth from what they come to be in their later activities. At a quite definite point of time in the life of this Bodhisattva, something like a revolution, a great transformation, always takes place. To express it in real terms, in some place or other there is a more or less gifted child, in whom it is not noticeable that they have to do anything special in preparation for the future evolution of humanity. Esoteric research confirms that no one during their childhood and youth gives so little sign of what they really are as the individual who is to incorporate a Bodhisattva. For at a certain point of time in their lives a great change comes over them. If an individuality from the remote past—Moses, for example— is incorporated, it is not the same with him as it was with the individuality of Christ, to whom Jesus of Nazareth left his sheaths. In the case of a Bodhisattva, there certainly will be something like an exchange, but the individuality remains in a certain sense, and the individuality who comes from the remote past—as Patriarch and so forth—and is to bring new forces for the evolution of humanity, descends, and the human being who receives him experiences an immense transformation. This transformation occurs particularly between the thirtieth and thirty-third years. It can never be known beforehand that this body will be taken possession of by the Bodhisattva. The change never shows itself in youth. The distinctive feature is precisely that the later years are so unlike the youthful ones.

He who was incorporated in Jeshu ben Pandira—the Bodhisattva who was repeatedly reincarnated, and who succeeded

Gautama Buddha—has prepared himself for his Bodhisattva-incarnation so that he can reappear and rise to the Buddha dignity exactly 5,000 years after the illumination of Gautama Buddha under the bodhi tree. Here again, esoteric investigation fully agrees with oriental tradition. So, 3,000 years from now, this Bodhisattva, looking back on all that has happened in the new epoch, and looking back on the Christ-Impulse and all that is connected with it, will speak in such a way that his speech will make into a reality what has just been characterized: intellectuality will become directly moral. The future Bodhisattva, who will place all that he has at the service of the Christ-Impulse, will be a bringer of the Good through the Word, through the Logos. He will speak in a language as yet possessed by no individual, but a language which is so holy that whoever speaks it can be called a bringer of the Good. This also will not show itself in their youth, but approximately in their thirty-first year, they will appear as a new individual, and will yield themselves up as the one who can be filled with a higher individuality. The experience of one single incarnation in the flesh holds good only for Jesus Christ. All Bodhisattvas go through various successive incarnations on the physical plane. This Bodhisattva, 3,000 years hence, will have advanced so far that they will be a bringer of the Good, a Maitreya Buddha, who will place his Words of Goodness at the service of the Christ-Impulse, which a sufficient number of humans will by then have made part of their lives. The perspective of the future development of humanity tells us this today.

What was necessary so that human beings could come gradually to this epoch of evolution? This we can make clear as follows.

If we wish to make a graphic picture of what happened in Ancient Lemuria for human earthly evolution, we can say: That was the time when we descended from divine heights: it was ordained for us that we should develop further in a certain way, but through the luciferic influence we were cast down more deeply into matter than we would have been without that influence. Thereby our path in evolution became different.

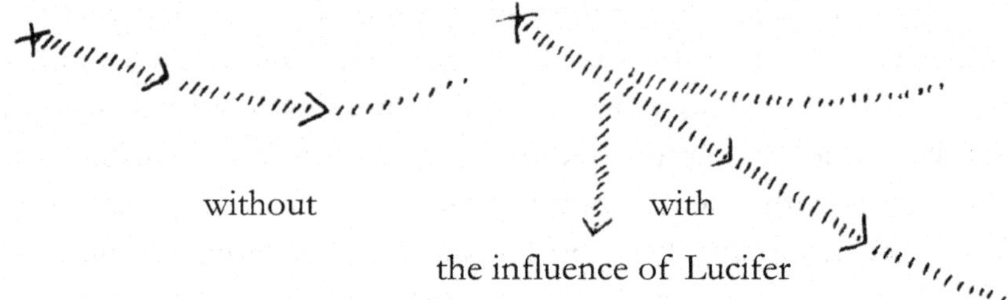

When an individual had gone downwards to the lowest stage, a powerful impetus in the upward direction was required. This impetus could come about only because in the higher worlds, the Being whom we designate as the Being of Christ had formed a resolution that He would not have needed to take for His own evolution. For the Being of Christ would also have attained His evolution if He had taken a path far, far above the path that humans were pursuing. He could have passed by, so to speak, far above the evolution of humanity. But if the upward impulse

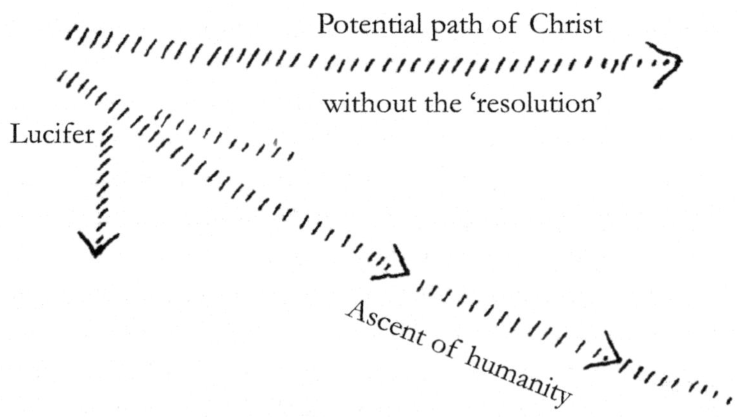

had not been given, human evolution would have been compelled to continue on its downward path. The Christ would have had an ascent, but humanity would have experienced a downfall. Only because the Being of Christ had taken the resolution to unite

Himself at the time of the events of Palestine with a human, to embody Himself in a human and to make the upward path possible for humanity—only this could bring about the redemption of humanity, as we may now call it: redemption from the impulse brought by the luciferic forces and designated symbolically in the Bible as 'original sin', the Temptation by the Serpent and the original sin that was its consequence. Christ accomplished something that was not necessary for Himself.

What kind of act was this?

It was an act of divine love! We must be quite clear that no human feeling is capable of realizing the intensity of love that was needed for a God to make a decision—a decision He had no need to make—to work upon Earth in a human body. Thereby, through an act of love, the most important event in human evolution was brought about. And when we grasp this act of love by a God, when we try to grasp it as a great ideal in contrast with which every human act of love can be but small, then, through this feeling of utter disproportion between human love and the divine love needed for the Mystery of Golgotha, they will draw near to the building up, to the giving birth within them, of those Imaginations which place before our spiritual gaze the momentous Event of Golgotha. Yes, verily, it is possible to attain to the Imagination of the mount on which the Cross was raised, that Cross on which hung a God in human body, a God who out of His own free will, out of Love, accomplished the act whereby the Earth and humanity could reach their goal.

If the God who is designated by the name of the Father had not at one time permitted the luciferic influences to come to humans, humans would not have developed the conditions for the free ego. With the luciferic influence, the conditions for the free ego were established. That had to be permitted by the Father-God. But just as the ego, for the sake of freedom, had to become entangled in matter, so then, in order that the ego might be freed from this entanglement, the entire love of the Son had to lead to the Act of Golgotha. Through this alone, human freedom, complete human dignity, first became possible. For the fact that we can be free beings, we have to thank a divine act of love. As humans we may feel that we are free beings, but we may never forget that for this freedom we have to thank this act of love. Then, in the midst of our feeling, the thought will arise: 'You can attain to the value, the dignity, of a human; but one thing you may not forget, that for being what you are you have to thank Him who has brought back to you your human prototype through the redemption on Golgotha.' Humans should not be able to lay hold of the thought of freedom without the thought of redemption through Christ: only then is the thought of freedom justified. If we will to be free, we must bring the offering of thanks to Christ for our freedom. Then only can we really perceive it. And those who consider that their human dignity is restricted when they thank Christ for it, should recognize that human opinions have no significance in face of cosmic facts, and that one day they will very willingly acknowledge that their freedom was won by Christ.

What we have been able to do in these lectures is not very much for gaining a closer understanding of the Christ-Impulse, and of the whole course of human evolution on Earth, from the standpoint of anthroposophy. We can only bring together single building-stones. But if the effect upon our souls is something like a renewed stimulus to further effort, to further development along the path of knowledge, then these stones will have done their work for the great spiritual temple of humanity. And the best we can carry away from an anthroposophical study such as this is that once more we have learnt something towards a certain goal, that we have again somewhat enriched our knowledge. And our high goal is this: that we may know more exactly how much we still need to know. Then we shall be more and more permeated with the truth of the old Socratic saying: 'The more a man learns, the more he knows how little he knows.' But this conviction is good only when it is not a confession of passive, easy-going resignation, but testifies to a living will and effort towards an ever-extending knowledge. We ought not to acknowledge how little we know by saying, 'Since we cannot know everything, we would rather learn nothing; so let us fold our hands in our lap.' That would be a false result of anthroposophical study. The right result is to be more and more inspired to further striving; to regard every new thing learnt as a step towards the attainment of yet higher stages.

In these lectures, we have perhaps had to say much about the thought of redemption without often using the word. This thought of redemption should be felt by a seeker after the spirit as it was felt by a great forerunner of anthroposophy: that it is related and entrusted to our souls only as a consequence of our striving after the highest goals of knowing, feeling, and willing. And as this great forerunner[64] connects the word 'redemption' with the word 'striving' and has expressed it in the line, '*Wer immer strebend sich bemüht, den können wir erlösen*'—'He who never gives up striving, he it is whom we can redeem'[65]—so should the anthroposophist always feel. The true redemption can be grasped and felt and willed in its own realm only by someone who never gives up.

May this lecture cycle—which has been specially laid upon my heart, because so much has to be said in it concerning the thought of redemption—be a stimulus to our further striving; may we find ourselves ever more and more united in our striving, during this incarnation and in later ones. May this be the fruit that comes from such studies. With this we will close, taking with us as a stimulus the thought that we must continually exert ourselves, in order that we may see what the Christ is, on the one hand, and on the other may draw nearer to redemption, which is being set free not merely from the lower earthly path and earthly fate, but free also from everything that hinders man from attaining his human dignity. But these things are written down truly only in the annals of the spiritual. For the script that can be read in spiritual realms is the only true writing. Let us therefore strive to read the chapter concerning human dignity and the mission of humanity, in the script where these things stand written in the spiritual worlds.

Public Lecture

Karlsruhe, 4 October 1911

As our subject is arousing the very widest interest everywhere, it seems justifiable to approach it from an anthroposophical standpoint. The manner in which it is being discussed and brought to public notice is, of course, very far removed from this point of view. If it is true that anthroposophy is little understood and liked today, it may be said at once that the treating of this theme in an anthroposophical manner presents peculiar difficulties. It is unusual in our age for the feelings to be so attuned as to appreciate anthroposophical truths bearing on the more obvious matters of spiritual life, and it is directly repugnant to our present-day consciousness when a topic has to be discussed which calls for the application of anthroposophy or spiritual science to the most difficult and holiest subjects.

It may be safely affirmed at the outset that the Being around whom our thoughts are about to centre has been for many centuries the turning point of all thought and feeling, and moreover that He has called forth widely differing judgments, emotions and opinions. Countless as are those who for centuries have held firmly as a rock to all that is connected with the Name of Christ and of Jesus, beyond number also are pictures of Him which have moved souls and occupied thoughtful human beings ever since the Event in Palestine. Always the picture has been modified according to the general views of the times, to what was felt and considered true at any given period. Thus, when the way had been prepared by the intellectual currents of thought of the eighteenth century, it came about in the course of the following century that what could be intellectually grasped as 'Christ' withdrew into the background as compared with what was called later the 'historical Jesus'. It is around the 'historical Jesus' that the widely extended controversy has arisen, and which has here in Karlsruhe its most important protagonists and its most vigorous combatants. For this reason, it is as well to give a short indication of the actual position of the controversy before entering on the subject of 'Christ Jesus'.

We might say that the historical Jesus of nineteenth-century thought originated under the influence of the intellectual current that takes a merely external view of spiritual life and judges it by means of external documents: that there is evidence of His having lived at the beginning of our era in Palestine, that He was crucified and, according to the faithful, rose again. It is quite in line with the character and nature of the present era, now approaching its termination, that in the case of theological research, faith limited itself to what it was thought could be confirmed by historical documents in the same way as any ordinary event is confirmed by independent writings. It may be said that all the historical written traditions elsewhere than in the New Testament could, in the opinion of one of the most important judges, be 'easily contained in a quarto page'. All the other references to the historical Jesus in any documents whatever, such for example as in Josephus or Tacitus, may be put out of court, for they can never be used from the standpoint of that historical science which holds good today. Beyond these there are only the Gospels and the Pauline Epistles. How did the historical research of the nineteenth century examine the Gospels? Regarded purely externally how do they appear? If taken like other records, such as those of military engagements and so forth, they seem to be very contradictory documents of the physical plane, the fourfold presentation of which cannot be brought into harmony. In face of what we call historical criticism these records fall to pieces. For it must be allowed that everything which the earnest and diligent research of the nineteenth century collected out of the Gospels themselves, in order to gain a true picture of Jesus of Nazareth, has crumbled away through the presentation of the kind of research brought forward by Professor Drews. As to all that can be said against the Gospels as facts of history, it is evident that nothing can come to light about the person of Jesus of Nazareth if we apply the methods whereby accurate science and strict criticism ratify other historical facts. We can only be considered very dilettante scientists if we do not make this concession to the science of the day.

Is it not the case that those who in the nineteenth century presented the teaching of Jesus of Nazareth, and wanted to arrive at an historical portrait of Him, had an entirely false conception of the Gospels? Were the Gospels really intended to be historical records in the sense understood in that century?

Whatever was to be said on this subject I endeavoured to state many years ago in my work, *Christianity as Mystical Fact*, and our present question, as to what was the real object of the Gospels, was intended to receive its answer not merely through the contents of that book but through the title itself. For the title was not 'The Mysticism of Christianity', nor 'The Mystical Contents of Christianity': its object was rather to show that Christianity in its origin and its whole being is not an external fact but a fact of the spiritual world, and one that can only be comprehended by an insight into a realm lying behind the world of sense and behind what can be corroborated by historical records. It was shown that the forces and causes which brought about the event of Palestine were not to be found in that region wherein external historical events take place, and thus that possibly not only may Christianity have a mystical content but that mysticism—the actual gazing into the spiritual—is necessary to disentangle the threads that were woven behind the Event in Palestine and made it possible.

In order to realize what Christianity is, and what it can and must be in the soul of man today if he is to understand it aright, let us see how deeply grounded in the spiritual facts of human development were the words of St Augustine: 'That which we now call the Christian religion already existed among the ancients and was never absent from the beginning of the human race up to the time when Christ appeared in the flesh, from which time forward the true religion which was already there received the name of the Christian religion.' Thus, does a standard authority point to the fact that it was not something new which came into humanity with the events of

Palestine, but that in a certain sense a transformation had taken place in that which from time immemorial the souls of human beings had sought and striven for as knowledge. Something was given to humanity which had always been in existence, though hitherto along other lines than the Christian. If we wish to test the other way in which the preceding ages could come to the truths and wisdom of Christianity, we are referred by the historical development of humanity to the Mysteries of Antiquity or the Ancient Mysteries. What is meant by these expressions is little understood today, but it will become clearer the more human beings grasp the conception of the cosmos as presented by spiritual science.

Not merely upon the external religions of the people of antiquity must attention be focused, but upon what was practised in pre-Christian times in those mystic abodes designated by the name of the Mysteries. In the book *Occult Science* is to be found an explanation from the aspect of spiritual science, and there are also numbers of secular writers who have declared publicly what was the secret of mankind in antiquity. We read that only a few were admitted to the schools which were designated 'The Mysteries', and that these schools were the homes of the cults. Also, there was a small circle of human beings admitted to the Mysteries by the priestly sages, and for them this meant a kind of retirement from the outer world: they realized that if they were to reach what was to be attained they must lead a different life than they had so far lived openly, and above all that they must accustom themselves to another way of thinking. These Mysteries existed all over the world, among the Greeks and Romans and other peoples, as may be confirmed by referring to extensive literature which still exists. The pupils admitted to the Mysteries were taught something comparable with what is now called science or knowledge, but they did not receive it in the same way, for by what they experienced they became quite other beings. To them came the conviction that in every human being there lives, deeply hidden and slumbering so that the ordinary consciousness knows it not, a higher human being. As the ordinary person looks through his eyes upon the world and with his thought-power thinks over what he experiences, so can this other person—at first unknown to external consciousness, but capable of being awakened in the depths of his nature recognize another world unattainable by external sight and thought. This was called 'The birth of the inner human being'. The expression is still used, though in these days it is dry and abstract in character and regarded lightly, but when the disciple of the Mysteries applied it to himself it stood for a tremendous event to be compared in some measure with being born in the physical sense. As man in the physical world is born out of a dark substratum (be it one of nature according to the materialistic idea, or a spiritual substratum in the view of spiritual science) so, physically speaking, there was really born through the processes of the Mysteries a higher human being who previously had been as little present as was the human being before birth or conception. The disciple was a new-born being. The present view of knowledge, as given everywhere in answer to a deeply philosophic question, is exactly the opposite of that which formed the central point of the whole idea and outlook of the Mysteries. It is now asked in the sense of Kant and Schopenhauer, 'Where lie the limits of knowledge? What is it in the power of man to know?' We need only take up a newspaper to meet the answer that here or there lie the limits and that beyond them it is impossible to go. Certainly, it was admitted in the Mysteries that there were problems which people could not solve, but it would never have been held in the sense of Kant or in Schopenhauer's *Theory of Cognition* that 'Man cannot know' this or that! What would have been appealed to was man's capability of development, to the powers lying dormant within him which must be evoked so that he might rise to higher capacities of knowledge. The question in those times resolved itself into what was to be done in order to get beyond that which in normal life is the boundary of knowledge; how to develop deeper powers in human nature.

Something more is needed if we are to feel the whole magic charm of the Mysteries that, like a breath, pervades the works of the exoteric writers, Plato, Aristides, Plutarch and Cicero. Here we must be clear that the kind of mental comprehension present in the forming of the disciples of the Mysteries was quite different from that of the people of today when they confront scientific truths. What we now call science is open to anybody and everybody in any condition of receptivity whatever. It is just here that we recognize the characteristic of truth, that it is independent of mood and feeling. For the pupil of the Mysteries the most necessary thing was that, before he was brought to the great Truths, he should go through something whereby his soul was transformed in his feelings and impressions. What today appears as a simple scientific truth would not have been put to him so that he could grasp it externally with his understanding, but his natural temperament would have been prepared beforehand so that he could draw near with reverential awe to what could approach him. Consequently, his preparation was not one of learning; it was a gradual and radical transformation and education of his soul. The question was how the soul approached the great truths and wisdom and how it reacted to them, and hence arose the conviction that through the Mysteries man was bound up and united with the very foundations of the Cosmos and with what flowed from the springs of all cosmic beginnings. Thus, was the disciple prepared for the experiencing of something which is described by Aristides. He who, according to what is to be found in my *Knowledge of the Higher Worlds and its Attainment* has lived through what these disciples experienced can himself bear witness. He knows that the words of Aristides correspond with the truth when he writes, 'I seemed to be approaching God, I seemed to feel His Presence, and I was in a state between waking and sleeping; my spirit was quite light—so light that no one who was uninitiated could describe or understand it.' There was a way, therefore, to the divine foundations of the universe which was neither science nor one-sided religion, but consisted in a thorough preparation of the soul for the realization of the ideas about the evolution of the universe so that it might draw near to God and those spiritual foundations. As we take in the external air with our breath and make it a part of our body, so did the disciple of the Mysteries receive into his soul that which pulsates spiritually through the universe until he was united with it and so became a new man permeated by the Divinity.

Now, however, anthroposophy or spiritual science shows that what was then possible was only an historical phenomenon in human evolution, and when the question arises as to whether the Ancient

Mysteries of pre-Christian times are still possible in the same way it can only be said that historical research verily proves that what has just been described did really exist but that it exists no longer in the same form. The pre-Christian method of Initiation is not now possible. A human being must indeed be short-sighted if he believes that the human soul is the same in all epochs, or that the spiritual path of the olden times holds good for the present. The path to the divine and primal sources of the world has now become another, and intellectual historical research shows that it did so in its very essence at the time ascribed by tradition to the events of Palestine. These events made a deep incision in the evolution of humanity. Something entered into human nature in the post-Christian period which was entirely differed from what was there before. Such a method of thinking as is possible nowadays—the method of drawing nearer to the universe through scientific thought—did not exist in pre-Christian ages. The Mysteries did not conduct man in the manner described to the very highest treasures of wisdom in order that he might do something in secret, or acquire something special for himself as a member of a small circle, but because our modern way of combining thoughts through logic was not possible at that time. A glance at the history of humanity will show that in the course of two centuries, during the time of the Greek philosophers, the present mode of thinking was gradually prepared, and that only now has it reached the point of embracing external nature so wonderfully. Thus, the entire form our consciousness takes and the way we create our conceptions of the universe differ entirely from pre-Christian times. For the moment we are only concerned with this fact as showing that human nature has changed. A careful review of human evolution makes it clear that the entire consciousness has altered in the course of evolution (the results arising from research are to be found in my *Occult Science*). The people of old did not regard things and think about them as we do with our senses and understanding; they had a kind of clairvoyance, but this was of a dim and dreamlike nature (not such as is described in my *The Way of Initiation*). Herein lies the import of evolution, that an old clairvoyance which in primitive times was spread over all humanity gave way to that form of thought which we possess today. The ordinary inhabitants of every country had this kind of clairvoyant power, and a path leading from that to higher stages was provided in the Mysteries. Thereby development was given to the normal soul-faculties of man.

Observation of the world by what we call reasoning and logic having displaced the old clairvoyance, the latter is no longer a natural faculty, but it lasted right through the historical period and reached its culmination in the Greco-Roman era during which the appearance of Christ occurred. At that point of time collective humanity everywhere had come so far in its evolution that the old clairvoyance had passed away and the old Mysteries were no longer possible. What then took the place of the old Mysteries and what did man acquire through the Mysteries?

These were of two kinds: the one proceeded from that centre of civilization which was afterwards occupied by the Ancient Persians, and the other was to be met with in its purest form in Egypt and Greece. They were entirely different throughout those times. It was the endeavour of all the Mysteries to produce in man an extension of his soul-powers, but this was achieved in a different way in Greece and Egypt, than in Persia. In the two former, which agreed essentially, the object was to effect in the disciples a transformation of their soul-powers. This transformation took place under a certain supposition which must be understood before anything else. It was that in the depths of the soul there slumbers another, a divine human being; that from the same sources whence the rock forms into crystal and the plants break forth in the spring the hidden human being originated. Plants, however, had already utilized all that was contained within them, whereas man, in so far as he had understood himself and worked with his own powers, had remained an imperfect being, and that which was within him had only come to the fore after much endeavour. Appeal, therefore, in the Egyptian and Greek Mysteries was made to a spiritual, a divine inner human being, and when this was referred to, allusion was made also to the powers within the Earth. For according to the views held, the Earth was not regarded as the lifeless cosmic body of modern astronomy, but as a spiritual planetary being. In Egypt reference was made to the wonderful spirit-forces and nature-forces, called by the names of Isis and Osiris, when it was desired to contemplate the origin and source of what could be experienced as manifestation in the inner human being. In Greece this primal source was referred to under the name of Dionysus. As a consequence of this, profane writers asserted that the nature and being of things were the objects sought for, and in the Greek Mysteries they called what was found of the forces of human nature the 'sub-earthly' portion of man, not the 'super-earthly'. The nature of the great 'Daemons' was spoken of, and under this title was represented all that worked on the Earth of the nature of spiritual forces. The nature of these daemons (in a good sense) was sought for through that which man was to bring forth from himself. Then the disciple had to go through all the feelings and perceptions that were possible for him in the course of evolution. He had to experience what was meant by 'going down into the depths of his soul'; to learn that a fundamental feeling so dominated all soul-being that in ordinary life no conception of it could be formed, and that that feeling was a deep egoism—the almost unconquerable selfishness lying within the inner recesses of a human being. By means of struggling against and conquering all selfishness and egoism the disciple had to go through something for which we have today only an abstract expression, i.e., the feeling of all-inclusive love and sympathy for people and beings. Sympathy, in so far as the human soul was capable of it, was to take the place of selfishness. It was clearly understood that if the disciple evoked this sympathy, which belonged in the first place to the hidden forces of the world of feeling, it could draw out from the depths of his soul the divine powers slumbering therein. It was held moreover that as he looked out upon the world with his ordinary understanding he must soon become aware of his powerlessness as a person with reference to the Cosmos, and that the further he projected his conceptions and ideas the stronger this feeling grew until in the end he was led to doubt what indeed could be called knowledge, i.e., Gnosis. Arrived at that point he must then overcome this feeling of emptiness in his soul whenever he desired to encompass the cosmos with his ideas. This consciousness of a void was accompanied by fear and anxiety, and consequently the Greek disciple of mysticism first filled himself with a dread of the unknown and then by coupling this with sympathy drew forth the divine powers lying within him. So did he learn to transform fear into awe and reverence, and to realize how the highest kind of awe and reverential devotion for all the phenomena of the universe was able to penetrate every substance and conception that lay beyond the scope of ordinary knowledge.

Thus, the Greek Mysteries, as also those of Isis and Osiris in the Egyptian Mysteries, worked outwards from the inmost nature of man and sought to lead him into the spiritual worlds. It was a living apprehension of the 'God in Man'. A real acquaintance was formed between man and God, and immortality ranked not as mere abstract theory and philosophy but as something known, something as firmly grounded as the knowledge of external colours, and this was experienced as an intimate connection with external things. With no less certainty was this experienced also in the Persian or Mithraic Mysteries. Whereas man was led in the Greek and Egyptian Mysteries through the unfettering of his soul-powers, he was confronted at once with the universe itself in the Mithraic Mysteries; not only did the universe work upon him through the great and mighty nature which is overlooked by those who regard the world in its external aspect, but by gaining a deep intimacy with nature, he could gaze upon phenomena that lay outside the limits of the human understanding. By the methods then used the most terrible and magnificent powers were brought before the pupil from universal space. Whereas the Greek disciple was affected by a deep feeling of reverence, to the Mithraic disciple alone was given the knowledge of the terrible and awe-inspiring powers in nature so that he felt himself infinitesimally small in comparison. So powerful was this impression, consequent upon his alienation from the primal source of being, that he felt that in its vastness the universe could at any moment overwhelm and annihilate him. The first impulse came from his being led through a comprehensive astronomy and science away from external things to the greatness of the phenomena of the universe, and what he further developed in the Mysteries was then more a consequence of the truth in all its ramifications when nature in her details (science in the old sense of the word) worked upon his soul. The Greek disciple became fearless through the setting free of his powers. The Mithraic disciple was brought so far that he drank in the greatness of cosmic thought, and thereby his soul also became strong and courageous. A knowledge of the dignity and value of a human being was gained, and with it a feeling for truth and fidelity; the disciple learned to recognize that man must always hold himself under control during his earthly existence.

Such were the benefits obtained especially through the Mithraic Mysteries, and whereas the Greek and Egyptian Mysteries are to be found spread over Greece and Egypt, the Mithraic are diffused from Persia as far as the Caspian Sea, along the Danube into Germany, and even to the South of France, to Spain and to England. Europe was indeed permeated by the Mithraic Mysteries, and everywhere it was seen clearly that something streamed into man from the universe if only he could learn to understand it, and this that could be received was Mithra, the God that streams through the world in all worlds. It was through this power of action that courage was aroused: the warriors, the Roman legionaries, were filled with the Mithraic service or cult of Mithra. Both leaders and men were initiated into the Mysteries. Thus was God sought on the one hand by the freeing of the individual soul-powers, and it was quite evident that through this process something streamed out from the depths of the soul. On the other hand, however, it was equally evident that when man sought God by devoting himself to the great cosmic phenomena, something streamed into his soul as the essence, the finest life-sap contained in the world. There were found the primordial forces of the universe. God came, as it were, into human souls through this development which was attained in the Mystery schools. A veritable process is to be seen here: each soul became a door for the entrance of the Godhead into human evolution on Earth. Few were able to undergo such a development, and a special preparation for it was necessary. The teaching consisted in showing that what was hidden in external nature (Mithra) as also in the inner man of the Greek, poured through the world as a stream of divine consecration.

The evolution of man has now changed, and the entire method of initiation is different. Here we touch upon what must be called the mystical fact of the Christ event. To penetrate deeply into history is to see that the early Christians were more or less dimly conscious that the same force which entered the soul only through devotion to the Mysteries, to the Divine Principle of the universe (streaming forth from cosmos as the Mithra or out of the depths of the soul as the Dionysus), was as the deed of a unique cosmic Divinity in one single fact in the evolution of the Earth. That which was sought for beyond this, and was not to be found except by those who alienated themselves from outer life in the Mysteries, was at a given time incorporated into the Earth by the Divinity. No human effort was needed, for the Divinity once and for all permeated the Being of the Earth, and henceforth even those who had lost the power to penetrate to the Divine Principle of the cosmos could meet Him in another way. The God who could now penetrate into the human soul (neither as Mithra from without nor Dionysus from within) was Himself a fusion of Mithra and Dionysus, and also was related to human nature in its depths. He was embraced and encompassed by the Name of CHRIST. Mithra and Dionysus were united in the Being who entered humanity in the event of Palestine, and Christianity was the confluence of both cults. The Hebrews, who were chosen that they might provide the necessary body through which this event might take place, had become acquainted with the Mithraic and Dionysian cults, but they remained far removed from either. The Greek thought of himself as a weak man who must develop deeper powers before he could penetrate into the depths of his soul, while the follower of Mithra felt that by letting the whole surrounding sphere of the air work upon him he might become united with the divine qualities of the universe. The Hebrew, on the other hand, held that the deeper human nature, with all that was hidden within it, was already there in the first human being, and the ancient Hebrews called this primal man Adam. According to old Hebraic ideas that which man could seek, and which joined him with the divine, was present originally in Adam, but in course of evolution the descendants of each generation became further and further removed from the source of existence. Being 'subject to original sin', as they put it, meant that man had not remained as he was and had been ejected from the sphere of the

Divine; regarding himself as standing below Adam he sought the reason in original sin. But though less than that which lived in the depths of human nature, he could unite himself with the deeper powers and thereby be raised again. This point of view, that once man had stood higher and that through the qualities connected with the blood-ties he had lost something, was an historical one. What the adherent of the Mithraic Mysteries saw in humanity as one whole the Hebrew saw in his own nation and was conscious that its original source had been lost. So that while among the Persians there was a kind of training of the consciousness, there was among the ancient Hebrews a consciousness of a historical development; Adam, by falling into sin, had fallen from the heights where he once stood. Consequently, the Hebrews were the best prepared for the thought that that which had happened at the initial point of evolution (and which had brought about a deterioration in humanity) could only be raised again through an historical event, i.e., by something actually taking place in the spiritual substrata of the Earth's being. The ancient Hebrew who rightly understood evolution felt that the Mithra God, equally with the God who is evoked from the depths of the human soul, could come down without man going through a development in the Mysteries.

Thus, in these people, and above all in the case of John the Baptist, there arose a consciousness of the fact that the same which the Mysteries had handed down in the form of Dionysus and Mithra was born at one and the same time in one man. Those of them who felt this in a deeper sense held that even as through Adam the descent of man into the world was brought about (all people having descended from one forefather and inherited from him all the deeper forces that lead to sin and error) so, through one Being who descends from the spiritual worlds as the union of Mithra and Dionysus, must the initial point be formed to which people can look when they have to rise again. As in the Mysteries, human nature was developed through the setting free of the deeper soul forces or through a view of the cosmos, the Hebrews now saw in the God who came down into physical being Him on whom the soul must look and believe, for whom it must develop the deepest love, and who as the great example could lead them back to their divine origin.

He who had the profoundest knowledge of this fact of Christianity was Paul. The Apostle recognized that as people looked to Adam as their physical progenitor they could, through the Christ Impulse, look to the Christ as the great example, and so attain to what was striven for in the Mysteries and must be born again if they were to know their own original nature. The knowledge that was kept within the recesses of the Temples, and could only be attained after ascetic training, was set forth neither in mundane document nor as some external fact but as having been accomplished as a mystical fact, the God who pervaded the world having actually appeared in one single form. What the disciples of the Mithraic Mysteries acquired through looking upon the greatest model had now been attained through Christ. The courage, self-control and energy acquired by those disciples had also to be acquired by those who could no longer be initiated in the old Mithraic sense; through the model of the historical Christ and the gazing upon Him the impulse towards this fortitude was now to pour itself out upon the soul. In the Mithraic Mysteries, as has been shown, the whole universe was in a certain sense born in the soul of the disciple, and the courageous soul was fired with all the inner forces of initiative. In the Baptism of John something was poured down from above of which human nature could be the vehicle; when a human being was permeated with the thought that his nature was capable of assimilating the profoundest harmony of the universe, the view of the Baptism aroused within him the understanding that Mithra could be born in human nature. Those, therefore, who grasped the original meaning of Christianity, acknowledged that the end of the Mysteries had come: the God who formerly had poured Himself into the Mysteries had now flowed directly into the being of the Earth through the personality who stood at the beginning of a new era (our present one).

The connection with the Greek or Dionysian Mysteries has now to be considered. Through the fact that the human gaze was guided to Jesus of Nazareth in whom Mithra lived and who then passed through death, an indication was given that Mithra (the bestower of courage, self-control and energy) had himself died with the death of Jesus. It was further seen that because Mithra had so vanished that which man found in his deepest nature, and had attained earlier through the Dionysian Mysteries, had now become in Jesus of Nazareth the immortal conqueror over death. Herein lies the true Christian meaning of the Resurrection if it is grasped in its spiritually scientific sense. The Baptism by John in [the] Jordan demonstrated that the old Mithra had entered into man, that thereby human nature had won the victory over death, and that by the example so created the soul could unite itself in the deepest love in order to come to that which lived in its own depths. In the Risen Christ was seen the fact that man, by living according to the event that had taken place in history, could rise above the level of ordinary humanity.

Thus, in the centre of the history of the world was set an historical event in the place of that which had been sought in the Mysteries times without number. The great revelation that came to St Paul was that human nature had thereby become different, and this was concealed within what is known as 'The Event of Damascus'. Writing of what he experienced before Damascus, the Apostle relates how he learned to understand, not from external documents but through a purely spiritual clairvoyant experience, that the moment when the Incarnation itself should take place in an historical personage had already passed. The existence of Christ as a real man could never be experienced by Paul through an external fact, and what he could learn in Palestine did not convince him that the Union of Mithra and Dionysus had lived in Jesus of Nazareth. But when, before Damascus, his spiritual sight was opened, it became clear that a God who could be called by the Name of Christ not only worked through the world as a super-sensible Being but had actually come to Earth and conquered death. Henceforth he preached that what for the initiates had previously been a streaming substance was now to be found as continuous historical fact. This lies at the basis of his words, 'If Christ be not risen then is our preaching vain, and your faith is also vain.'

Such was the path by which Paul came to Jesus by the indirect way of Christ, it being clear to him that something had taken place in Palestine which previously could only be experienced in the Mysteries. And this still applies today. Because Christ is the focus of all human development and the highest example for the inmost powers of the soul the bond established with Him must be of the most inti-mate kind. To become a disciple, it is required of a man that he set little value upon his own life, and so it must be regarded as of small importance to lay aside all documentary evidence and historical tra-ditions in order to come to Christ. Indeed, there is cause for thank-fulness that the fact that there ever was an historical Christ Jesus cannot be established, for no document could prove that He was the most significant of all that has passed into humanity.

The connection between Christ and the ancient Mysteries is there-fore quite clear. The disciples of the latter had to go through what may be called intimate soul experiences in order to come to God; their inner feelings and sensations were livelier and more intense than those of the ordinary person, and so they became aware that they were set fast in a lower nature which hindered them from arriving at the sources of being. This lower nature was indeed a seducer leading them away from the upward path, and that which so allured them had also become their own lower nature, and herein lay the 'Temp-tation' that came to every disciple of the Mysteries. At the moment when God awoke within them they became aware also of their lower or sensual natures. It was as though some strange unknown being were urging them not to follow the unsubstantial and airy heights of the spiritual world, but to seize the coarse and material things that lay close at hand. Each disciple had to pass through a time when everything spiritual seemed unreal in comparison with the ordinary way of looking at things, and all that was connected with the senses appeared alluring as against the stress of spiritual effort. At another stage in mystic development these lower forces were overcome, a higher outlook being attained with the growth of invigorated pow-ers of courage and so forth. All this teaching was clothed in cer-tain instructions that may be verified from the writings of exoteric authors, as also in the methods of initiation given by spiritual science and set forth in *Occult Science*. There were various methods both in the Greek and the Mithraic Mysteries. Finally, the disciples experi-enced the 'at-one-ment' with Him who was the Divine Man, but here the methods were different and varied widely in the many countries where initiation existed.

In my *Christianity as Mystical Fact* the purpose is to show that in the Gospels nothing is to be met with but a rebirth of old initiation instructions. What took place externally had already taken place similarly in the course of the Mysteries, and therefore the Divine Being who was in Jesus of Nazareth after the descent of the Mithra Being had to experience the 'Temptation'. As the tempter came on a small scale to the pupil of the Mysteries so did he also confront the God become man. All that was true in the Mysteries is to be found repeated in the Gospel records which were new versions of the old inscriptions and instructions given in the initiations. The writers of the Gospels saw that once that which hitherto had lain only in the Mysteries had been enacted on the plane of cosmic history, it was permissible to describe it in the same words as those in which their directions for initiation were recorded. It is for this very reason that the Gospels were not intended to be biographies of Him who was the vehicle for the Christ. This is just the mistake of all modern criticisms of the Gospels. At the time they were written the sole object was to lead the human soul to a real love for the Great Soul, the source of the world's existence. Strangely enough a clear consciousness of this prevailed almost to the end of the eighteenth century. It is pointed out in isolated writings of remarkable interest that through the Gospels the soul can be so transformed as to find the Christ. Old Meister Eckhardt writes, 'Some people want to look at God with their eyes as they look at a cow, and want to love God as they love a cow. They love God as an outward possession and an inward comfort, but these people do not love Him aright ... Simple folk imagine they ought to see God as if He stood there and they here; it is not so; God and I are One in recognition.' In another passage he writes:

> A Master says, 'God has become man, and thereby the whole human race is raised in dignity. We may rejoice that Christ our brother has through His own power passed beyond the choir of angels, and sits at the right hand of the Father.' This Master has spoken rightly, but verily I do not pay much attention to it. What help would it be to me if I had a brother who was a rich man, and I was at the same time a poor one? How would it help me if I had a brother who was a wise man, and I myself a fool? ... The heavenly Father begat His only Son in Himself

> and in me. Why in Himself and in me? I am one with Him, and it is not possible for Him to exclude me. In the same work the Holy Ghost received His Being, and is from me as from God. Why? I am in God, and if the Holy Ghost does not receive His Being from me neither does he receive it from God. I am in no way excluded.

That is the point: that man through mystic development, without external mysteries but through the simple evolution of the soul, will in later times be able to experience that which was once experienced in the Mysteries. This, however, will only be possible because the Christ Event took place. Even if there were no Gospels, no records and no traditions, he who experiences the Christ in himself along with the being filled with Christ has the certainty, as St Paul had it, that at the beginning of our era Christ was incarnated in a physical body. An historical biography of Jesus of Nazareth can never be gathered out of the Gospels, but through the right unfolding of his soul powers man can and must raise himself up to the Christ, and through the Christ to Jesus. Thus only can be understood what was the aim of the Gospels and what was lacking in the whole of the nineteenth-century researches on the subject of Jesus. The picture of the Christ was allowed to recede into the background in order to present a tangible Jesus quite externally from the historical records. The Gospels were misunderstood, and consequently the methods of investigation crumbled to pieces.

Herewith the way is at the same time made clear to spiritual science. Its object is to show what are the deeper powers that have lain in man since the coming of Christ, and which he can develop. Not in the depths of externally appointed Mysteries, but in the stillness of his room, man can attain by devoting himself to what happened in Palestine that which was attained by the disciples of the Mysteries. By experiencing the Christ within himself he gains in courage and energy and in a consciousness of his dignity as man, and comes to the knowledge of how he has to take his place in humanity in the right sense. And at the same time he experiences, as could the adherent of the Greek Mysteries, the universal love which lives in Christ and embraces all external creatures. He learns never to be afraid or to despair in face of the world, and in full freedom and at the same time humility is sensible of devotion to the secrets of the universe.

All this comes to the man who permeates himself with the mystical fact of Christianity, the successor of the old mysteries. Simply through a cognitional development of these fundamental thoughts the historical Jesus becomes a fact for those who have a deep knowledge of Christ. In Western philosophy it was said that without eyes none could see colour nor hear without ears; the universe would be without light and sound. True as this is with regard to seeing and hearing, it is equally true that without light no eye could have come into existence nor could man have had any perceptions connected with it. As Goethe says, 'If the eye were not born of like nature to the sun it could never look upon the sun,' and 'The eye is a creation of the light.'

The Mystical Christ, spoken of by those whose spiritual sight is opened and who behold Him as Paul did, was not always in man. In pre-Christian times He was unattainable in any development through the Mysteries in the way in which He was to be found after the Mystery of Golgotha. That there might be an inner Christ and that the higher man could be born an historical Christ was needed, the Incarnation of the Christ in the Jesus. As the eye can originate only through the effect of light, so in order that there could be a Mystical Christ the historical Christ must have been there. Had there been no documents containing a biography of Jesus of Nazareth this could still be said and felt, for Jesus is not to be recognized through external writings. This fact was long known in the evolution of the West and will again be known. Spiritual science will so formulate that it can draw together from out its various spheres what will lead to a real understanding of the Christ, and thereby to an understanding of Jesus. It has come about that Jesus has been actually alienated from the world and the methods of the Jesus investigations have melted away, but the deepening of ourselves in the Christ Being (in the Christ as a Being) will lead to a recognition of the greatness of Jesus of Nazareth.

This path, by which the Christ is first recognized through inward soul experience, leads through what really has developed out of the soul to the understanding of the mystical fact of Christianity, and of the gradual development of humanity, as being such that the Christ event must take place within it as the most significant point in the evolution of man. The way leads through the Christ to Jesus. The Christ idea bears fruitful seed that will bring humanity not merely to the apprehension of a general pantheistic cosmic spirit, but the individual man to the understanding of his own history; as he feels his Earth to be bound up with all cosmic existence so will he recognize that his past is bound up with a super-sensible and super-historical Event. This Event is that the Christ Being stands as a super-sensible mystical fact at the middle point of human evolution, and that so will He be recognized by the humanity of the future apart from all external historical research and documents. Christ will remain the strong cornerstone of mankind's evolution. Man will bring the forces out of himself to renew his own history, and therewith also the history of the evolution of the world.

APPENDICES

Appendix 1

ROSICRUCIANISM

'Rosicrucianism is a spiritual and cultural movement which arose in Europe in the early 17th century after the publication of several texts which purported to announce the existence of a hitherto unknown esoteric order to the world and made seeking its knowledge attractive to many. ...

'The manifestos do not elaborate extensively on the matter, but clearly combine references to Kabbalah, Hermeticism, alchemy, and Christian mysticism. The Rosicrucian manifestos heralded a "universal reformation of mankind", through a science allegedly kept secret for decades until the intellectual climate might receive it. ...

'Between 1614 and 1617, three anonymous manifestos were published, first in Germany and later throughout Europe, These were the *Fama Fraternitatis RC* (*The Fame of the Brotherhood of RC*, 1614), the *Confessio Fraternitatis* (*The Confession of the Brotherhood of RC*, 1615), and the *Chymical Wedding of Christian Rosicross anno 1459* (1617)'. [*Wikipedia*]

See Frances Yates, *The Rosicrucian Enlightenment* (London: Routledge, 1972); Paul Allen, ed., *A Christian Rosenkreutz Anthology* (Great Barrington, Massachusetts: Lindisfarne, 1996); Rudolf Steiner, *The Secret Stream: Christian Rosenkreutz and Rosicrucianism*, edited by Christopher Bamford (Great Barrington, Massachusetts: Anthroposophic Press, 2000); and CW 233a; Rudolf Steiner, *Rosicrucianism and Modern Initiation* (Forest Row: Rudolf Steiner Press, 2020).

Appendix 2

LESSING

Gotthold Ephraim Lessing (1729–1781) was a major dramatist, philosopher, and theologian. Lessing was a fascinating figure, who hardly fits the stereotype of 'Enlightenment rationalist' so often foisted upon him. A posthumous report that he had been a closet Spinozist (tantamount to an atheist in the minds of many) started a huge controversy that involved many of the major writers of the day, Goethe included. A passionate lottery player, he bet the number of his age on his deathbed.

A discussion of six of his major works follows. *Laocoon: An Essay on the Limits of Painting and Poetry* (1767)[66] is one of the greatest treatises in the history of Germans aesthetics. In it, Lessing disagrees with his contemporary, the renowned Johann Winckelmann, about the interpretation of the Hellenistic sculpture 'Laocoon,' which shows the Trojan priest and his sons about to be strangled by serpents. He uses this to work out a fundamental distinction between poetry and painting. Whereas painting is limited to a single spatial and temporal moment, and therefore must render the single, expressive climax of a chain of events, poetry's excellence consists in its ability to describe temporal and spatial movement.

After having been turned down by Frederick the Great for the position of Royal Librarian, Lessing accepted the offer of some Hamburg merchants to serve as advisor and critic of their project to found a national theatre. Even though the project did not succeed, his reviews of more than 50 performances were published as *The Hamburg Dramaturgy* (1767–1769),[67] consisting of 104 brief essays on the basic principles of drama. 'Topics covered by Lessing in the series of essays include Aristotle's theory of tragedy, acting theory, the role of theatre in society, the means by which theatre achieves its emotional effects, criticism of the actor and the play, issues of translation, and a nascent theory of the psychology of emotions.' The work defined the new field of dramaturgy, and also introduced the term.[68]

How the Ancients Depicted Death (1769) is a polemic, and begins with a defence of polemic as a path to the truth. Lessing's opponent is Christian Adolph Klotze, who maintained that Lessing had denied the ancients' depiction of death as a skeleton. He adduces many ancient depictions of skeletons to disprove this. Lessing freely admits that the skeleton was depicted in antiquity, but he denies they depicted death. He goes on to describe beautifully the many alternative pictures of death in antiquity.

Ernst and Falk: Dialogues for Freemasons (1778)[69] is divided into five parts, and contains in dialogic form precepts for Masonic activity in the world. The immediate occasion of the dialogue was Lessing's acceptance into the Hamburg Lodge in 1770. He became interested in Masonic ideas, and read around the basic texts. He decided that a systematic presentation of Masonic ideas was lacking. The dialogues are an attempt to remedy that situation.

Nathan the Wise (1779)[70] is a play that constitutes a passionate appeal for tolerance. The central episode is 'the parable of the ring,' which Nathan tells when asked the treacherous question whether Christianity, Islam, or Judaism is the true religion. He narrates that there once was a man who possessed a ring that made him 'agreeable to God and human beings'. The ring was passed down through generations of heirs, until it reached someone who loved three sons equally, and had promised the ring to each. When death approached, he asked a jeweller to make two identical copies. Upon his death, each son received a ring, and not knowing which was authentic, they quarrelled among themselves. They went before a judge, who, recalling the true ring's property, asked which of the sons the other two loved most. They were silent, which led the judge to think that none of the rings was authentic. He reminded them of their father's equal love, and told them each to act as though he had the authentic ring; each must seek to make himself agreeable to God and human beings. Perhaps some future judge would be wise enough to give the answer.

Anthroposophists will be intrigued to learn that late in life (ca. 1780) Lessing argued that humans must necessarily have more than five senses, and that we seem to be restricted to five only because the other, higher senses have not yet evolved. Lessing also published a late treatise, *The Education of the Human Race* (1777–1780),[71] in which he attempts to reconcile the tensions between the religion of the Old Testament, the New Testament, and 'the Christianity of reason' (as he termed it) by invoking the idea of reincarnation. The relevant passages come at the very end, and deserve to be quoted in full:

86

> It will certainly come, the time of a *new, eternal gospel,* which is promised to us even in the primers of the New Covenant. ...

93

> Exactly so! Every individual—one sooner, another later—must first have traversed the same route whereby the race attains its perfection. But can he have traversed it in one and the same lifetime? Can he, in this life, have been both a sensual Jew and the spiritual Christian? Can he have overtaken both of them in the same life?

94

Well, surely not!—But why should every individual not have been present more than once in this world?

95

Is this hypothesis so ridiculous just because it is the oldest one? Because the human understanding hit upon it at once, before was distracted and weakened by the sophistry of the schools?

96

Why should I not likewise have already taken all the steps here towards my perfection which merely temporal rewards and punishments can lead mankind to take?

97

And why should I not, on another occasion, have taken all those steps which the prospects of eternal rewards give us so strong an incentive to take?

98

Why should I not come back as often as I am able to acquire new knowledge and new accomplishments? Do I take away so much on one occasion that it may not be worth the trouble coming back?

99

Should I not come back because of this?—Or because I forget that I have been here before? It is as well that I should forget. The memory of my previous states would only permit me to make a poor use of the present one. And does what I must forget for the present have to be forgotten forever?

100

Or am I not to return because too much time would be lost in so doing?—Lost?—And what exactly do I have to lose? Is not the whole of eternity mine?

Appendix 3

THE ETHERIC AND THE ASTRAL BODIES

'E$_{\text{THERIC}}$ body' is Steiner's early, theosophical term for the subtle body of supra-physical forces that sustains life. Later he would also refer to it variously as 'the life body', or the 'formative forces body', or (echoing Spinoza's distinction between *natura naturans* and *natura naturata*) the realm of 'living working' as opposed to the physical realm of 'finished work'.

The etheric body is known through Imagination, and first reveals itself to strengthened thinking as supra-sensible pictures. The etheric body consists of centrifugal forces, expresses itself in all aqueous processes, and flows in great currents through the cosmos. The etheric is a 'time body'; here time becomes space. It is a unity that is always there as a temporal totality, right up to the present moment.

The individual etheric body is precipitated out of a vast cosmic ether. It can be subdivided further into warmth ether, light ether, chemical or tone ether, and life ether. Theodor Schwenk's *Sensitive Chaos: The Creation of Flowing Forms in Water and Air* (London: Rudolf Steiner Press, 1996) is a scientifically compelling and aesthetically beautiful exploration of these forces.

'Astral body' is Steiner's early, theosophical term for the subtle body that corresponds generally to 'soul' or 'psyche'. Like Freud and Jung, he sees it as internally differentiated and gradually transformed by the activity of the higher faculty of the 'I' or 'ego'. The astral body reveals itself to Inspiration, and emerges in a sense from behind Imagination. (The traditional concept of the Music of the Spheres is an experience of macrocosmic astrality.) It consists of centripetal forces, and expresses itself in breathing and in the airy element generally. It also expresses itself as the human nervous system. The astral body has remained behind in time, and casts its beams forward into the present incarnation; it remains in the spiritual world before conception and birth.

The *locus classicus* for both of these bodies among Steiner's introductory works is the uncharacteristically schematic and static description in his early book *Theosophy* (1904; many English editions are available, including now a very inexpensive ebook edition). A much more dynamic (but also much more difficult) account is to be found in the middle four lectures of Rudolf Steiner, *A Psychology of Body, Soul, & Spirit* (New York: SteinerBooks, 1999), which includes a valuable introduction by Robert Sardello. See also Lecture 5 (2 February, 1924) of the cycle GA 234; *Anthroposophy: An Introduction*, trans. and Intro. Owen Barfield (London: Anthroposophical Publishing Co., 1961; also, *Anthroposophy and the Inner Life*, Rudolf Steiner Press, Bristol 1994).

Appendix 4

IMMANUEL KANT

IMMANUEL Kant (1724–1804) was surely the most important modern philosopher, a great revolutionary who changed philosophy utterly and irrevocably. In his First and Second Critiques (1781 and 1788), Kant effected a 'Copernican revolution', whereby the autonomous subject was firmly placed in the centre of the universe. His Third Critique (1790) was even more revolutionary: he identified the aesthetic faculty as the primary agent in both epistemology and ethics. He argued for the spontaneity of the imagination, and launched modern aesthetics by defining art as disinterested contemplation. Hans-Georg Gadamer has gone so far as to argue that all subsequent philosophy has been little more than a series of attempts to rewrite Kant's Third Critique.

Kant was the founder and the inspiration of both German Idealism and German philosophical Romanticism, and the German philosophers within those movements who influenced Steiner most directly (Goethe, Fichte, Schiller, and Hegel) were all profoundly indebted to Kant while simultaneously criticizing what they saw as shortcomings in his philosophy. Fichte and Schiller both described their philosophical work as attempts to rewrite the letter of Kant in the spirit of Kant.

As a philosopher, Steiner was also both indebted to Kant and at the same time critical of him, although his most trenchant criticisms are usually directed not at Kant's actual positions, but rather at the reductive neo-Kantianism of Steiner's contemporaries. For more on Steiner's difficult relationship to Kant, see Frederick Amrine, 'Rudolf Steiner as a Philosopher,' *Research Bulletin* [of the Research Institute for Waldorf Education], 19, No. 1 (2014), pp. 7–18; reprinted in *Kicking Away the Ladder* (Waldorf Publications, 2019).

Appendix 5

GNOSIS/GNOSTICISM

Gnosticism (from the Greek word for 'knowledge') is a modern name for a variety of ancient religious ideas and systems, originating in Jewish-Christian milieus in the first and second century CE. These systems believed that the material world is created by an emanation of the highest God, trapping the divine spark within the human body.

This divine spark could be liberated by *gnosis*. Gnostics considered the principal element of salvation to be direct knowledge of the supreme divinity in the form of mystical or esoteric insight. Many Gnostic texts deal not in concepts of sin and repentance, but with illusion and enlightenment.

Some of the core teachings include the following:

1. All matter is evil, and the non-material, spiritual realm is good.
2. There is an unknowable God, who gave rise to many lesser spirit beings called Aeons.
3. One evil, lower spirit being is the creator who made the universe.
4. Gnosticism does not deal with 'sin,' only ignorance.
5. To achieve salvation, one needs to get in touch with secret knowledge.

Until 1945, Gnostic writings were known chiefly by quotes from early Church Fathers declaring them heretical, and all 'heretical' texts were seemingly eliminated. However, a collection of Coptic Gnostic codices was discovered in Nag Hammadi, Egypt, in 1945. The discovery has revolutionized the field, and caused us to question many long-held assumptions about the earliest development of Christianity. The study of this library has led certain scholars to question the existence of any unified movement called 'Gnosticism' (see Michael Allen Williams, *Rethinking 'Gnosticism': An Argument For Dismantling A Dubious Category* [Princeton University Press 1996]). More compelling is Andrew Welburn's book *Gnosis: The Mysteries and Christianity* (Edinburgh: Floris, 1994), which argues for a discontinuity between Judaism and Christianity, and that the influence of especially the Mysteries has been obscured. The texts from Nag Hammadi fill these gaps, witnessing the great intellectual ferment of the earliest years of Christianity, when people still were trying to make sense of the great event that had taken place.

After the second century, a decline set in, but Gnosticism persisted throughout the centuries as an undercurrent of Western culture, resurfacing for example in the Hermetic writings in the Renaissance. In the Persian Empire, Gnosticism spread as far as China with Manicheism, while Mandaeism, a Gnostic monotheistic religion, is still alive in Iraq.

[sources: *Wikipedia*; *The Internet Encyclopedia of Philosophy*; Andrew Welburn, *Gnosis*]

Appendix 6

HELENA BLAVATSKY

Helena Petrovna Blavatsky (1831–1891) was a Russian spiritualist and author. Born into an aristocratic family of Russian-German descent, 'Blavatsky traveled widely around the empire as a child. Largely self-educated, she developed an interest in Western esotericism during her teenage years. She became interested in occultism and spiritualism and for many years traveled extensively throughout Asia, Europe, and the United States; she also claimed to have spent several years in India and Tibet studying under Hindu gurus. In 1873 she went to New York City, where she met and became a close companion of Henry Steel Olcott, and in 1875 they and several other prominent persons founded the Theosophical Society. In 1877 her first major work, *Isis Unveiled,* was published. In this book she criticized the science and religion of her day and asserted that mystical experience and doctrine were the means to attain true spiritual insight and authority. .... *The Voice of Silence* (1889) and her most important work, *The Secret Doctrine* (1888) [were published], which was an overview of theosophical teachings. It was followed in 1889 by her *Key to Theosophy.* Her *Collected Writings* were published in 15 volumes (1950–91)'. [*Brittanica*]

Appendix 7

Cosmic Evolution

Steiner's account of cosmic evolution is grand beyond all imagining. Steiner affirmed the reality of evolution, but not as Darwin understood it. He honoured Darwin's theory, which was the inspiration and the precondition for Steiner's own research into what one might better term evolutionary cosmology. The same process Darwin describes from an earthly perspective as a gradually *ascending* evolution of increasingly complex biological forms, Steiner describes from a spiritual perspective as a gradual *descent* of spiritual entities into ever more adequate material vessels. In other places, Steiner offers additional perspectives on his cosmology, complementing the 'outer' view of the finished products in *Esoteric Science*, for example, with an especially sublime cycle of five short lectures offering, as it were, an 'Elohim's-eye view' of the same unfolding process.

In Steiner's account, humanity was created from the top down, but it has evolved from the bottom up, over successive 'incarnations' of Earth evolution proper, which was preceded by Saturn, Sun, and Moon, and shall be followed by Jupiter, Venus, and Vulcan. Evolution allows us to approach multiple goals: over many aeons, we have been guided from simplicity toward complexity, from unconsciousness toward consciousness, from passivity toward activity, and from necessity toward freedom. Having received the gift of wisdom, our task is now to internalize that wisdom and transform it into active love. The paradox of freedom implies that the further we progress towards these goals, the less certain is the outcome of the process, which will increasingly be placed into our own hands.

The central texts are:

- Chapter 4 of CW 13, *An Outline of Esoteric Science* (Great Barrington. Massachusetts: SteinerBooks, 1997);
- CW 132, *Inner Experiences of Evolution* (Great Barrington, Massachusetts: SteinerBooks, 2009);
- CW 136, *Spiritual Beings in the Heavenly Bodies and in the Kingdoms of Nature* (Great Barrington, Massachusetts: SteinerBooks, 2012);
- CW 110, *The Spiritual Hierarchies and the Physical World: Zodiac, Planets and Cosmos*, trans. René M. Querido (Great Barrington, NY: SteinerBooks, 2008);
- and GA 122, *Genesis: Secrets of Creation* (2002; London: Rudolf Steiner Press, 2012).

Appendix 8

The Hierarchies

Steiner's complex and highly esoteric ontology affirms the longstanding spiritual teaching that humans occupy a developmental stage between animals 'beneath' and angelic beings 'above' us. ('Beneath' and 'above' are meant to indicate relatively lower and higher levels of consciousness, developmental complexity, and power.) Arthur O. Lovejoy's eponymous study of 1936, which is widely viewed as the founding document of modern intellectual history, called this idea 'The Great Chain of Being', and that is now the conventional term for this set of ideas. This idea is in keeping with a Christian tradition extending back through Thomas Aquinas to Dionysius the Areopagite (late fifth or early sixth century CE; now referred to as 'Pseudo-Dionysius' to distinguish him from his much-earlier namesake), and ultimately to St Paul. In his treatise *On the Celestial Hierarchy* (Pseudo-Dionysius, *The Complete Works* [Mahwah, NJ: Paulist Press, 1987], pp. 143–192), Pseudo-Dionysius had distinguished nine ranks of beings 'above' humans in the spiritual or intelligible world: in ascending order, he terms them 'Angels', 'Archangels', and 'Principalities' (together the 'Third Hierarchy'); 'Authorities', 'Powers', and 'Dominions' (among other current translations; together the 'Second Hierarchy'); and 'Thrones', 'Cherubim', and 'Seraphim' (together the First Hierarchy). Steiner tends to refer to the Third and Second Hierarchies by their Greek names: 'Angeloi', 'Archangeloi', 'Archai'; 'Exousiai', 'Dynameis', and 'Kyriotetes'. Another set of terms Steiner often employs is 'Spirits of Form' (rather than 'Exousiai'), 'Spirits of Movement' (rather than 'Dynameis'), 'Spirits of Wisdom' (rather than 'Kyriotetes'), and 'Spirits of Will' (rather than 'Thrones'). Among Steiner's many discussions of the Hierarchies, the most fundamental are Ch. 4 of CW 13: *An Outline of Esoteric Science*, trans. Catherine E. Creeger (Great Barrington, MA: SteinerBooks, 1997); CW 136: *Spiritual Beings in the Heavenly Bodies and in the Kingdoms of Nature* (Great Barrington, MA: SteinerBooks, 2012); and CW 110: *The Spiritual Hierarchies and the Physical World: Zodiac, Planets and Cosmos*, trans. René M. Querido (Great Barrington, NY: SteinerBooks, 2008).

Appendix 9

AHRIMAN AND LUCIFER

Lucifer

Ahriman

Rudolf Steiner spoke often about the dual nature of evil, ascribing its source to supersensible beings he calls Lucifer and Ahriman. Lucifer might be termed the 'red devil', who tempts humans to sin on the side of *superbia*: pride, anger, egotism, erotic passions, etc. 'Ahriman' is a traditional name for a black demon, beginning with the Zoroastrian figure Angra Mainyu, opponent of the Sun God Ahura Mazda. Ahriman's temptations are those of *acedia*: laziness, greed, and denial of the Spirit generally.

Lucifer incarnated in the third millennium BCE, in the distant East. Ahriman will incarnate in the twenty-first century, in the West. Lucifer wants us to live in the past, while Ahriman cuts us off from the past. Lucifer wants us to flee the Earth; Ahriman wants to bind us to the Earth. Lucifer is responsible for the glories of pagan culture, which however provided no moral impulses. He longs for his cosmic home, which is the planet Venus. Ahriman seeks to subvert culture by promoting materialism, utility, nationalism, and literalism. He wants to reduce the freedom of the spiritual-cultural sphere to politics and economics. He wants to reduce all qualities to quantities.

Steiner argues that the assaults of these beings are providential: only by overcoming their resistance and holding them in proper balance can humanity become inwardly strong enough to develop genuine freedom, knowledge and love. Both figures are represented in Steiner's monumental sculpture 'The Group' (from which these photos have been taken). In 'The Group', Christ as the Representative of Humanity shows us how to hold the balance: He does not vanquish Lucifer and Ahriman, but He keeps each in their place, restricting their activity.

For an excellent discussion of Steiner's ideas as applied to Goethe's *Faust*, see Alan P. Cottrell, *Goethe's View of Evil and the Search for a New Image of Man in our Time* (Edinburgh: Floris Press, 1982). Mephistopheles in Goethe's *Faust* exhibits traits of both beings by turns, and Steiner was critical of Goethe for having conflated them. Lucifer and Ahriman also appear as characters in Steiner's own expressionist *Mystery Dramas* (1910–1913): see GA 14, Rudolf Steiner, *Four Mystery Dramas*, trans. Ruth and Hans Pusch (Great Barrington, MA: SteinerBooks, 2007).

APPENDIX 10

THE KANT-LAPLACE HYPOTHESIS

THE Kant-Laplace hypothesis is an important cosmogonic theory that is also known as the 'nebular hypothesis'. It is the ancestor of our contemporary 'solar nebular disk model'. The theory hypothesizes that the solar system was formed when a primordial nebula began to spin and formed planets through the resultant centrifugal force, and many found the explanation compelling because it seemed to explain the planets' circular and roughly coplanar orbits moving in the same direction as the Sun's rotation. It was first expounded fully by Immanuel Kant in his *Universal Natural History and Theory of the Heavens* [1755; multiple English editions available]. Pierre-Simon, Marquis de Laplace (1749–1827), the great French mathematician and astronomer who extended the Newtonian paradigm in his five-volume *Celestial Mechanics* (1799–1825) and other writings, developed the same theory independently and published it in his *System of the World* [1796; many English translations available]. Steiner often derides this hypothesis, so often demonstrated in school classrooms, for failing to account for the teacher-demiurge who sets the nebula in motion in the first place. (See e.g. the end of the lecture of January 18, 1921 in CW 323; *Interdisciplinary Astronomy* [Keryx, 2017].)

NOTES

Textual sources: It is not known which stenographer took down these lectures. Neither an original stenogram nor a typewritten transcription by the stenographer in plain text has survived. The only textual basis is therefore the first printed manuscript from 1912 and the first published edition by Marie Steiner from 1933. The text was revised for the following (German) editions and a few changes were made in the notes. For the seventh edition (1988), the volume was reviewed by David Hoffmann and revised with extended notes, new references and a detailed index of names.

The title of the lecture cycle was given by Rudolf Steiner.

The words 'theosophy' and 'theosophical' used in the lectures at the time are always to be understood in the sense of anthroposophically-oriented spiritual science (anthroposophy). Due to a later explicit instruction by Rudolf Steiner, they are replaced here, where appropriate, by 'anthroposophy' and 'anthroposophical' or 'spiritual science' and 'spiritual scientific'.

Works by Rudolf Steiner within the Complete Edition (GA) are indicated in the notes with the bibliography number. See also the overview at the end of the volume.

1   The Society of Jesus was founded in 1540 by Ignatius of Loyola with the approval of Pope Paul III.

2   *Maya* is a theosophical term that Steiner uses frequently. It is a contraction of the Sanskrit terms *maha* [great], *a* [not or non-, like 'alpha privative' in Ancient Greek; cf. 'apolitical'], and *ya* [being]; hence, 'maya' means literally 'the great non-being'. It is illusory because it seems to exist, but ultimately does not.

3   Steiner means the second person of the Trinity.

4   See Appendix 1.

5   Steiner refers frequently to Imagination, Inspiration, and Intuition. Like Wordsworth, Steiner saw Imagination as more than reason, as 'reason in its most exalted mood'. A good way to understand Imagination, Inspiration,

and Intuition is to recall, and then expand, Plato's Allegory of the Cave, in which everyday thoughts are revealed to be but the shadows of a higher, more active and intuitive thinking activity. Steiner followed the German Idealists and the Romantics in calling this mode of intuitive thinking Imagination. By the same token, Steiner argued that there are higher modes of cognition of which everyday feeling and willing are but the shadows of Inspiration and Intuition respectively. For a brief introduction, see Rudolf Steiner, *Imagination, Inspiration, and Intuition*, trans. and ed. Frederick Amrine, Keryx, 2018. The most systematic treatment is arguably GA 12; *The Stages of Higher Knowledge: Imagination, Inspiration, Intuition* (Great Barrington, MA: SteinerBooks, 2009).

6 CW 10; *How to Know Higher Worlds: A Modern Path of Initiation*, trans. Christopher Bamford, Classics in Anthroposophy (Great Barrington, MA: Anthroposophic Press, 1994).

7 Rudolf Steiner wrote and directed four Mystery Dramas: *The Portal of Initiation* (1910), *The Soul's Probation* (1911), *The Guardian of the Threshold* (1912) and *The Souls' Awakening* (1913). See GA 14, Rudolf Steiner, *Four Mystery Dramas*, trans. Ruth and Hans Pusch (Great Barrington, MA: SteinerBooks/Anthroposophic Press, 2007); also *The Four Mystery Plays*, trans. Adam Bittleston (London: Rudolf Steiner Press, 1982) and *Four Modern Mystery Dramas*, trans. Richard Ramsbotham (Rudolf Steiner Press, 2023). All four were performed originally in Munich, which had become the centre of the artistic avant-garde in Central Europe, and they are in many ways typically Expressionist. Kandinsky and Schönberg among many others experienced the Mystery Dramas and were influenced by them during these last years leading up to World War I.

8 See Appendix 2.

9 Maximilian Droßbach (1810–1884). The work referred to, *Rebirth, or the Solution of the Question of Immortality in an Empirical Manner in Accordance with Well-Known Laws of Nature*, appeared in 1849.

10 Gustav Widenmann (1812–1876) was a Swabian doctor.

11 'Reinkarnation und Karma, vom Standpunkte der modernen Naturwissenschaft notwendige Vorstellungen' was published in 1903 in Rudolf Steiner's magazine *Lucifer-Gnosis*. It is collected in GA 34, which remains untranslated at this date (2022).

12 CW 9; *Theosophy* (1904; many English editions are available, including now a very inexpensive ebook edition). This early work presents the basics of Steiner's spiritual psychology using the terminology of theosophy. A much more dynamic (but also much more difficult) account is to be found in the middle four lectures of Rudolf Steiner, *A Psychology of Body, Soul, & Spirit* (New York: SteinerBooks, 1999), which includes a valuable Introduction by Robert Sardello.

13 See Appendix 3.

14 Steiner's main introductory treatment of this topic is in Ch. 10 of his basic book CW 10, *How to Know Higher Worlds: A Modern Path of Initiation* (Great Barrington, MA: Anthroposophic Press, 1994). He describes the Guardian as a wise being who blocks our access to the spiritual world until we have achieved an appropriate stage of spiritual and especially moral development.

15 'The Mystery of Golgotha' is Steiner's favoured term for all that is more conventionally referred to as the Incarnation, the Passion, and the Resurrection. One of Steiner's earliest publications, his book *Christianity as Mystical Fact*, situates Christianity squarely within the context of ancient mystery religions (rather than mysticism, which the title might seem to imply). This important text is now volume 8 of Steiner's *Complete Works* in English, and the latest edition (New York: Anthroposophic Press, 1997) was both translated and introduced by a scholar and anthroposophist of great stature, Andrew Welburn. In the same spirit, Steiner also refers to 'the Easter Mystery'.

16 *Kamaloka* is the period after death when the soul is freeing itself from its inclination toward physical existence in order to follow the laws of the spiritual world. See CW 9; *Theosophy* (1904; many English editions are available, including now a very inexpensive ebook edition), Chapter 3, or Chapter 3 of CW 13; *An Outline of Esoteric Science*, trans. Catherine E. Creeger (Great Barrington, MA: Steiner-Books, 1997).

17 *die Christus-Entwickelung der Menschheit.*

18 Apollonius of Tyana (3 BCE–c. 97 CE) was a Greek Neopythagorean philosopher from the town of Tyana in the Roman province of Cappadocia in Anatolia. Some theosophists have maintained that Apollonius of Tyana was the reincarnation of the being they call the Master Jesus. Helena Blavatsky in 1881 refers to Apollonius of Tyana as 'the great thaumaturgist of the second century AD'.

19 Steiner's fullest accounts of epochs such as Lemuria in the remote past of human evolution are to be found in Ch. 4 of CW 13, *An Outline of Esoteric Science*, trans. Catherine E. Creeger (Great Barrington, Massachusetts: Steiner-Books, 1997), and in CW 11; *Cosmic Memory: Atlantis and Lemuria* (San Francisco: HarperCollins, 1981).

20 Blaise Pascal (1623–1662) was a prominent mathematician, scientist, and Catholic theologian. He argued in his book *Pensées* a religious doctrine that sought the experience of God through the heart, through intuition, rather than through reason.

21 Pascal was of course a rationalist in his mathematical and scientific work; Steiner is referring solely to his theological writings.

22 Vladimir Solovyov (1853–1900) was an important Russian philosopher and theologian. A close friend of Dostoevsky, he wrote about his encounters with

Sophia, whom he conceived as the merciful unifying feminine wisdom of God. His thought was especially influential among the Symbolist movement after his death.

23 See Appendix 4.

24 *Der deutsche Monistenbund* was a scientific society founded in Jena in 1906 under the leadership of the eminent biologist Ernst Haeckel. It was a complex organization with competing factions, but its general tenor was materialist and anti-religious.

25 'Impulse' is one of Steiner's favourite words. It crops up everywhere, and it is always (but only mildly) metaphorical. Because the term is so resolutely mechanistic, but its referent is invariably spiritual or cultural, the effect can be jarring. As is so easily done in German, Steiner will frequently coin new terms by conjoining them with other words, e.g. 'Faust-impulse', 'Resurrection-impulse', and 'I-impulse'. 'Christ-Impulse' occurs very frequently, and it makes sense in the context of Steiner's view of Christianity as something that intervenes in the physical world to effect human evolution, as opposed to a series of ideas to be understood.

26 Saint Augustine of Hippo (354–430) 'was a Roman African, early Christian theologian and philosopher from Numidia whose writings influenced the development of Western Christianity and Western philosophy. He was the bishop of Hippo Regius in North Africa and is viewed as one of the most important Church Fathers in Western Christianity for his writings in the Patristic Era. Among his most important works are *The City of God*, *On Christian Doctrine* and *Confessions*'. [*Wikipedia*]

27 Justin Martyr (c. 100 CE–c. 165 CE), also known as Justin the Philosopher, was an early Christian apologist and philosopher.

28 Socrates (470-399 BCE), although he wrote nothing, had an enormous influence on the subsequent history of philosophy. A consummate rationalist, he was the teacher of Plato—indeed, many of Plato's dialogues feature Socrates in a starring role. Despite his vast influence, he was in many ways an enigmatic and controversial figure.

29 The darkly obscure pre-Socratic philosopher Heraclitus was a native of Ephesus (ca. 535–ca. 475 BCE). *Fragments: The Collected Wisdom of Heraclitus* (New York: Viking, 2001) is an excellent English translation. The standard English-language treatment of the pre-Socratics remains G. S. Kirk and J. E. Raven, *The Presocratic Philosophers: A Critical History with a Selection of Texts* (Cambridge: Cambridge UP, 1971).

30 See Appendix 5.

31 Richard Wagner (1813–1883) was a German composer and theorist who is especially well known for his operas or 'music dramas', as he called them. He is considered a late Romantic. Among his most important works are the four-opera cycle *The Ring of the Nibelungs, Tristan and Isolde,* and *Parsifal.*

32 CW 8; *Christianity as Mystical Fact and the Mysteries of Antiquity,* trans. Andrew Welburn, ed. Christopher Bamford (Great Barrington: SteinerBooks, 2006).

33 'The Mysteries' is the Greek term for schools and rites that were esoteric in the strong sense: neophytes were forbidden to divulge their teachings—in some cases (such as the Pythagoreans) on pain of death. The most important Mystery centres were in Eleusis, Samothrace, and Ephesus.

34 The Akashic Record is a symbolic, spiritual script in which everything is recorded that has ever happened on Earth. It can be read by an initiate, and this is how the spiritual researcher can speak of things about which no historical records survive.

35 See Appendix 6.

36 Saint Jerome (c. 345 CE–c. 420 CE) is best known for his translation of the Bible into Latin (the translation that became known as the Vulgate) and his commentaries on the whole Bible.

37 The Ebionites were a Jewish Christian sect of the early centuries CE that viewed poverty as a blessing.

38 See Appendix 7.

39 Steiner's theosophical term for Antiquity; he sees it as having lasted from 747 BCE to 1413 CE. He also terms it the Greco-Roman age or the Greco-Latin period. The name implies that Greece and Rome were the 'vanguard' cultures during the period, i.e. the loci of innovation and progress. He sees other cultures such as ancient India, Persia, and Egypt having been the leaders during even earlier periods. Steiner's terminology is idiosyncratic here, but the underlying thoughts are commonplaces of intellectual history.

40 Inspired and deeply religious, Aeschylus (c. 525–456 BCE) was the eldest of the great triumvirate of Athenian tragic dramatists; he has been called 'the father of tragedy'.

41 'Egypto-Chaldean' is Steiner's theosophical term for a long epoch he sees as having ended ca. 747 BCE. He also calls it the third post-Atlantean epoch or age. The implication of the term is that the Egyptian, Sumerian and Babylonian cultures were in the vanguard of human cultural evolution during that period—quite a conventional notion after all, despite the idiosyncrasy of the label. Because it has become a standard anthroposophical term, 'Chaldean' stands here rather that Sumerian and/or Babylonian, which would be more conventional in English.

42   Pericles (495–429 BCE) was the Athenian statesman most responsible for the full development of Athenian democracy and the Athenian Empire. The Acropolis was built during his reign.

43   Nāgasena was a Sarvastivadan Buddhist sage who lived around 150 BCE. His answers to questions about Buddhism posed by the Indian King Milinda were recorded.

44   David Friedrich Strauß (1808–1874) 'was a German liberal Protestant theologian and writer, who influenced Christian Europe with his portrayal of the "historical Jesus", whose divine nature he denied. His work was connected to the Tübingen School, which revolutionized study of the New Testament, early Christianity, and ancient religions'. [*Wikipedia*]

45   See Appendix 8.

46   See Appendix 9.

47   Translated as CW 13; *An Outline of Esoteric Science*, trans. Catherine E. Creeger (Great Barrington, MA: SteinerBooks, 1997). An otherwise excellent earlier translation by George Adams bore the unfortunate title *Occult Science*. At the time of writing, Steiner was the head of the Theosophical Society in Germany, and the word *Geheimwissenschaft* in his title was meant to echo Blavatsky's tome, *The Secret Doctrine*. Thus *The Secret Science* would be a far more accurate translation. CW 13 is now considered one of the four 'basic books' of anthroposophy.

48   Steiner's fullest accounts of epochs such as Atlantis in the remote past of human evolution are to be found in Ch. 4 of CW 13, *An Outline of Esoteric Science*, trans. Catherine E. Creeger (Great Barrington, Massachusetts: SteinerBooks, 1997), and in CW 11, *Cosmic Memory: Atlantis and Lemuria* (San Francisco: HarperCollins, 1981). Because Steiner uses theosophical rather than modern geological terms, it is difficult to date this epoch, but Atlantis seems to correspond to the end of the Pleistocene, when the transition to the much warmer temperatures of the Holocene would have led to the massive flooding of areas that had previously been dry land. The Biblical myth of the Flood may represent an archetypal recollection of this primordial transition.

49   *Volks-Ich*

50   *Volks-Gruppen-Ich*

51   CW 129; *Wonders of the World, Trials of the Soul, Revelations of the Spirit* (Forest Row: Rudolf Steiner Press, 2020).

52   *Formleib*

53   GA 15; *The Spiritual Guidance of the Individual and Humanity*, Classics in Anthroposophy (Hudson, New York: Anthroposophic Press, 1991). This beautiful

booklet, worked up from three lectures Steiner had given earlier, is one of the best introductions to anthroposophy.

54 Steiner comments briefly on two different translations of this passage into German.

55 Johann Albrecht Bengel (24 June 1687–2 November 1752), also known as *Bengelius*, was a Lutheran pietist clergyman and scholar of Greek known for his edition and critical exegesis of the Greek New Testament.

56 Friedrich Christoph Oetinger (1702–1782) was a German Lutheran theologian and theosophist.

57 Richard Rothe (1799–1867) was a German Lutheran theologian.

58 See Appendix 10.

59 Nicolaus Copernicus (1473–1543) was the first astronomer to publish a comprehensive and persuasive heliocentric account of the universe, *On the Revolutions of the Heavenly Spheres* (1543).

60 Kant pronounced the German mathematician and astronomer Johannes Kepler (1571–1630) the most rigorous thinker who ever lived. He is most famous for discovering and mathematically modelling the elliptical motions of the planets, and for major contributions toward the theory of gravitation eventually formalized by Newton.

61 Galileo Galilei (1564–1642), the Italian physicist, astronomer, philosopher, and mathematician 'who made fundamental contributions to the sciences of motion, astronomy, and strength of materials and to the development of the scientific method. His formulation of (circular) inertia, the law of falling bodies, and parabolic trajectories marked the beginning of a fundamental change in the study of motion. His insistence that the book of nature was written in the language of mathematics changed natural philosophy from a verbal, qualitative account to a mathematical one in which experimentation became a recognized method for discovering the facts of nature. Finally, his discoveries with the telescope revolutionized astronomy and paved the way for the acceptance of the Copernican heliocentric system, but his advocacy of that system eventually resulted' in his being brought before the Inquisition. [*Britannica*]

62 GA 103; *The Gospel of John* (Hudson, NY: SteinerBooks, 2022).

63 GA 123; *According to Matthew: The Gospel of Christ's Humanity* (Great Barrington: SteinerBooks, 2003).

64 The 'great forerunner' is Goethe.

65 These words are spoken by the Angels after Faust's death and resurrection.

66 Gotthold Ephraim Lessing, *Laocoön: An Essay on the Limits of Painting and Poetry*, translated by Edward Allen McCormick (Baltimore: Johns Hopkins, 1984).

67   G. E. Lessing, *The Hamburg Dramaturgy*, trans. Wendy Arons and Sara Figal; ed. Natalya Baldyga (New York: Routledge, 2018).

68   *Britannica, Wikipedia*

69   Gotthold Ephraim Lessing, *Philosophical and Theological Writings*, ed. H. B. Nisbet (Cambridge: Cambridge University Press, 2005), pp. 184–216.

70   Gotthold Ephraim Lessing, *Nathan the Wise with Related Documents*, trans. and ed. by Ronald Schechter (Boston: Bedford/St. Martins. 2004).

71   *Philosophical and Theological Writings*, pp. 217–240.

Rudolf Steiner's Collected Works

The German Edition of Rudolf Steiner's Collected Works (the *Gesamtausgabe* [GA], published by Rudolf Steiner Verlag, Dornach, Switzerland) will be completed in the year 2025. The works are organized either by type of work (written, spoken, artistic creations), chronology, audience (public or other), or subject (education, art, etc.). For ease of comparison, the Collected Works in English (CW), listed below, follows the German organization and numbering.

The volumes that have so far been published in the English Collected Works edition appear *in italics with their published titles*; all other volumes, including those that have appeared in editions other than the CW, are set in Roman type with *literal translations* of the German titles. Published English titles are not necessarily the same as the German.

This list is current as of the date of this volume's publication.

A. Written Works

I. Writings 1884–1925

CW 1	Introductions and Selected Commentary on Goethe's Natural-scientific Writings
CW 1a–e	Goethe's Natural-scientific Writings
CW 1f	Editorial Afterwords to Goethe's Natural-scientific Writings in the Weimar Edition (1891–1896)
CW 2	*Goethe's Theory of Knowledge: An Outline of the Epistemology of His Worldview*
CW 3	Truth and Science
CW 4	The Philosophy of Freedom
CW 4a	Documents to "The Philosophy of Freedom"
CW 5	Friedrich Nietzsche, A Fighter against His Own Time

CW 6 Goethe's Worldview

CW 7 Mysticism at the Dawn of Modern Spiritual Life and Its Relationship with Modern Worldviews

CW 8 *Christianity as Mystical Fact and the Mysteries of Antiquity*

CW 9 Theosophy: An Introduction into Supersensible World Knowledge and Human Purpose

CW 10 How Does One Attain Knowledge of Higher Worlds?

CW 11 From the Akasha-Chronicle

CW 12 Levels of Higher Knowledge

CW 13 Occult Science in Outline

CW 14 *Four Modern Mystery Dramas*

CW 15 The Spiritual Guidance of the Individual and Humanity

CW 16/17 *A Way of Self-Knowledge & The Threshold of the Spiritual World*

CW 18 The Riddles of Philosophy in Their History, Presented as an Outline

CW 18a Views of the World and of Life in the Nineteenth Century

CW 19 Thoughts during the Time of War (1915) and Further Texts on the Events of the World War (1917–1921)

CW 20 The Riddles of the Human Being: Articulated and Unarticulated in the Thinking, Views and Opinions of a Series of German and Austrian Personalities

CW 21 The Riddles of the Soul

CW 22 Goethe's Spiritual Nature and Its Revelation in "Faust" and through the "Fairy Tale of the Snake and the Lily"

CW 23 The Central Points of the Social Question in the Necessities of Life in the Present and the Future

CW 24 Essays Concerning the Threefold Division of the Social Organism and the Period 1915–1921

CW 25 Three Steps of Anthroposophy. Philosophy – Cosmology – Religion

CW 26 Anthroposophical Leading Thoughts

CW 27 Fundamentals for Expansion of the Art of Healing according to Spiritual-Scientific Insights

CW 28 *Autobiography: Chapters in the Course of My Life: 1861–1907*

II. Collected Essays

CW 29 Collected Essays on Dramaturgy, 1889–1900

CW 30 Methodical Foundations of Anthroposophy: Collected Essays on Philosophy, Natural Science, Aesthetics and Psychology, 1884–1901

CW 31 Collected Essays on Culture and Current Events, 1887–1901

CW 32 Collected Essays on Literature, 1884–1902

CW 33 Biographies and Biographical Sketches, 1894–1905

CW 34	Lucifer-Gnosis: Foundational Essays on Anthroposophy and Reports from the Periodicals "Luzifer" and "Lucifer-Gnosis," 1903–1908
CW 35	Philosophy and Anthroposophy: Collected Essays, 1904–1923
CW 36	The Goetheanum-Idea in the Middle of the Cultural Crisis of the Present: Collected Essays from the Periodical "Das Goetheanum," 1921–1925
CW 37	Writings on the History of the Anthroposophical Movement and Society 1902–1925

III. Publications from the Literary Estate

CW 38/1	Complete Letters, Vol. 1: Weimar Period 1879–1890
CW 38/2	Complete Letters, Vol. 2: Weimar Period 1890–1897
CW 38/3	Complete Letters, Vol. 3: Early Berlin Period 1897–1905 [forthcoming]
CW 38/4	Complete Letters, Vol. 4: Activity within the Theosophical Society 1905–1912 [forthcoming]
CW 38/5	Complete Letters, Vol. 5: From the Founding of the Anthroposophical Society to the Opening of the Goetheanum 1913–1920 [forthcoming]
CW 38/6	Complete Letters, Vol. 6: The Last Years 1920–1925 [forthcoming]
CW 40	Truth-Wrought Words
CW 40a	Sayings, Poems and Mantras; Supplementary Volume
CW 41a	Translations and Free Renderings from the Old and New Testaments
CW 41b	Translations and Free Renderings of Various Works
CW 42	Stage Adaptations I: Dramas by Edouard Schuré
CW 43	Stage Adaptations II: The Oberufer Christmas Plays
CW 44	Sketches, Fragments and Paralipomena on the Four Mystery Dramas
CW 45	Anthroposophy: A Fragment from the Year 1910
CW 46	Posthumous Essays and Fragments 1879–1924
CW 47/48	Notebooks and Notepads (digital edition)
CW 49	Notes for and about Helmuth and Eliza von Moltke and Relatives, 1904–1924 [forthcoming]
CW 50	[Blank number]

B. Lectures

I. Public Lectures

CW 51	*On Philosophy, History, and Literature: Lectures at the Worker Education School and the Independent College, Berlin, 1901–1905*
CW 52	Spiritual Teachings Concerning the Soul and Observation of the World

CW 53	The Origin and Goal of the Human Being
CW 54	The Riddles of the World and Anthroposophy
CW 55	Knowledge of the Supersensible in Our Times and Its Meaning for Life Today
CW 56	Knowledge of the Soul and of the Spirit
CW 57	Where and How Does One Find the Spirit?
CW 58	The Metamorphoses of the Soul Life. Paths of Soul Experiences: Part One
CW 59	The Metamorphoses of the Soul Life. Paths of Soul Experiences: Part Two
CW 60	The Answers of Spiritual Science to the Biggest Questions of Existence
CW 61	Human History in the Light of Spiritual Research
CW 62	*Results of Spiritual Research*
CW 63	Spiritual Science as a Treasure for Life
CW 64	Out of Destiny-Burdened Times
CW 65	Out of Central European Spiritual Life
CW 66	Spirit and Matter, Life and Death
CW 67	The Eternal in the Human Soul. Immortality and Freedom
CW 68a	On the Being of Christianity
CW 68b	The Cycle of the Human Being within the Sense-, Soul-, and Spirit-World
CW 68c	Goethe and the Present
CW 68d	The Being of Man in the Light of Spiritual Science
CW 69a	Truths and Errors of Spiritual Research. Spiritual Science and the Future of Mankind
CW 69b	Knowledge and Immortality
CW 69c	New Christ-Experience
CW 69d	Death and Immortality in the Light of Spiritual Science
CW 69e	Spiritual Science and the Spiritual Goals of Our Time
CW 70a	Human Soul, Destiny and Death
CW 70b	Paths to the Knowledge of the Eternal Powers of the Human Soul
CW 71a	Soul Immortality [forthcoming]
CW 71b	The Human Being as a Soul and Spirit Being
CW 72	Freedom – Immortality – Social Life
CW 73	The Supplementing of the Modern Sciences through Anthroposophy
CW 73a	Specialized Fields of Knowledge and Anthroposophy
CW 74	The Philosophy of Thomas Aquinas
CW 75	*Anthroposophy and the Natural Sciences: Foundations and Methods*
CW 76	The Fructifying Effect of Anthroposophy on Specialized Fields
CW 77a	The Task of Anthroposophy in Relation to Science and Life: The Darmstadt College Course
CW 77b	Art and Anthroposophy. The Goetheanum-Impulse

CW 78   Anthroposophy, Its Roots of Knowledge and Fruits for Life

CW 79   The Reality of the Higher Worlds

CW 80a   The Being of Anthroposophy

CW 80b   The Inner Realm of Nature and the Being of the Human Soul

CW 80c   Anthroposophical Spiritual Science and the Great Civilizational Questions of the Present

CW 81   *Reimagining Academic Studies: Science, Philosophy, Education, Social Science, Theology, Theory of Language*

CW 82   *Becoming Fully Human: The Significance of Anthroposophy in Contemporary Spiritual Life*

CW 83   *The Tension between East and West*

CW 84   *The Aims of Anthroposophy and the Purpose of the Goetheanum*

CW 85   Supplementary Volume: Individual Public Lectures I [forthcoming]

CW 86   Supplementary Volume: Individual Public Lectures II [forthcoming]

II. Lectures to the Members of the Anthroposophical Society

CW 87   Ancient Mysteries and Christianity

CW 88   *Concerning the Astral World and Devachan*

CW 89   Consciousness–Life–Form. Fundamental Principles of a Spiritual-Scientific Cosmology

CW 90a   Self-knowledge and Knowledge of the Divine, Vol. I. Theosophy, Christology, and Mythology

CW 90b   Self-knowledge and Knowledge of the Divine, Vol. II. Theosophy, Christology, and Mythology

CW 90c   Theosophy and Occultism

CW 91   Cosmology and Human Evolution. Introduction to Theosophy – Theory of Colours

CW 92   *The Occult Truths of Myths and Legends: Greek and Germanic Mythology: Richard Wagner in the Light of Spiritual Science*

CW 93   The Temple Legend and the Golden Legend as a Symbolic Expression of Past and Future Secrets of Human Development. From the Contents of the Esoteric School

CW 93a   Fundamentals of Esotericism

CW 94   Cosmogony. Popular Occultism. The Gospel of John. Theosophy Based on the Gospel of John

The Theosophy in the Gospel of John

CW 95   At the Gates of Theosophy

CW 96   Origin-Impulses of Spiritual Science. Christian Esotericism in the Light of New Spirit-knowledge

CW 97   The Christian Mystery
CW 98   *Nature Beings and Spirit Beings: Their Activity in Our Visible World*
CW 99   The Theosophy of the Rosicrucians
CW 100   *True Knowledge of the Christ: Theosophy and Rosicucianism—The Gospel of John*
CW 101   Myths and Legends. Occult Signs and Symbols
CW 102   *Good and Evil Spirits and Their Influence on Humanity*
CW 103   *The Gospel of John*
CW 104   The Apocalypse of John
CW 104a   From the Picture-Script of the Apocalypse of John
CW 105   *Universe, Earth, Human Being: Their Relationship to Egyptian Myths and Modern Civilization*
CW 106   Egyptian Myths and Mysteries in Relation to the Active Spiritual Forces of the Present
CW 107   *Disease, Karma, and Healing: Spiritual-scientific Enquiries into the Nature of the Human Being*
CW 108   Answering the Questions of Life and the World through Anthroposophy
CW 109   The Principle of Spiritual Economy in Connection with the Question of Reincarnation. An Aspect of the Spiritual Guidance of Humanity
CW 110   *The Spiritual Hierarchies and the Physical World: Zodiac, Planets, and Cosmos*
CW 111   Introduction to the Foundations of Theosophy
CW 112   The Gospel of John in Relation to the Three Other Gospels, Especially the Gospel of Luke
CW 113   The Orient in the Light of the Occident. The Children of Lucifer and the Brothers of Christ
CW 114   The Gospel of Luke
CW 115   Anthroposophy – Psychosophy – Pneumatosophy
CW 116   *The Christ-Impulse and the Development of Ego-Consciousness*
CW 117   *Deeper Secrets of Human Evolution in Light of the Gospels*
CW 117a   The Gospel of John and the Three Other Gospels
CW 118   The Event of the Christ-Appearance in the Etheric World
CW 119   *Macrocosm and Microcosm: The Greater and the Lesser World: Questions Concerning the Soul, Life and the Spirit*
CW 120   The Revelations of Karma
CW 121   *The Mission of Folk Souls*
CW 122   The Secrets of the Biblical Creation-Story. The Six-Day Work in the First Book of Moses
CW 123   The Gospel of Matthew
CW 124   *Background to the Gospel of St Mark*
CW 125   *Paths and Goals of the Spiritual Human Being: Life Questions in the Light of Spiritual Science*

CW 126   Occult History. Esoteric Observations of the Karmic Relation-ships of Personalities and Events of World History

CW 127   *The Mission of the New Spiritual Revelation: The Pivotal Nature of the Christ Event in Earth Evolution*

CW 128   An Occult Physiology

CW 129   *Wonders of the World: Trials of the Soul, Revelations of the Spirit*

CW 130   Esoteric Christianity and the Spiritual Guidance of Humanity

CW 131   *From Jesus to Christ*

CW 132   *Inner Experiences of Evolution*

CW 133   The Earthly and the Cosmic Human Being

CW 134   *The World of the Senses and the World of the Spirit*

CW 135   Reincarnation and Karma and Their Meaning for the Culture of the Present

CW 136   *Spiritual Beings in the Heavenly Bodies and in the Kingdoms of Nature*

CW 137   The Human Being in the Light of Occultism, Theosophy and Philosophy

CW 138   On Initiation. On Eternity and the Passing Moment. On the Light of the Spirit and the Darkness of Life

CW 139   The Gospel of Mark

CW 140   Occult Investigation into the Life between Death and New Birth. The Living Interaction between Life and Death

CW 141   *Between Death and Rebirth: In Relation to Cosmic Facts*

CW 142/46 *The Bhagavad Gita and the West: The Esoteric Significance of the Bhagavad Gita and Its Relation to the Epistles of Paul*

CW 143   *Three Paths to Christ: Experiencing the Supersensible*

CW 144   *The Mysteries of Initiation: From Isis to the Holy Grail*

CW 145   What Significance Does Occult Development of the Human Being Have for the Sheaths–Physical Body, Etheric Body, Astral Body, and Self?

CW 146   [See CW 142/46]

CW 147   The Secrets of the Threshold

CW 148   The Fifth Gospel

CW 149   *Christ and the Spiritual World: The Quest for the Holy Grail*

CW 150   *How the Spiritual World Projects into Physical Existence: The Influence of the Dead*

CW 151   *Human and Cosmic Thought*

CW 152   *Approaching the Mystery of Golgotha*

CW 153   The Inner Being of Man and Life Between Death and New Birth

CW 154   How does One Gain an Understanding of the Spiritual World? The Flowing in of Spiritual Impulses from out of the World of the Deceased

CW 155   *Christ and the Human Soul: The Meaning of Life – The Spiritual Foundation of Morality – Anthroposophy and Christianity*

CW 156   *Inner Reading and Inner Hearing: And How to Achieve Existence in the World of Ideas*

CW 157   Human Destinies and the Destiny of Peoples

CW 157a   The Formation of Destiny and the Life after Death

CW 158   *Our Connection with the Elemental World: Kalevala – Olaf Åsteson – the Russian People: The World as the Result of Balancing Influences*

CW 159   *The Mystery of Death: The Nature and Significance of Central Europe and the European Folk-Spirits*

CW 160   [Blank number]

CW 161   *Artistic Sensitivity as a Spiritual Approach to Knowing Life and the World*

CW 162   Questions of Art and Life in Light of Spiritual Science

CW 163   Coincidence, Necessity and Providence. Imaginative Knowledge and the Processes after Death

CW 164   *The Value of Thinking for a Cognition that Satisfies the Human Being: The Relationship between Spiritual Science and Natural Science*

CW 165   *Unifying Humanity Spiritually through the Christ Impulse*

CW 166   Necessity and Freedom in World Events and in Human Action

CW 167   *The Human Spirit Past and Present: Occult Fraternities and the Mystery of Golgotha*

CW 168   *The Connection between the Living and the Dead*

CW 169   World-being and Selfhood

CW 170   The Riddle of the Human Being. The Spiritual Background of Human History

CW 171   Inner Development-Impulses of Humanity. Goethe and the Crisis of the 19th Century.

CW 172   The Karma of the Vocation of the Human Being in Connection with Goethe's Life

CW 173a   Observations of Modern History, Vol. I: Paths to an Objective Judgment

CW 173b   Observations of Modern History, Vol. II: The Karma of Untruthfulness

CW 173c   Observations of Modern History, Vol. III: The Reality of Occult Impulses

CW 174a   *Europe Between East and West in Cosmic and Human History*

CW 174b   *The Spiritual Background to the First World War*

CW 175   *Building Stones for an Understanding of the Mystery of Golgotha: Human Life in a Cosmic Context*

CW 176   *The Karma of Materialism: Aspects of Human Evolution*

CW 177   *The Fall of the Spirits of Darkness: The Spiritual Background to the Outer World: Spiritual Beings and Their Effects*

CW 178   Individual Spiritual Beings and Their Influence in the Soul of the Human Being

CW 179   *The Influence of the Dead on Destiny*

CW 180   Mystery Truths and Christmas Impulses. Ancient Myths and their Meaning

CW 181   *Dying Earth and Living Cosmos: The Living Gifts of Anthroposophy: The Need for New Forms of Consciousness*

CW 182   Death as Transformation of Life

CW 183   *Human Evolution: A Spiritual-Scientific Quest*

CW 184   *Eternal and Transient Elements in Human Life: The Cosmic Past of Humanity and the Mystery of Evil*

CW 185   Historical Symptomology

CW 185a   Historical-Developmental Foundations for Forming a Social Judgment

CW 186   The Fundamental Social Demands of Our Time. In Changed Times

CW 187   How Can Humanity Find the Christ Again? The Threefold Shadow-Existence of our Time and the New Christ-Light

CW 188   *Goetheanism, an Impulse of Transformation and Resurrection*

CW 189   *Conscious Society: Anthroposophy and the Social Question*

CW 190   *Past and Future Impulses in Societal Events*

CW 191   *Understanding Society through Spiritual-Scientific Knowledge: Social Three-folding, Christ, Lucifer, and Ahriman*

CW 192   Spiritual-Scientific Treatment of Social and Pedagogical Questions

CW 193   *Problems of Society: An Esoteric View, from Luciferic Past to Ahrimanic Future*

CW 194   *Michael's Mission: Revealing the Essential Secrets of Human Nature*

CW 195   *Cosmic New Year: Thoughts for New Year 1920*

CW 196   *What Is Necessary in These Urgent Times*

CW 197   *Polarities in the Evolution of Humanity: West and East — Materialism and Mysticism — Knowledge and Belief*

CW 198   *Healing the Social Organism*

CW 199   Spiritual Science as Knowledge of the Foundational Impulses of Social Formation

CW 200   The New Spirituality and the Christ-Experience of the 20th Century

CW 201   The Correspondences Between Microcosm and Macrocosm. The Human Being — A Hieroglyph of the Universe

CW 202   *Universal Spirituality and Human Physicality: Bridging the Divide: The Search for the New Isis and the Divine Sophia*

CW 203   The Responsibility of Human Beings for the Development of the World through their Spiritual Connection with the Planet Earth and the World of the Stars

CW 204   Perspectives of the Development of Humanity. The Materialistic Knowledge-Impulse and the Task of Anthroposophy

CW 205   Human Development, World-Soul, and World-Spirit. Part One: The Human Being as a Being of Body and Soul in Relationship to the World

CW 206   Human Development, World-Soul, and World-Spirit. Part Two: The Human Being as a Spiritual Being in the Process of Historical Development

CW 207   Anthroposophy as Cosmosophy. Part One: Characteristic Features of the Human Being in the Earthly and the Cosmic Realms

CW 208   Anthroposophy as Cosmosophy. Part Two: The Forming of the Human Being as the Result of Cosmic Influence

CW 209   *The Language of the Cosmos: Cosmic Influences and the Spiritual Task of Northern Europe*

CW 210   Old and New Methods of Initiation. Drama and Poetry in the Change of Consciousness in the Modern Age

CW 211   *The Sun Mystery and the Mystery of Death and Resurrection: Exoteric and Esoteric Christianity*

CW 212   *Life of the Human Soul: And Its Relation to World Evolution*

CW 213   *Human Questions and Cosmic Answers*

CW 214   The Mystery of the Trinity: The Human Being in Relationship with the Spiritual World in the Course of Time

CW 215   Philosophy, Cosmology, and Religion in Anthroposophy

CW 216   *Supersensible Impulses in the Historical Development of Humanity*

CW 217   *Becoming the Archangel Michael's Companions: Rudolf Steiner's Challenge to the Younger Generation*

CW 217a   *Youth and the Etheric Heart: Rudolf Steiner Speaks to the Younger Generation*

CW 218   *Spirit as Sculptor of the Human Organism*

CW 219   The Relationship of the World of the Stars to the Human Being, and of the Human Being to the World of the Stars. The Spiritual Communion of Humanity

CW 220   *Awake! For the Sake of the Future*

CW 221   Earth-Knowing and Heaven-Insight

CW 222   *The Driving Force of Spiritual Powers in World History*

CW 223   The Cycle of the Year as Breathing Process of the Earth and the Four Great Festival-Seasons. Anthroposophy and the Human Heart (*Gemüt*)

CW 224   The Human Soul and its Connection with Divine-Spiritual Individualities. The Internalization of the Festivals of the Year

CW 225   *Three Perspectives of Anthroposophy: Cultural Phenomena from the Point of View of Spiritual Science*

CW 226   Human Being, Human Destiny, and World Development

CW 227　Initiation-Knowledge

CW 228　*Initiation Science: And the Development of the Human Mind*

CW 229　The Experiencing of the Course of the Year in Four Cosmic Imaginations

CW 230　The Human Being as Harmony of the Creative, Building, and Formative World-Word

CW 231　The Supersensible Human Being, Understood Anthroposophically

CW 232　The Forming of the Mysteries

CW 233　*World History and the Mysteries in the Light of Anthroposophy*

CW 233a　*Rosicrucianism and Modern Initiation: Mystery Centres of the Middle Ages: The Easter Festival and the History of the Mysteries*

CW 234　Anthroposophy. A Summary after 21 Years

CW 235　Esoteric Observations of Karmic Relationships in 6 Volumes, Vol. 1

CW 236　Esoteric Observations of Karmic Relationships in 6 Volumes, Vol. 2

CW 237　Esoteric Observations of Karmic Relationships in 6 Volumes, Vol. 3: The Karmic Relationships of the Anthroposophical Movement

CW 238　Esoteric Observations of Karmic Relationships in 6 Volumes, Vol. 4: The Spiritual Life of the Present in Relationship to the Anthroposophical Movement

CW 239　Esoteric Observations of Karmic Relationships in 6 Volumes, Vol. 5

CW 240　Esoteric Observations of Karmic Relationships in 6 Volumes, Vol. 6

CW 241　[Blank number]

CW 242　[Blank number]

CW 243　*True and False Paths of Spiritual Research*

CW 244　Answers to Questions, and Interviews

CW 245　[Blank number]

CW 246　Supplementary Volume I: Individual Members Lectures

CW 247　Supplementary Volume II: Individual Members Lectures

CW 248　[Blank number]

CW 249　[Blank number]

CW 250　On the History of the German Section of the Theosophical Society 1902–1913. Lectures, Speeches, Reports, and Minutes

CW 251　On the History of the Anthroposophical Society 1913–1922

CW 252　On the History of the Building Association and the Goetheanum Association 1911–1924

CW 253　*Sexuality, Inner Development, and Community Life: Ethical and Spiritual Dimensions of the Crisis in the Anthroposophical Society in Dornach, 1915*

CW 254   The Occult Movement in the 19th Century and Its Relationship to
            World Culture. Significant Points from the Exoteric Cultural Life
            around the Middle of the 19th Century
CW 255b   Anthroposophy and Its Opponents
CW 256   [Blank number]
CW 257   Anthroposophical Community-Building
CW 258   *The Anthroposophic Movement: The History and Conditions of the Anthro-
            posophical Movement in Relation to the Anthroposophical Society: An
            Encouragement for Self-Examination*
CW 259   The Year of Destiny 1923 in the History of the Anthroposophical
            Society. From the Burning of the Goetheanum to the Christmas
            Conference
CW 260   The Christmas Conference for the Founding of the General
            Anthroposophical Society 1923/24
CW 260a   The Constitution of the General Anthroposophical Society and
            the School for Spiritual Science. The Rebuilding of the Goethe-
            anum
CW 261   *Our Dead: Memorial, Funeral, and Cremation Addresses 1906–1924*
CW 262   Rudolf Steiner and Marie Steiner-von Sivers: Correspondence and
            Documents, 1901–1925
CW 263/1   Rudolf Steiner and Edith Maryon: Correspondence: Letters,
            Verses, Sketches, 1912–1924
CW 264   *From the History and Contents of the First Section of the Esoteric School:
            Letters, Documents, and Lectures: 1904–1914*
CW 265   *Freemasonry and Ritual Work: The Misraim Service*
CW 265a   Teaching and Instruction Lessons for Members of the Knowl-
            edge-Cultic Section of the Esoteric School 1904–1914 [forthcoming]
CW 266/1   *From the Esoteric School: Esoteric Lessons 1904–1909*
CW 266/2   *From the Esoteric School: Esoteric Lessons 1910–1912*
CW 266/3   *From the Esoteric School: Esoteric Lessons 1913–1923*
CW 267   *Soul Exercises: Word and Symbol Meditations*
CW 268   *Mantric Sayings: Meditations 1903–1925*
CW 269   Ritual Texts for the Celebration of the Free Christian Religious
            Instruction. The Collected Verses for Teachers and Students of
            the Waldorf School
CW 270   Esoteric Instructions for the First Class of the School for Spiritual
            Science at the Goetheanum 1924, 4 Volumes

III. Lectures and Courses on Specific Realms of Life Lectures on Art

CW 271   *Art and Theory of Art: Foundations of a New Aesthetics*
CW 272   *Anthroposophy in the Light of Goethe's* Faust: *Volume One of Spiritu-
            al-Scientific Commentaries on Goethe's* Faust

CW 273   *Goethe's* Faust *in the Light of Anthroposophy: Volume Two of Spiritual-Scientific Commentaries on Goethe's* Faust

CW 274   Addresses for the Christmas Plays from the Old Folk Traditions

CW 275   Art in the Light of Mystery Wisdom

CW 276   *The Arts and Their Mission*

CW 277a   The Origin and Development of Eurythmy 1912–1918

CW 277b   The Origin and Development of Eurythmy 1918–1920

CW 277c   The Origin and Development of Eurythmy 1920–1922 [forthcoming]

CW 277d   The Origin and Development of Eurythmy 1923–1924 [forthcoming]

CW 278   Eurythmy as Visible Song

CW 279   *Eurythmy as Speech Made Visible: Speech Eurythmy Course*

CW 280   The Method and Nature of Speech Formation

CW 281   The Art of Recitation and Declamation

CW 282   Speech Formation and Dramatic Art

CW 283   The Nature of the Musical Element and the Experience of Tone in the Human Being

CW 284   *Rosicrucianism Renewed: The Unity of Art, Science & Religion: The Theosophical Congress of Whitsun 1907*

CW 285   [Blank number]

CW 286   Paths to a New Style of Architecture. "And the Building Becomes Man"

CW 287   *Architecture as Peacework: The First Goetheanum, Dornach, 1914*

CW 288   *Architecture, Sculpture, and Painting of the First Goetheanum*

CW 289   The Building-Idea of the Goetheanum: Lectures with Slides from the Years 1920–1921

CW 290   *Toward a New Theory of Architecture: The First Goetheanum in Pictures [no longer in the German GA]*

CW 291   The Being of Colours

CW 291a   Knowledge of Colours. Supplementary Volume to "The Being of Colours"

CW 292   *Art History as a Reflection of Inner Spiritual Impulses*

Lectures on Education

CW 293   General Knowledge of the Human Being as the Foundation of Pedagogy

CW 294   The Art of Education: Methodology and Didactics

CW 295   The Art of Education: Seminar Discussions and Lectures on Lesson Planning

CW 296   The Question of Education as a Social Question

CW 297   The Idea and Practice of the Waldorf School

CW 297a   Education for Life: Self-Education and the Practice of Pedagogy
CW 298   Rudolf Steiner in the Waldorf School
CW 299   Spiritual-Scientific Observations on Speech
CW 300a   Conferences with the Teachers of the Free Waldorf School in Stuttgart, 1919 to 1924, in 3 Volumes, Vol. 1
CW 300b   Conferences with the Teachers of the Free Waldorf School in Stuttgart, 1919 to 1924, in 3 Volumes, Vol. 2
CW 300c   Conferences with the Teachers of the Free Waldorf School in Stuttgart, 1919 to 1924, in 3 Volumes, Vol. 3
CW 301   The Renewal of Pedagogical-Didactical Art through Spiritual Science
CW 302   Knowledge of the Human Being and the Forming of Class Lessons
CW 302a   Education and Teaching from a Knowledge of the Human Being
CW 303   The Healthy Development of the Human Being
CW 304   Methods of Education and Teaching Based on Anthroposophy
CW 304a   Anthroposophical Knowledge of the Human Being and Pedagogy
CW 305   The Soul-Spiritual Foundational Forces of the Art of Education. Spiritual Values in Education and Social Life
CW 306   Pedagogical Praxis from the Viewpoint of a Spiritual-Scientific Knowledge of the Human Being. The Education of the Child and Young Human Beings
CW 307   The Spiritual Life of the Present and Education
CW 308   The Method of Teaching and the Life-Requirements for Teaching
CW 309   Anthroposophical Pedagogy and Its Prerequisites
CW 310   The Pedagogical Value of a Knowledge of the Human Being and the Cultural Value of Pedagogy
CW 311   The Art of Education from an Understanding of the Being of Humanity

Lectures on Medicine

CW 312   *Introducing Anthroposophical Medicine*
CW 313   *Illness and Therapy: Spiritual-Scientific Aspects of Healing*
CW 314   *Physiology and Healing: Treatment, Therapy, and Hygiene*
CW 315   Curative Eurythmy
CW 316   *Understanding Healing: Meditative Reflections on Deepening Medicine through Spiritual Science*
CW 317   *Education for Special Needs: The Curative Education Course*
CW 318   The Working Together of Doctors and Pastors
CW 319   *The Healing Process: Spirit, Nature & Our Bodies*

Lectures on Natural Science

CW 320 Spiritual-Scientific Impulses for the Development of Physics 1: The First Natural-Scientific Course: Light, Colour, Tone, Mass, Electricity, Magnetism

CW 321 Spiritual-Scientific Impulses for the Development of Physics 2: The Second Natural-Scientific Course: Warmth at the Border of Positive and Negative Materiality

CW 322 The Borders of the Knowledge of Nature

CW 323 *Interdisciplinary Astronomy: Third Scientific Course*

CW 324 Nature Observation, Mathematics, and Scientific Experimentation and Results from the Viewpoint of Anthroposophy

CW 324a The Fourth Dimension in Mathematics and Reality

CW 325 Natural Science and the World-Historical Development of Humanity since Ancient Times

CW 326 The Moment of the Coming Into Being of Natural Science in World History and Its Development Since Then

CW 327 *Agriculture: Spiritual-Scientific Foundations for Agricultural Renewal*

Lectures on Social Life and the Threefold Arrangement of the Social Organism

CW 328 The Social Question

CW 329 The Liberation of the Human Being as the Foundation for a New Social Form

CW 330 The Renewal of the Social Organism

CW 331 Work-Council and Socialization

CW 332a The Social Future

CW 332b Lectures and Speeches on Social and Economic Issues

CW 333 *Freedom of Thought and Societal Forces: Implementing the Demands of Modern Society*

CW 334 From the Unified State to the Threefold Social Organism

CW 335 The Crisis of the Present and the Path to Healthy Thinking

CW 336 The Great Questions of the Times and Anthroposophical Spiritual Knowledge

CW 337a Social Ideas, Social Realities, Social Practice, Vol. 1: Question-and-Answer Evenings and Study Evenings of the Alliance for the Threefold Social Organism in Stuttgart, 1919–1920

CW 337b Social Ideas, Social Realities, Social Practice, Vol. 2: Discussion Evenings of the Swiss Alliance for the Threefold Social Organism

CW 338   *Communicating Anthroposophy: The Course for Speakers to Promote the Idea of Threefolding*
CW 339   Anthroposophy, Threefold Social Organism, and the Art of Public Speaking
CW 340/41   *Rethinking Economics: Lectures and Seminars on World Economics*

Lectures and Courses on Christian Religious Work

CW 342   *First Steps in Christian Religious Renewal: Preparing the Ground for The Christian Community*
CW 343   Lectures and Courses on Christian Religious Work, Vol. 2: Spiritual Knowledge – Religious Feeling – Cultic Doing
CW 344   Lectures and Courses on Christian Religious Work, Vol. 3: Lectures at the Founding of The Christian Community
CW 345   Lectures and Courses on Christian Religious Work, Vol. 4: Concerning the Nature of the Working Word
CW 346   Lectures and Courses on Christian Religious Work, Vol. 5: The Apocalypse and the Work of the Priest

Lectures for Workers at the Goetheanum

CW 347   The Knowledge of the Nature of the Human Being According to Body, Soul and Spirit. On Earlier Conditions of the Earth
CW 348   On Health and Illness. Foundations of a Spiritual-Scientific Doctrine of the Senses
CW 349   On the Life of the Human Being and of the Earth. On the Nature of Christianity
CW 350   Rhythms in the Cosmos and in the Human Being. How Does One Come To See the Spiritual World?
CW 351   The Human Being and the World. The Influence of the Spirit in Nature. On the Nature of Bees
CW 352   Nature and the Human Being Observed Spiritual-Scientifically
CW 353   The History of Humanity and the World-Views of the Folk Cultures
CW 354   The Creation of the World and the Human Being. Life on Earth and the Influence of the Stars

C. Artistic Works

CW A 1–10; 57 The Architectural Work I: The Goetheanum and Its Predecessors
CW A 11   The Sculptural Work
CW A 12   The Goetheanum Windows. The Speech of Light. Sketches and Studies

CW A 13–16;
52–56   Painting Work
CW A 14   Sketches for the Painting of the Small Dome of the First Goethe-
               anum
CW A 27–43 The Architectural Work II: Commercial and Residential Buildings
               in Dornach and Other Places [forthcoming]
CW A 45   The Graphic Work
CW A 48   The Drawing Work
CW A 51   The Art of Jewellry as a Goethean Language of Form
CW A 54.0   A Path of Training in Painting. Pastel Sketches and Watercolours
CW A 54.1   Nature Moods. Nine Training Sketches for Painters

Eurythmy Figures

CW A 26   Skectches of the Eurythmy Figures
CW A 26a   The Eurythmy Figures of Rudolf Steiner, Artistically Executed by
               Annemarie Bäschlin
CW A 26b   Eurythmy Figures from the Time When They Were Created

Eurythmy Forms

CW A 23/1   Volume I: Eurythmy Forms for Poems by Rudolf Steiner
CW A 23/2   Volume II: Eurythmy Forms for the Calendar of the Soul by
               Rudolf Steiner
CW A 23/3   Volume III: Euythmy Forms for Poems by J. W. von Goethe
CW A 23/4   Volume IV: Eurythmy Forms for Poems by Christian Morgen-
               stern
CW A 23/5   Volume V: Eurythmy Forms for Poems by Albert Steffen
CW A 23/6   Volume VI: Eurythmy Forms for German Poems by Fercher von
               Steinwand, Hamerling, Hebbel, C. F. Meyer, Nietzsche, among oth-
               ers
CW A 23/7   Volume VII: Eurythmy Forms for English Poems
CW A 23/8   Volume VIII: Eurythmy Forms for French and Russian Poems
CW A 24   Volume IX: Eurythmy Forms for Tone Eurythmy

Blackboard Drawings from Lectures

CW A 58/1   Volume I: 20 Plates from Public Lectures 1920–1924 in CWs 73a,
               74, 76, and 84
CW A 58/2   Volume II: 38 Plates from Lectures in 1919 in CWs 191 and 194
CW A 58/3   Volume III: 34 Plates from Lectures in 1920 in CWs 196 and 198
CW A 58/4   Volume IV: 33 Plates from Lectures in 1920 in CWs 199 and 200
CW A 58/5   Volume V: 31 Plates from Lectures in 1920 in CW 201
CW A 58/6   Volume VI: 46 Plates from Lectures 1920–1921 in CWs 202–204

CW A 58/7   Volume VII: 38 Plates from Lectures in 1921 in CWs 205 and 206

CW A 58/8   Volume VIII: 42 Plates from Lectures in 1921 in CWs 207–209

CW A 58/9   Volume IX: 40 Plates from Lectures in 1922 in CWs 210–212

CW A 58/10   Volume X: 35 Plates from Lectures in 1922 in CWs 213–215

CW A 58/11   Volume XI: 41 Plates from Lectures 1922–1923 in CWs 216, 218–220

CW A 58/12   Volume XII: 37 Plates from Lectures in 1923 in CWs 221–225

CW A 58/13   Volume XIII: 38 Plates from Lectures in 1923 in CWs 227–230

CW A 58/14   Volume XIV: 36 Plates from Lectures in 1923 in CWs 232 and 233

CW A 58/15   Volume XV: 37 Plates from Lectures in 1924 in CWs 233a, 234, and 243

CW A 58/16   Volume XVI: 56 Plates from the "Karma Lectures" in CWs 235–238 and 240

CW A 58/17   Volume XVII: 21 Plates from Lectures on the History of the Anthroposophical Society in CWs 257, 258, 260, and 260a

CW A 58/18   Volume XVIII: 33 Plates from Lectures on Art in CWs 271, 276, 283, 288–290, and 291

CW A 58/19   Volume XIX: 41 Plates from Lectures on Eurythmy in CWs 278, 279, and 315

CW A 58/20   Volume XX: 27 Plates from Lectures on Speech Formation in CWs 281 and 282

CW A 58/21   Volume XXI: 42 Plates from Lectures on Education in CWs 296, 303, 304, 306, and 311

CW A 58/22   Volume XXII: 46 Plates from Lectures on Medicine in CWs 312–315

CW A 58/23   Volume XXIII: 48 Plates from Lectures in 1924 in CWs 316–318

CW A 58/24   Volume XXIV: 39 Plates from Lectures on Natural Science and the Social Question in CWs 322, 326, 327, 339, and 340

CW A 58/25   Volume XXV: 33 Plates from the "Workers Lectures" (Volumes 1 and 2) in CWs 347 and 348

CW A 58/26   Volume XXVI: 51 Plates from the "Workers Lectures" (Volumes 3 and 4) in CWs 349 and 350

CW A 58/27   Volume XXVII: 35 Plates from the "Workers Lectures" (Volumes 5 and 6) in CWs 351 and 352

CW A 58/28   Volume XXVIII: 42 Plates from the "Workers Lectures" (Volumes 7 and 8) in CWs 353 and 354

CW A 58/29   Volume XXIX: 43 Plates from Lectures and Courses on Christian Religious Activity in CWs 342–344 and 346

CW A 58/30   Volume XXX: 27 Plates from CWs 255b, 324a, 337b, and 340, Corrigenda, Plates without CW Assignment, Copies

SIGNIFICANT EVENTS IN THE LIFE OF
RUDOLF STEINER

1829:   June 23: birth of Johann Steiner (1829–1910)—Rudolf Steiner's father—in Geras, Lower Austria.

1834:   May 8: birth of Franciska Blie (1834–1918)—Rudolf Steiner's mother—in Horn, Lower Austria. 'My father and mother were both children of the glorious Lower Austrian forest district north of the Danube.'

1860:   May 16: marriage of Johann Steiner and Franciska Blie.

1861:   February 25: birth of *Rudolf Joseph Lorenz Steiner* in Kraljevec, Croatia, near the border with Hungary, where Johann Steiner works as a telegrapher for the South Austria Railroad. Rudolf Steiner is baptized two days later, February 27, the date usually given as his birthday.

1862:   Summer: the family moves to Mödling, Lower Austria.

1863:   The family moves to Pottschach, Lower Austria, near the Styrian border, where Johann Steiner becomes stationmaster. 'The view stretched to the mountains . . . majestic peaks in the distance and the sweet charm of nature in the immediate surroundings.'

1864:   November 15: birth of Rudolf Steiner's sister, Leopoldine (d. November 1, 1927). She will become a seamstress and live with her parents for the rest of her life.

1866:   July 28: birth of Rudolf Steiner's deaf-mute brother, Gustav (d. May 1, 1941).

1867:   Rudolf Steiner enters the village school. Following a disagreement between his father and the schoolmaster, whose wife falsely accused the boy of causing a commotion, Rudolf Steiner is taken out of school and taught at home.

1868:   A critical experience. Unknown to the family, an aunt dies in a distant town. Sitting in the station waiting room, Rudolf Steiner sees her 'form', which speaks to him, asking for help. 'Beginning with this experience, a new soul life began in the boy, one in which not only the outer trees and mountains spoke to him, but also the worlds that lay behind them. From this moment on, the boy began to live with the spirits of nature . . .'

1869:   The family moves to the peaceful, rural village of Neudorfl, near Wiener Neustadt in present-day Austria. Rudolf Steiner attends the village school. Because of the 'unorthodoxy' of his writing and spelling, he has to do 'extra lessons'.

1870:   Through a book lent to him by his tutor, he discovers geometry: 'To grasp something purely in the spirit brought me inner happiness. I know that I first learned happiness through geometry.' The same tutor allows him to draw, while other students still struggle with their reading and writing. 'An artistic element' thus enters his education.

1871:   Though his parents are not religious, Rudolf Steiner becomes a 'church child', a favourite of the priest, who was 'an exceptional character'. 'Up to the age of ten or eleven, among those I came to know, he was far and away the most significant.' Among other things, he introduces Steiner to Copernican, heliocentric cosmology. As an altar boy, Rudolf Steiner serves at Masses, funerals, and Corpus Christi processions. At year's end, after an incident in which he escapes a thrashing, his father forbids him to go to church.

1872:   Rudolf Steiner transfers to grammar school in Wiener-Neustadt, a five-mile walk from home, which must be done in all weathers.

1873–75:   Through his teachers and on his own, Rudolf Steiner has many wonderful experiences with science and mathematics. Outside school, he teaches himself analytic geometry, trigonometry, differential equations, and calculus.

1876:   Rudolf Steiner begins tutoring other students. He learns bookbinding from his father. He also teaches himself stenography.

1877:   Rudolf Steiner discovers Kant's *Critique of Pure Reason,* which he reads and rereads. He also discovers and reads von Rotteck's *World History.*

1878:   He studies extensively in contemporary psychology and philosophy.

1879:   Rudolf Steiner graduates from high school with honours. His father is transferred to Inzersdorf, near Vienna. He uses his first visit to Vienna 'to purchase a great number of philosophy books'—Kant, Fichte, Schelling, and Hegel, as well as numerous histories of philosophy. His aim: to find a path from the 'I' to nature.

October
1879–1883:   Rudolf Steiner attends the Technical College in Vienna—to study mathematics, chemistry, physics, mineralogy, botany, zoology,

biology, geology, and mechanics—with a scholarship. He also attends lectures in history and literature, while avidly reading philosophy on his own. His two favourite professors are Karl Julius Schröer (German language and literature) and Edmund Reitlinger (physics). He also audits lectures by Robert Zimmermann on aesthetics and Franz Brentano on philosophy. During this year he begins his friendship with Moritz Zitter (1861–1921), who will help support him financially when he is in Berlin.

1880: Rudolf Steiner attends lectures on Schiller and Goethe by Karl Julius Schröer, who becomes his mentor. Also 'through a remarkable combination of circumstances', he meets Felix Koguzki, a 'herb gatherer' and healer, who could 'see deeply into the secrets of nature'. Rudolf Steiner will meet and study with this 'emissary of the Master' throughout his time in Vienna.

1881: January: '... I didn't sleep a wink. I was busy with philosophical problems until about 12:30 a.m. Then, finally, I threw myself down on my couch. All my striving during the previous year had been to research whether the following statement by Schelling was true or not: *Within everyone dwells a secret, marvellous capacity to draw back from the stream of time—out of the self clothed in all that comes to us from outside— into our innermost being and there, in the immutable form of the Eternal, to look into ourselves.* I believe, and I am still quite certain of it, that I discovered this capacity in myself; I had long had an inkling of it. Now the whole of idealist philosophy stood before me in modified form. What's a sleepless night compared to that!'
Rudolf Steiner begins communicating with leading thinkers of the day, who send him books in return, which he reads eagerly.

July: 'I am not one of those who dives into the day like an animal in human form. I pursue a quite specific goal, an idealistic aim— knowledge of the truth! This cannot be done offhandedly. It requires the greatest striving in the world, free of all egotism, and equally of all resignation.'

August: Steiner puts down on paper for the first time thoughts for a 'Philosophy of Freedom'. 'The striving for the absolute: this human yearning is freedom.' He also seeks to outline a 'peasant philosophy', describing what the worldview of a 'peasant'—one who lives close to the earth and the old ways—really is.

1881–1882: Felix Koguzki, the herb gatherer, reveals himself to be the envoy of another, higher initiatory personality, who instructs Rudolf Steiner to penetrate Fichte's philosophy and to master modern scientific thinking as a preparation for right entry into the spirit. This 'Master' also teaches him the double (evolutionary and involutionary) nature of time.

1882:   Through the offices of Karl Julius Schröer, Rudolf Steiner is asked by Joseph Kürschner to edit Goethe's scientific works for the *Deutsche National-Literatur* edition. He writes 'A Possible Critique of Atomistic Concepts' and sends it to Friedrich Theodor Vischer.

1883:   Rudolf Steiner completes his college studies and begins work on the Goethe project.

1884:   First volume of Goethe's *Scientific Writings* (CW 1) appears (March). He lectures on Goethe and Lessing, and Goethe's approach to science. In July, he enters the household of Ladislaus and Pauline Specht as tutor to the four Specht boys. He will live there until 1890. At this time, he meets Josef Breuer (1842–1925), the co-author with Sigmund Freud of *Studies in Hysteria,* who is the Specht family doctor.

1885:   While continuing to edit Goethe's writings, Rudolf Steiner reads deeply in contemporary philosophy (Eduard von Hartmann, Johannes Volkelt, and Richard Wahle, among others).

1886:   May: Rudolf Steiner sends Kürschner the manuscript of *Outlines of Goethe's Theory of Knowledge* (CW 2), which appears in October, and which he sends out widely. He also meets the poet Marie Eugenie Delle Grazie and writes 'Nature and Our Ideals' for her. He attends her salon, where he meets many priests, theologians, and philosophers, who will become his friends. Meanwhile, the director of the Goethe Archive in Weimar requests his collaboration with the *Sophien* edition of Goethe's works, particularly the writings on colour.

1887:   At the beginning of the year, Rudolf Steiner is very sick. As the year progresses and his health improves, he becomes increasingly 'a man of letters', lecturing, writing essays, and taking part in Austrian cultural life. In August–September, the second volume of Goethe's *Scientific Writings* appears.

1888:   January–July: Rudolf Steiner assumes editorship of the 'German Weekly' *(Deutsche Wochenschrift).* He begins lecturing more intensively, giving, for example, a lecture titled 'Goethe as Father of a New Aesthetics'. He meets and becomes soul friends with Friedrich Eckstein (1861–1939), a vegetarian, philosopher of symbolism, alchemist, and musician, who will introduce him to various spiritual currents (including Theosophy) and with whom he will meditate and interpret esoteric and alchemical texts.

1889:   Rudolf Steiner first reads Nietzsche *(Beyond Good and Evil).* He encounters Theosophy again and learns of Madame Blavatsky in the theosophical circle around Marie Lang (1858–1934). Here he also meets well-known figures of Austrian life, as well as esoteric figures like the occultist Franz Hartmann and Karl Leinigen-Billigen (translator of C.G. Harrison's *The Transcendental Universe*). During this period, Steiner first reads A.P. Sinnett's *Esoteric Buddhism* and Mabel Collins's *Light on the Path*. He also begins travelling, visiting Budapest, Weimar, and Berlin (where he meets philosopher Eduard von Hartmann).

1890:   Rudolf Steiner finishes Volume 3 of Goethe's scientific writings. He begins his doctoral dissertation, which will become *Truth and Science* (CW 3). He also meets the poet and feminist Rosa Mayreder (1858–1938), with whom he can exchange his most intimate thoughts. In September, Rudolf Steiner moves to Weimar to work in the Goethe-Schiller Archive.

1891:   Volume 3 of the Kürschner edition of Goethe appears. Meanwhile, Rudolf Steiner edits Goethe's studies in mineralogy and scientific writings for the *Sophien* edition. He meets Ludwig Laistner of the Cotta Publishing Company, who asks for a book on the basic question of metaphysics. From this will result, ultimately, *The Philosophy of Freedom* (CW 4), which will be published not by Cotta but by Emil Felber. In October, Rudolf Steiner takes the oral exam for a doctorate in philosophy, mathematics, and mechanics at Rostock University, receiving his doctorate on the twenty-sixth. In November, he gives his first lecture on Goethe's 'Fairy Tale' in Vienna.

1892:   Rudolf Steiner continues work at the Goethe-Schiller Archive and on his *Philosophy of Freedom*. *Truth and Science,* his doctoral dissertation, is published. Steiner undertakes to write Introductions to books on Schopenhauer and Jean Paul for Cotta. At year's end, he finds lodging with Anna Eunike, née Schulz (1853–1911), a widow with four daughters and a son. He also develops a friendship with Otto Erich Hartleben (1864–1905) with whom he shares literary interests.

1893:   Rudolf Steiner begins his habit of producing many reviews and articles. In March, he gives a lecture titled 'Hypnotism, with Reference to Spiritism'. In September, volume 4 of the Kürschner edition is completed. In November, *The Philosophy of Freedom* appears. This year, too, he meets John Henry Mackay (1864–1933), the anarchist, and Max Stirner, a scholar and biographer.

1894:   Rudolf Steiner meets Elisabeth Fürster Nietzsche, the philosopher's sister, and begins to read Nietzsche in earnest, beginning with the as yet unpublished *Antichrist*. He also meets Ernst Haeckel (1834–1919). In the fall, he begins to write *Nietzsche, A Fighter against His Time* (CW 5).

1895:   May, *Nietzsche, A Fighter against His Time* appears.

1896:   January 22: Rudolf Steiner sees Friedrich Nietzsche for the first and only time. Moves between the Nietzsche and the Goethe-Schiller

Archives, where he completes his work before year's end. He falls out with Elisabeth Förster Nietzsche, thus ending his association with the Nietzsche Archive.

1897: Rudolf Steiner finishes the manuscript of *Goethe's Worldview* (CW 6). He moves to Berlin with Anna Eunike and begins editorship of the *Magazin für Literatur*. From now on, Steiner will write countless reviews, literary and philosophical articles, and so on. He begins lecturing at the 'Free Literary Society'. In September, he attends the Zionist Congress in Basel. He sides with Dreyfus in the Dreyfus affair.

1898: Rudolf Steiner is very active as an editor in the political, artistic, and theatrical life of Berlin. He becomes friendly with John Henry Mackay and poet Ludwig Jacobowski (1868–1900). He joins Jacobowski's circle of writers, artists, and scientists—'The Coming Ones' (*Die Kommenden*)—and contributes lectures to the group until 1903. He also lectures at the 'League for College Pedagogy'. He writes an article for Goethe's sesquicentennial, 'Goethe's Secret Revelation', on the 'Fairy Tale of the Green Snake and the Beautiful Lily'.

1898–99: 'This was a trying time for my soul as I looked at Christianity. . . . I was able to progress only by contemplating, by means of spiritual perception, the evolution of Christianity. . . . Conscious knowledge of real Christianity began to dawn in me around the turn of the century. This seed continued to develop. My soul trial occurred shortly before the beginning of the twentieth century. It was decisive for my soul's development that I stood spiritually before the Mystery of Golgotha in a deep and solemn celebration of knowledge.'

1899: Rudolf Steiner begins teaching and giving lectures and lecture cycles at the Workers' College, founded by Wilhelm Liebknecht (1826–1900). He will continue to do so until 1904. Writes: *Literature and Spiritual Life in the Nineteenth Century; Individualism in Philosophy; Haeckel and His Opponents; Poetry in the Present;* and begins what will become (fifteen years later) *The Riddles of Philosophy* (CW 18). He also meets many artists and writers, including Käthe Kollwitz, Stefan Zweig, and Rainer Maria Rilke. On October 31, he marries Anna Eunike.

1900: 'I thought that the turn of the century must bring humanity a new light. It seemed to me that the separation of human thinking and willing from the spirit had peaked. A turn or reversal of direction in human evolution seemed to me a necessity.' Rudolf Steiner finishes *World and Life Views in the Nineteenth Century* (the second part of what will become *The Riddles of Philosophy)* and dedicates it to

Ernst Haeckel. It is published in March. He continues lecturing at *Die Kommenden,* whose leadership he assumes after the death of Jacobowski. Also, he gives the Gutenberg Jubilee lecture before 7,000 typesetters and printers. In September, Rudolf Steiner is invited by Count and Countess Brockdorff to lecture in the Theosophical Library. His first lecture is on Nietzsche. His second lecture is titled 'Goethe's Secret Revelation.' October 6, he begins a lecture cycle on the mystics that will become *Mystics after Modernism* (CW 7). November–December: 'Marie von Sivers appears in the audience. . . .' Also in November, Steiner gives his first lecture at the Giordano Bruno Bund (where he will continue to lecture until May, 1905). He speaks on Bruno and modern Rome, focusing on the importance of the philosophy of Thomas Aquinas as monism.

1901: In continual financial straits, Rudolf Steiner's early friends Moritz Zitter and Rosa Mayreder help support him. In October, he begins the lecture cycle *Christianity as Mystical Fact* (CW 8) at the Theosophical Library. In November, he gives his first 'theosophical lecture' on Goethe's 'Fairy Tale' in Hamburg at the invitation of Wilhelm Hubbe-Schleiden. He also attends a gathering to celebrate the founding of the Theosophical Society at Count and Countess Brockdorff's. He gives a lecture cycle, 'From Buddha to Christ,' for the circle of the *Kommenden.* November 17, Marie von Sivers asks Rudolf Steiner if Theosophy needs a Western–Christian spiritual movement (to complement Theosophy's Eastern emphasis). 'The question was posed. Now, following spiritual laws, I could begin to give an answer. . . .' In December, Rudolf Steiner writes his first article for a theosophical publication. At year's end, the Brockdorffs and possibly Wilhelm Hubbe-Schleiden ask Rudolf Steiner to join the Theosophical Society and undertake the leadership of the German section. Rudolf Steiner agrees, on the condition that Marie von Sivers (then in Italy) work with him.

1902: Beginning in January, Rudolf Steiner attends the opening of the Workers' School in Spandau with Rosa Luxemberg (1870–1919). January 17, Rudolf Steiner joins the Theosophical Society. In April, he is asked to become general secretary of the German Section of the Theosophical Society, and works on preparations for its founding. In July, he visits London for a theosophical congress. He meets Bertram Keightly, G.R.S. Mead, A.P. Sinnett, and Annie Besant, among others. In September, *Christianity as Mystical Fact* appears. In October, Rudolf Steiner gives his first public lecture on Theosophy ('Monism and Theosophy') to about three hundred people at the Giordano Bruno Bund. On October 19–21, the

German Section of the Theosophical Society has its first meeting; Rudolf Steiner is the general secretary, and Annie Besant attends. Steiner lectures on practical karma studies. On October 23, Annie Besant inducts Rudolf Steiner into the Esoteric School of the Theosophical Society. On October 25, Steiner begins a weekly series of lectures: 'The Field of Theosophy'. During this year, Rudolf Steiner also first meets Ita Wegman (1876–1943), who will become his close collaborator in his final years.

1903:   Rudolf Steiner holds about 300 lectures and seminars. In May, the first issue of the periodical *Luzifer* appears. In June, Rudolf Steiner visits London for the first meeting of the Federation of the European Sections of the Theosophical Society, where he meets Colonel Olcott. He begins to write *Theosophy* (CW 9).

1904:   Rudolf Steiner continues lecturing at the Workers' College and elsewhere (about 90 lectures), while lecturing intensively all over Germany among theosophists (about 140 lectures). In February, he meets Carl Unger (1878–1929), who will become a member of the board of the Anthroposophical Society (1913). In March, he meets Michael Bauer (1871–1929), a Christian mystic, who will also be on the board. In May, *Theosophy* appears, with the dedication: 'To the spirit of Giordano Bruno'. Rudolf Steiner and Marie von Sivers visit London for meetings with Annie Besant. June: Rudolf Steiner and Marie von Sivers attend the meeting of the Federation of European Sections of the Theosophical Society in Amsterdam. In July, Steiner begins the articles in *Luzifer-Gnosis* that will become *How to Know Higher Worlds* (CW 10) and *Cosmic Memory* (CW 11). In September, Annie Besant visits Germany. In December, Steiner lectures on Freemasonry. He mentions the High Grade Masonry derived from John Yarker and represented by Theodore Reuss and Karl Kellner as a blank slate 'into which a good image could be placed'.

1905:   This year, Steiner ends his non-theosophical lecturing activity. Supported by Marie von Sivers, his theosophical lecturing—both in public and in the Theosophical Society—increases significantly: 'The German Theosophical Movement is of exceptional importance.' Steiner recommends reading, among others, Fichte, Jacob Boehme, and Angelus Silesius. He begins to introduce Christian themes into Theosophy. He also begins to work with doctors (Felix Peipers and Ludwig Noll). In July, he is in London for the Federation of European Sections, where he attends a lecture by Annie Besant: 'I have seldom seen Mrs Besant speak in so inward and heartfelt a manner... Through Mrs Besant I have found the way to H.P. Blavatsky.' September to October, he gives a course of 31 lectures for a small group of esoteric students. In October, the annual meeting of the German Section of the Theosophical Society, which still remains very small, takes place. Rudolf Steiner reports membership has risen from 121 to 377 members. In November, seeking to establish esoteric 'continuity', Rudolf Steiner and Marie von Sivers participate in a 'Memphis-Misraim' Masonic ceremony. They pay 45 marks for membership. 'Yesterday, you saw how little remains of former esoteric institutions.' 'We are dealing only with a "framework" … for the present, nothing lies behind it. The occult powers have completely withdrawn.'

1906:   Expansion of theosophical work. Rudolf Steiner gives about 245 lectures, only 44 of which take place in Berlin. Cycles are given in Paris, Leipzig, Stuttgart, and Munich. Esoteric work also intensifies. Rudolf Steiner begins writing *An Outline of Esoteric Science* (CW 13). In January, Rudolf Steiner receives permission (a patent) from the Great Orient of the Scottish A & A Thirty-Three Degree Rite of the Order of the Ancient Freemasons of the Memphis-Misraim Rite to direct a chapter under the name 'Mystica Aeterna.' This will become the 'Cognitive-Ritual Section' (also called 'Misraim Service') of the Esoteric School. (See: *Freemasonry and Ritual Work: The Misraim Service,* CW 265.) During this time, Steiner also meets Albert Schweitzer. In May, he is in Paris, where he visits Édouard Schuré. Many Russians attend his lectures (including Konstantin Balmont, Dimitri Mereszkovski, Zinaida Hippius, and Maximilian Woloshin). He attends the General Meeting of the European Federation of the Theosophical Society, at which Col Olcott is present for the last time. He spends the year's end in Venice and Rome, where he writes and works on his translation of H.P. Blavatsky's *Key to Theosophy.*

1907:   Further expansion of the German Theosophical Movement according to the Rosicrucian directive to 'introduce spirit into the world'—in education, in social questions, in art, and in science. In February, Col Olcott dies in Adyar. Before he dies, Olcott indicates that 'the Masters' wish Annie Besant to succeed him: much politicking ensues. Rudolf Steiner supports Besant's candidacy. April–May: preparations for the Congress of the Federation of European Sections of the Theosophical Society—the great, watershed Whitsun 'Munich Congress,' attended by Annie Besant and others. Steiner decides to separate Eastern and Western (Christian–Rosicrucian) esoteric schools. He takes his esoteric school out of the Theosophical Society (Besant and Rudolf Steiner are 'in harmony' on this). Steiner makes his first lecture tours to Austria and

Hungary. That summer, he is in Italy. In September, he visits Édouard Schuré, who will write the Introduction to the French edition of *Christianity as Mystical Fact* in Barr, Alsace. Rudolf Steiner writes the autobiographical statement known as the 'Barr Document.' In *Luzifer-Gnosis*, 'The Education of the Child' appears.

1908: The movement grows (membership: 1,150). Lecturing expands. Steiner makes his first extended lecture tour to Holland and Scandinavia, as well as visits to Naples and Sicily. Themes: St John's Gospel, the Apocalypse, Egypt, science, philosophy, and logic. *Luzifer-Gnosis* ceases publication. In Berlin, Marie von Sivers (with Johanna Mücke (1864–1949) forms the *Philosophisch-Theosophisch* (after 1915 *Philosophisch-Anthroposophisch) Verlag* to publish Steiner's work. Steiner gives lecture cycles titled *The Gospel of St John* (CW 103) and *The Apocalypse* (104).

1909: *An Outline of Esoteric Science* appears. Lecturing and travel continues. Rudolf Steiner's spiritual research expands to include the polarity of Lucifer and Ahriman; the work of great individualities in history; the Maitreya Buddha and the Bodhisattvas; spiritual economy (CW 109); the work of the spiritual hierarchies in heaven and on earth (CW 110). He also deepens and intensifies his research into the Gospels, giving lectures on the Gospel of St Luke (CW 114) with the first mention of two Jesus children. Meets and becomes friends with Christian Morgenstern (1871–1914). In April, he lays the foundation stone for the Malsch model—the building that will lead to the first Goetheanum. In May, the International Congress of the Federation of European Sections of the Theosophical Society takes place in Budapest. Rudolf Steiner receives the Subba Row medal for *How to Know Higher Worlds*. During this time, Charles W. Leadbeater discovers Jiddu Krishnamurti (1895–1986) and proclaims him the future 'world teacher,' the bearer of the Maitreya Buddha and the 'reappearing Christ.' In October, Steiner delivers seminal lectures on 'anthroposophy,' which he will try, unsuccessfully, to rework over the next years into the unfinished work, *Anthroposophy (A Fragment)* (CW 45).

1910: New themes: *The Reappearance of Christ in the Etheric* (CW 118); *The Fifth Gospel; The Mission of Folk Souls* (CW 121); *Occult History* (CW 126); the evolving development of etheric cognitive capacities. Rudolf Steiner continues his Gospel research with *The Gospel of St Matthew* (CW 123). In January, his father dies. In April, he takes a month-long trip to Italy, including Rome, Monte Cassino, and Sicily. He also visits Scandinavia again. July–August, he writes the first Mystery Drama, *The Portal of Initiation* (CW 14). In November, he gives 'psychosophy' lectures. In December, he submits 'On the

<table>
<tr><td>1911:</td><td>

Psychological Foundations and Epistemological Framework of Theosophy' to the International Philosophical Congress in Bologna. The crisis in the Theosophical Society deepens. In January, 'The Order of the Rising Sun,' which will soon become 'The Order of the Star in the East,' is founded for the coming world teacher, Krishnamurti. At the same time, Marie von Sivers, Rudolf Steiner's co-worker, falls ill. Fewer lectures are given, but important new ground is broken. In Prague, in March, Steiner meets Franz Kafka (1883–1924) and Hugo Bergmann (1883–1975). In April, he delivers his paper to the Philosophical Congress. He writes the second Mystery Drama, *The Soul's Probation* (CW 14). Also, while Marie von Sivers is convalescing, Rudolf Steiner begins work on *Calendar 1912/1913*, which will contain the 'Calendar of the Soul' meditations. On March 19, Anna (Eunike) Steiner dies. In September, Rudolf Steiner visits Einsiedeln, birthplace of Paracelsus. In December, Friedrich Rittelmeyer, future founder of The Christian Community, meets Rudolf Steiner. The *Johannes-Bauverein*, the 'building committee,' which would lead to the first Goetheanum (first planned for Munich), is also founded, and a preliminary committee for the founding of an independent association is created that, in the following year, will become the Anthroposophical Society. Important lecture cycles include *Occult Physiology* (CW 128); *Wonders of the World* (CW 129); *From Jesus to Christ* (CW 131). Other themes: esoteric Christianity; Christian Rosenkreutz; the spiritual guidance of humanity; the sense world and the world of the spirit.

</td></tr>
<tr><td>1912:</td><td>

Despite the ongoing, now increasing crisis in the Theosophical Society, much is accomplished: *Calendar 1912/1913* is published; eurythmy is created; both the third Mystery Drama, *The Guardian of the Threshold* (CW 14) and *A Way of Self-Knowledge* (CW 16) are written. New (or renewed) themes included life between death and rebirth and karma and reincarnation. Other lecture cycles: *Spiritual Beings in the Heavenly Bodies and in the Kingdoms of Nature* (CW 136); *The Human Being in the Light of Occultism, Theosophy, and Philosophy* (CW 137); *The Gospel of St Mark* (CW 139); and *The Bhagavad Gita and the Epistles of Paul* (CW 142). On May 8, Rudolf Steiner celebrates White Lotus Day, H.P. Blavatsky's death day, which he had faithfully observed for the past decade, for the last time. In August, Rudolf Steiner suggests the 'independent association' be called the 'Anthroposophical Society.' In September, the first eurythmy course takes place. In October, Rudolf Steiner declines recognition of a Theosophical Society lodge dedicated to the Star of the East and decides to expel all Theosophical Society members belonging to the order.

</td></tr>
</table>

Also, with Marie von Sivers, he first visits Dornach, near Basel, Switzerland, and they stand on the hill where the Goetheanum will be built. In November, a Theosophical Society lodge is opened by direct mandate from Adyar (Annie Besant). In December, a meeting of the German section occurs at which it is decided that belonging to the Order of the Star of the East is incompatible with membership in the Theosophical Society. December 28: informal founding of the Anthroposophical Society in Berlin.

1913:   Expulsion of the German section from the Theosophical Society. February 2–3: Foundation meeting of the Anthroposophical Society. Board members include: Marie von Sivers, Michael Bauer, and Carl Unger. September 20: Laying of the foundation stone for the *Johannes Bau* (Goetheanum) in Dornach. Building begins immediately. The fourth Mystery Drama, *The Soul's Awakening* (CW 14), is completed. Also: *The Threshold of the Spiritual World* (CW 147). Lecture cycles include: *The Bhagavad Gita and the Epistles of Paul* and *The Esoteric Meaning of the Bhagavad Gita* (CW 146), which the Russian philosopher Nikolai Berdyaev attends; *The Mysteries of the East and of Christianity* (CW 144); *The Effects of Esoteric Development* (CW 145); and *The Fifth Gospel* (CW 148). In May, Rudolf Steiner is in London and Paris, where anthroposophical work continues.

1914:   Building continues on the *Johannes Bau* (Goetheanum) in Dornach, with artists and co-workers from seventeen nations. The general assembly of the Anthroposophical Society takes place. In May, Rudolf Steiner visits Paris, as well as Chartres Cathedral. June 28: assassination in Sarajevo ('Now the catastrophe has happened!'). August 1: War is declared. Rudolf Steiner returns to Germany from Dornach—he will travel back and forth. He writes the last chapter of *The Riddles of Philosophy*. Lecture cycles include: *Human and Cosmic Thought* (CW 151); *Inner Being of Humanity between Death and a New Birth* (CW 153); *Occult Reading and Occult Hearing* (CW 156). December 24: marriage of Rudolf Steiner and Marie von Sivers.

1915:   Building continues. Life after death becomes a major theme, also art. Writes: *Thoughts during a Time of War* (CW 24). Lectures include: *The Secret of Death* (CW 159); *The Uniting of Humanity through the Christ Impulse* (CW 165).

1916:   Rudolf Steiner begins work with Edith Maryon (1872–1924) on the sculpture 'The Representative of Humanity' ('The Group'— Christ, Lucifer, and Ahriman). He also works with the alchemist Alexander von Bernus on the quarterly *Das Reich*. He writes *The Riddle of Humanity* (CW 20). Lectures include: *Necessity and Freedom in World History and Human Action* (CW 166); *Past and Present in the*

Human Spirit (CW 167); *The Karma of Vocation* (CW 172); *The Karma of Untruthfulness* (CW 173).

1917: Russian Revolution. The U.S. enters the war. Building continues. Rudolf Steiner delineates the idea of the 'threefold nature of the human being' (in a public lecture March 15) and the 'threefold nature of the social organism' (hammered out in May–June with the help of Otto von Lerchenfeld and Ludwig Polzer-Hoditz in the form of two documents titled *Memoranda,* which were distributed in high places). August–September: Rudolf Steiner writes *The Riddles of the Soul* (CW 20). Also: commentary on 'The Chymical Wedding of Christian Rosenkreutz' for Alexander Bernus (Das *Reich*). Lectures include: *The Karma of Materialism* (CW 176); *The Spiritual Background of the Outer World: The Fall of the Spirits of Darkness* (CW 177).

1918: March 18: peace treaty of Brest-Litovsk—'Now everything will truly enter chaos! What is needed is cultural renewal.' June: Rudolf Steiner visits Karlstein (Grail) Castle outside Prague. Lecture cycle: *From Symptom to Reality in Modern History* (CW 185). In mid-November, Emil Molt, of the Waldorf-Astoria Cigarette Company, has the idea of founding a school for his workers' children.

1919: Focus on the threefold social organism: tireless travel, countless lectures, meetings, and publications. At the same time, a new public stage of Anthroposophy emerges as cultural renewal begins. The coming years will see initiatives in pedagogy, medicine, pharmacology, and agriculture. January 27: threefold meeting: 'We must first of all, with the money we have, found free schools that can bring people what they need.' February: first public eurythmy performance in Zurich. Also: 'Appeal to the German People' (CW 24), circulated March 6 as a newspaper insert. In April, *Towards Social Renewal* (CW 23) appears—'perhaps the most widely read of all books on politics appearing since the war'. Rudolf Steiner is asked to undertake the 'direction and leadership' of the school founded by the Waldorf-Astoria Company. Rudolf Steiner begins to talk about the 'renewal' of education. May 30: a building is selected and purchased for the future Waldorf School. August–September, Rudolf Steiner gives a lecture course for Waldorf teachers, *The Foundations of Human Experience (Study of Man)* (CW 293). September 7: Opening of the first Waldorf School. December (into January): first science course, the *Light Course* (CW 320).

1920: The Waldorf School flourishes. New threefold initiatives. Founding of limited companies *Der Kommende Tag* and *Futurum A.G.* to infuse spiritual values into the economic realm. Rudolf Steiner also focuses on the sciences. Lectures: *Introducing Anthroposophical*

Medicine (CW 312); *The Warmth Course* (CW 321); *The Boundaries of Natural Science* (CW 322); *The Redemption of Thinking* (CW 74). February: Johannes Werner Klein—later a co-founder of The Christian Community—asks Rudolf Steiner about the possibility of a 'religious renewal,' a 'Johannine church.' In March, Rudolf Steiner gives the first course for doctors and medical students. In April, a divinity student asks Rudolf Steiner a second time about the possibility of religious renewal. September 27–October 16: anthroposophical 'university course.' December: lectures titled *The Search for the New Isis* (CW 202).

1921:   Rudolf Steiner continues his intensive work on cultural renewal, including the uphill battle for the threefold social order. 'University' arts, scientific, theological, and medical courses include: *The Astronomy Course* (CW 323); *Observation, Mathematics, and Scientific Experiment* (CW 324); the *Second Medical Course* (CW 313); *Colour.* In June and September–October, Rudolf Steiner also gives the first two 'priests' courses' (CW 342 and 343). The 'youth movement' gains momentum. Magazines are founded: *Die Drei* (January), and—under the editorship of Albert Steffen (1884–1963)—the weekly, *Das Goetheanum* (August). In February–March, Rudolf Steiner takes his first trip outside Germany since the war (Holland). On April 7, Steiner receives a letter regarding 'religious renewal,' and May 22–23, he agrees to address the question in a practical way. In June, the Klinical-Therapeutic Institute opens in Arlesheim under the direction of Dr Ita Wegman. In August, the Chemical-Pharmaceutical Laboratory opens in Arlesheim (Oskar Schmiedel and Ita Wegman are directors). The Clinical Therapeutic Institute is inaugurated in Stuttgart (Dr Ludwig Noll is director); also the Research Laboratory in Dornach (Ehrenfried Pfeiffer and Gunther Wachsmuth are directors). In November–December, Rudolf Steiner visits Norway.

1922:   The first half of the year involves very active public lecturing (thousands attend); in the second half, Rudolf Steiner begins to withdraw and turn toward the Society—'The Society is asleep.' It is 'too weak' to do what is asked of it. The businesses—*Der Kommende Tag* and *Futurum A.G.*—fail. In January, with the help of an agent, Steiner undertakes a twelve-city German lecture tour, accompanied by eurythmy performances. In two weeks he speaks to more than 2,000 people. In April, he gives a 'university course' in The Hague. He also visits England. In June, he is in Vienna for the East–West Congress. In August–September, he is back in England for the Oxford Conference on Education. Returning to Dornach, he gives the lectures *Philosophy, Cosmology, and*

Religion (CW 215), and gives the third priests' course (CW 344). On September 16, The Christian Community is founded. In October–November, Steiner is in Holland and England. He also speaks to the youth: *The Youth Course* (CW 217). In December, Steiner gives lectures titled *The Origins of Natural Science* (CW 326), and *Humanity and the World of Stars: The Spiritual Communion of Humanity* (CW 219). December 31: Fire at the Goetheanum, which is destroyed.

1923: Despite the fire, Rudolf Steiner continues his work unabated. A very hard year. Internal dispersion, dissension, and apathy abound. There is conflict—between old and new visions—within the Society. A wake-up call is needed, and Rudolf Steiner responds with renewed lecturing vitality. His focus: the spiritual context of human life; initiation science; the course of the year; and community building. As a foundation for an artistic school, he creates a series of pastel sketches. Lecture cycles: *The Anthroposophical Movement; Initiation Science* (CW 227) (in Wales at the Penmaenmawr Summer School); *The Four Seasons and the Archangels* (CW 229); *Harmony of the Creative Word* (CW 230); *The Supersensible Human* (CW 231), given in Holland for the founding of the Dutch Society. On November 10, in response to the failed Hitler-Ludendorff putsch in Munich, Steiner closes his Berlin residence and moves the *Philosophisch-Anthroposophisch Verlag* (Press) to Dornach. On December 9, Steiner begins the serialization of his *Autobiography: The Course of My Life* (CW 28) in *Das Goetheanum*. It will continue to appear weekly, without a break, until his death. Late December–early January: Rudolf Steiner re-founds the Anthroposophical Society (about 12,000 members internationally) and takes over its leadership. The new board members are: Marie Steiner, Ita Wegman, Albert Steffen, Elisabeth Vreede, and Gunther Wachsmuth. (See *The Christmas Meeting for the Founding of the General Anthroposophical Society*, CW 260.) Accompanying lectures: *Mystery Knowledge and Mystery Centres* (CW 232); *World History in the Light of Anthroposophy* (CW 233). December 25: the Foundation Stone is laid (in the hearts of members) in the form of the 'Foundation Stone Meditation.'

1924: January 1: having founded the Anthroposophical Society and taken over its leadership, Rudolf Steiner has the task of 'reforming' it. The process begins with a weekly newssheet ('What's Happening in the Anthroposophical Society') in which Rudolf Steiner's 'Letters to Members' and 'Anthroposophical Leading Thoughts' appear (CW 26). The next step is the creation of a new esoteric class, the 'first class' of the 'University of Spiritual Science' (which was to have been followed, had Rudolf Steiner lived longer, by two more advanced classes). Then comes a new language for

Anthroposophy—practical, phenomenological, and direct; and Rudolf Steiner creates the model for the second Goetheanum. He begins the series of extensive 'karma' lectures (CW 235–40); and finally, responding to needs, he creates two new initiatives: biodynamic agriculture and curative education. After the middle of the year, rumours begin to circulate regarding Steiner's health. Lectures: January–February, *Anthroposophy* (CW 234); February: *Tone Eurythmy* (CW 278); June: *The Agriculture Course* (CW 327); June–July: *Speech Eurythmy* (CW 279); *Curative Education* (CW 317); August: (England, 'Second International Summer School'), *Initiation Consciousness: True and False Paths in Spiritual Investigation* (CW 243); September: *Pastoral Medicine* (CW 318). On September 26, for the first time, Rudolf Steiner cancels a lecture. On September 28, he gives his last lecture. On September 29, he withdraws to his studio in the carpenter's shop; now he is definitively ill. Cared for by Ita Wegman, he continues working, however, and writing the weekly instalments of his *Autobiography* and *Letters to the Members/ Leading Thoughts* (CW 26).

1925:   Rudolf Steiner, while continuing to work, continues to weaken. He finishes *Extending Practical Medicine* (CW 27) with Ita Wegman. On March 30, around ten in the morning, Rudolf Steiner dies.

Index

A

abstract idealism, 132

Adam, 117

    body of, 108

    ego of, 118

    first, 88–90, 109

    organism of, 108

    second, 88–91

Aeschylus, 69

Akashic Record, 60, 118, 120

    aid of, 63

    reading of, 58, 105

    version from, 59

anthroposophy

    application of, 163

    development of, 63

    great forerunner of, 161

    path of, 57

    realm of, 1

    standpoint of, 92, 160

    teachings of, 153

Apocalypse, 81–82

Apollonius of Tyana, 39–40,
    62–63, 85

Aristides, 167–168

astral body

    active in, 115

    development of, 101, 122

    extract of, 94

    ideal, 121

    power of, 66, 116

    remnants of, 98

    rest of, 94

    sheath of, 40–41

Augustine, 52

B

Baptism of John, 51, 63, 176

    in Jordon, 41, 112, 122, 177

    moment of, 38

Being of Christ, 54

    actual sight of, 9

    bearer of, 37

    comprehensible theory of, 88

    cosmic, 123

    depths of, 15

    idea of, 52

    incarnation of, 148

    supra-sensible nature
        of, 65

Bengel, Johann Albrecht, 129

Bible, 5, 27, 96, 105, 117–118,
    141, 159

Bodhisattva, 155

    re-embodiment of, 156

Buddha

    forces of, 115–117, 154

    powers of, 116

    stream, 99

    truths of, 70

Buddhism/Buddhist
  adherent of, 71
  disciples of, 76
  essence of, 75
  kernel of, 70
  teaching, 100
  theory, 73

C

Christ/Jesus Christ
  appearance of, 152, 170
  bearer of, 38, 98, 108, 113, 141
  blood of, 56
  body of, 90, 108, 110
  contemporary of, 39
  deep knowledge of, 181
  element of, 15
  epoch, 33
  etheric form of, 35
  existence of, 177
  exoteric path to, 141
  historical appearance of, 1, 48,
      164, 176, 178, 181
  Imaginative picture of, 27
  incarnation of, 43
  indirect way of, 177
  Individuality of, 54, 156
  inner experience of, 51
  judgement of, 35
  life of, 41–42, 85–86
  living, 46
  Mystical, 181
  mystical fact of, 174
  name of, 163, 174, 177
  nature of, 112
  objective, 131
  personal, 45–46
  picture of, 29, 36, 180
  principle of, 1, 62, 136
  real nature of, 37

  recognition of, 48
  Resurrection of, 83–84, 91–92,
      99, 127
  Risen Body of, 109, 111
  significance of, 9
  substance of, 122
  teaching of, 111
  thought of, 139–140
  union of, 122, 138
  vision of, 32, 46, 51, 137
  whole nature of, 100
  working of, 11
  wounds of, 146
Christ-Event
  birth of, 50
  facts of, 32
  idea of, 1
  interpretation of, 63
  Mysteries of, 31
  nature of, 51
  renewal of, 32, 128
  supra-sensible experience of, 143
  understanding of, 57
  vision of, 153
Christ-Experience, 50
Christianity
  epoch of, 63
  essence of, 81–82
  essential question of, 83
  evolution of, 31, 35
  exoteric teachings of, 18
  impulse of, 11
  mysteries of, 31, 55
  mystical fact of, 181–182
  nature of, 43, 82
  opinion of, 139
  proclaimer of, 99
  sole ideal of, 15
  strength of, 15
  true, 15

truths of, 55, 166
    whole of, 83
    wisdom of, 166
Christ-Impulse
    beginning of, 140
    essential nature of, 99
    influence of, 64
    relationship of, 142
    service of, 157
    understanding of, 160
    widening of, 139
    world with, 129
Cicero, 167
civilization
    Ancient Persian, 113, 121
    earthly, 151
    epochs of, 20, 68
    European, 116
    fruits of, 151
    Western, 34, 116
clairvoyance, 45, 94
    dreamlike, 150
    old, 136, 169–170
    ordinary, 93
    power of, 53
cognition
    anthroposophical, 74
    conscious, 3–4, 8
    esoteric, 25
    external physical, 67
    human powers of, 32
    independent instrument of, 23
    realm of, 3–4, 6–7
consciousness
    Ancient Hebrew, 79
    Buddhistic, 70
    clairvoyant, 31, 101, 143
    earthly, 104
    external, 166–167
    European, 151

    folk-, 68
    Greek, 69
    human, 5, 33, 68, 104
    inner, 29, 48
    modern, 8, 90–91
    non-clairvoyant, 35
    normal, 4
    ordinary religious, 31
    of ego, 101–102, 105, 110–111
    of people, 72
    of seer, 48
    threshold of, 5
    training of, 175
    of void, 171
    Western, 150
Copernicus, Nicolaus, 137
Cosmic Being, 100, 123

D
Damascus
    event of, 88, 91, 125, 177
    experience of, 89
Deed on Golgotha, 56
Divine Being, 42, 76, 107, 135, 179
Divine Ego, 76–77
divine love, 159
    unfolding of, 126
divine spirits, 95, 105
divinity, 168
    cosmic, 174
Droßbach, Maximilian, 19, 21, 151

E
Earth
    Being of, 174, 176
    development on, 66
    elements of, 68, 79, 95
    embodiments of, 67, 101
    epoch, 105
    external substances of, 97

forces of, 97
human culture on, 114
human existence on, 96, 97
human race on, 107
incarnation on, 115, 117
kingdoms of, 13–14
physical, 74, 115
portion of, 13
spiritual atmosphere of, 54, 126
substances of, 94
whole, 13–14
Ebionites, 62
earthly evolution
achievement of, 108
beginning of, 148
course of, 148
of humans, 117, 127, 157
principles of, 2
Eckhardt, Meister, 179
ego, 72, 74
companion of, 66
conditions for free, 159
consciousness of, 78–79
dawn of, 74–75
external form of, 75
folk-group-, 101
germ of, 101
Greek, 77
group-, 101
human. *See* human ego
identification of, 77
nature of, 100
real being of, 100
-substance, 117
unfolding of, 101
value of, 76
Egyptian Mysteries, 172–173
element
cognitional, 2
cosmic, 68

destructive, 108
divine, 135
earthly, 124–125
holy, 17
human, 119
material, 123
moral, 155
second, 4
of Son, 11
of Spirit, 9
spiritual, 10, 18
subconscious, 5
substances and, 93
third, 4
truths, 61
unconscious, 9
of will, 6–7, 14
Epistles of John, 81
esoteric sight, 66, 110
etheric body
development of, 101
effect on, 23
ideal, 121
independence of, 23
main part of, 34
purest form of, 125
rest of, 66
separation of, 34
sheaths of, 41
Evangelists, 9, 143
Event in Palestine, 163, 165
Event of Damascus, 88,
91, 177
Event of Golgotha
objectivity of, 135
true significance of, 63
evolution
Christian, 36, 51, 62, 88, 111
concrete idea of, 135
cosmic, 106

direction of inner, 154
downward, 109
Earth, 80, 95, 101, 107–108
earthly. *See* earthly evolution
epoch of, 157
external, 62
historical, 21
human. *See* human evolution
import of, 169
intent of, 155
of man, 173, 182
of nineteenth century, 132
objective, 36
path of, 96
physical, 108
planetary, 105
process of, 110
progressive, 42
Saturn, 67
spiritual, 84
stage of, 20–21
of universe, 168
of West, 181
whole, 4, 42, 108, 142
of the world, 182

F
feeling
of contempt, 12
content of, 6
of contrition, 12
dominant, 70
effects of, 133
of emptiness, 171
fundamental, 171
Greek, 91
honest inner, 57
human, 159
of humility, 12, 144
independent, 20

instrument of, 23
intuitive, 136
of love, 25
and mood, 63, 168
mystical, 146
and perception, 23, 54
point of view of, 70
psychic forces of, 23
requisite exercises of, 147
of reverence, 172
tragic, 77, 91
for truth and fidelity, 173
universal, 25
world of, 21, 171
freedom
human, 159
love and, 42
sake of, 159
thought of, 160

G
Galileo, Galilei, 137
Gautama Buddha, 99, 107, 155
in East, 116
forces of, 122
illumination of, 157
God
compassionate, 13
forsaken, 12
knowledge of, 44
will of, 4
Gospel of Luke, 39, 58,
118, 121
Gospel of Mark, 58
Gospel of Matthew, 39, 55, 58
Gospel of St John, 9, 81–82, 85,
143–144
Grace
concept of, 55
realm of, 46

Greek Mysteries, 172–173,
178, 180
Guardian of the Threshold, 27

H
Heraclitus, 52
Holy Communion, 141
foundation of, 138
institution of, 137
symbol of, 139
Holy Spirit, 10
human body
anabolic forces in, 106
external form of, 91
material of, 94, 124
physical, 92–93, 95
training of, 69
human ego
being of, 107
ordinary, 100
rescue of, 110
human evolution
crisis of, 112
deepest truths of, 55
destinies of, 16
divine ordering of, 58
epoch of, 20, 57
Godhead into, 173
historical phenomenon
in, 168
periods of, 8, 68
picture of, 99
principles of, 110
whole of, 21, 65
humanity
Christ-development of, 35
Christian, 32
collective progress of, 148, 170
earthly, 56, 105
education of, 20

epoch of, 59–60
European, 116
exoteric path for, 137
faith led, 47
fourfold being of, 82
gradual development of, 182
heritage of, 1
historical development of, 166
mission of, 162
ordinary, 177
physical reproduction of, 89
redemption of, 159
salvation of, 153
spiritual life of, 128
spiritual temple of, 161
whole of, 21, 33, 151
human phantom
form of, 96
perfect, 126
rescue of, 112
restoration of, 127
human responsibility, 134
human soul
depths of, 175
individual, 142
with nature, 46, 104
progress of, 16–17
transformation of, 153

I
imagination, 10
of danger, 14
living, 13
vivid, 12–13
impulses
Christian, 152
moral, 3, 154–155
nature of, 127
subconscious, 7, 10
upward, 158

of will, 6
incarnation
    Bodhisattva-, 157
    earthly, 118, 155
    repetition of, 148
initiation
    character of, 61
    Christian, 16, 51, 143–147
    form of, 16
    gate of, 50
    method of, 173, 178
    modern, 17, 24
    path of, 26, 29
    rebirth of old, 179
    regions of, 10
    of Rose-Cross, 16
    Rosicrucian, 16, 18, 28, 147
    writings of, 84
inspiration, 10, 19
intuition, 10, 25

J
Jerome, 60, 62
Jerusalem, 14
Jeshu ben Pandira, 155–156
Jesuitism, 2
    degrees of, 12
    esoteric part of, 11
    pupil of, 11
Jesus of Nazareth, 1, 13
    birth of, 39
    body of, 38, 41, 98, 124
    development of, 37
    depreciation of, 37
    greatness of, 181
    historical biography of,
        180–181
    idea of, 121
    life of, 41, 113

nature of, 122
organism of, 121
personality of, 54
person of, 1, 165
teaching of, 165
true picture of, 164
John the Baptist, 53, 135, 175

K
Kant, Immanuel, 47, 167
karma
    concepts of, 128
    consequence of, 134
    earthly, 149
    foundation of, 134
    idea of, 18–19, 22–23
    matter of, 134
    recognition of, 18
    teaching of, 18
Kepler, Johannes, 137
kingdom
    animal, 4, 123
    of Grace, 46
    mineral, 4, 123, 144
    plant, 4, 123
King of the Worlds, 12–13
knowledge
    boundary of, 167
    clairvoyant, 31
    deeper, 64, 181
    of dignity, 173
    esoteric, 18, 68
    extent of, 114
    path of, 10, 26
    source of, 32
    spiritual, 68
    theosophical, 36
    valid, 47
    way of, 22

L
Lessing, Gotthold Ephraim, 19–22, 151
   The Education of the Human Race,
     19–20
Logos, 52, 157
Lord of Karma, 33–34, 148, 153–154
love and sympathy, 122, 171
Lucifer
   banner of, 14
   hosts of, 14
   influence of, 96–97
   working of, 106
Luke Jesus-child, 118–120

M
Macrocosm, 132–134
   external world of, 131
   spirituality of, 122
Maitreya Buddha, 157
Martyr, Justin, 52
Microcosm, 132, 134
Mithra and Dionysus, 174–175, 177
Mithraic Mysteries, 172–173,
    175–176, 178
Mount of Olives, 29, 38, 84
mystical death, 18, 146

N
Nathan Jesus-child, 115–117,
    119–120, 154
New Testament, 8, 13, 20, 33,
    50, 164

O
Oetinger, Friedrich Christoph, 129–131
Old Testament, 20–21, 42, 105

P
Pascal, Blaise, 44–46, 48
Pauline Epistles, 55, 65, 87, 164

phantom
   connection of, 124
   defective, 111
   destruction of, 105, 109
   disorganization of, 105
   domain of, 96
   human. *See* human phantom
   invisible, 95–96
   physical, 111
   pure, 108–109
   strength of, 105
physical body
   annihilation of, 107
   attributes of, 108
   beginning of, 101
   combination of, 96
   death of, 105
   decadence of, 106–107
   destiny of, 83
   destruction of, 106
   development of, 122
   dissolution of, 105
   external, 69, 75, 80, 91, 105
   fate of, 82
   forces of, 111
   form of, 107
   human, 74–75, 92, 95, 126
   ideal, 121
   independent of, 125–126
   instrument of, 26
   nature of, 104
   ordinary interweaving of, 22
   phantom belongs to, 94–96,
    105–106, 108
   real prototype of, 147
   sheath of, 41, 104
   significance of, 79
   threefold bodily organization
    of, 114
   whole working of, 26, 94

Plato, 167
Plutarch, 167

R
realm
    of air, 4
    of common life, 8
    cosmic, 121
    dark, 6
    of esoteric, 141
    of Grace, 46
    material, 136
    moral, 3
    psychic life in, 4
    of spirit, 5–9
    spiritual, 162
    subconscious, 7–8
    of Son, 8
    whole, 4
    of will, 6
redemption
    act of, 134, 136
    human, 131
    individual, 151
    thought of, 160–161
    true, 161
    work of, 143
reincarnation
    idea of, 22, 53, 129, 152
    question of, 22
    recognition of, 18, 21–22
    teaching of, 18, 73, 150–151
    thought of, 151–152
religious life, 1
Risen One, 87–88, 125
Rosicrucianism, 2, 15, 18, 24, 35
    principle of, 17
    sources of, 17
    true, 17
Rothe, Richard, 129

S
Schopenhauer, Arthur, 167
science
    esoteric, 1, 8, 53, 96, 115, 118
    external, 45
    historical, 154
    natural, 20, 22, 46, 141
    spiritual. *See* spiritual science
sheath
    bodily, 70–71, 74
    external, 26, 41, 70
    human, 100
    spiritual, 53
sleep
    dreamless, 6
    unconsciousness of, 3
    waking and, 168
Socrates, 52, 154
Solomon Jesus-child, 113–114, 119
Solovyov, Vladimir, 45–48
Son
    element of, 11
    of the Gods, 39
    individual working of, 9
    love of, 159
    power of, 10
    principle of, 5–6
    realm of, 8
soul
    -being, 171
    conscious life of, 5
    courageous, 176
    depths of, 173–174
    elemental part of, 6
    Great, 179
    Greek, 69–70
    healthy life of, 7
    heart and, 50
    human. *See* human soul
    immortality of, 19, 22

inner development of, 132
inner path of, 131
of Jesuit, 12, 14
oceanic life of, 4
-powers, 170, 172–173,
177–178
sanctuary of, 24
subconscious impulses of, 10
subconscious life of, 3–4
unconscious life of, 6
world of, 34
spirit
Christian and Jesuit way of, 11
Communion in, 139
conscious human, 6
cosmic, 28, 182
of the Cosmos, 28
element of, 9, 138–139
Greek, 69
knowledge of, 10, 139
and matter, 137–138
mind and, 65
realm of, 5–9
Sun, 121
spiritual life
cognitive, 3
conscious, 4, 7
epoch for, 128
esoteric, 1
external view of, 164
German, 19
modern, 17
path of, 30
progress of, 4
questions of, 1
true, 130
spiritual science
anthroposophical, 17
aspect of, 166
view of, 167

spiritual world
doors of, 149
fact of, 165
rest of, 115
understanding of, 56
Strauß, David Friedrich, 84

T
Tanakh, 42, 105
temptation, 27–29, 84, 159,
178–179
theoretical materialism, 132
theosophy
aim of, 138–139
deepening of, 131
exoteric, 24
path of, 128
spirit of, 141
of time, 130
whole of, 17
truth
characteristic of, 168
distortion of, 55
esoteric, 66
and fidelity, 173
life of, 46
scientific, 168
ways of, 2

U
universe
atomistic conception of, 137
divine foundations of, 168
divine qualities of, 174
harmony of, 176
material, 136
phenomena of, 172
primordial forces of, 173
secrets of, 181
whole, 176

W
Wagner, Richard, 56
willing, 23, 161
worldview
    anthroposophical, 154
    Christian, 82
    modern, 140

Z
Zarathustra
    great faculties of, 114
    individuality of, 37, 41, 113–114,
        119–122
    indwelling of, 122